CRISIS COMMUNICATIONS

CRISIS COMMUNICATIONS
Lessons from September 11

Edited by
A. Michael Noll

ROWMAN & LITTLEFIELD PUBLISHERS, INC.
Lanham • Boulder • New York • Toronto • Oxford

P
96
.T47
C75
2003

ROWMAN & LITTLEFIELD PUBLISHERS, INC.

Published in the United States of America
by Rowman & Littlefield Publishers, Inc.
A Member of the Rowman & Littlefield Publishing Group
4501 Forbes Boulevard, Suite 200, Lanham, Maryland 20706
www.rowmanlittlefield.com

PO Box 317
Oxford
OX2 9RU, UK

British Library Cataloguing in Publication Information Available

Library of Congress Cataloging-in-Publication Data

Crisis communications : lessons from September 11 / edited by A. Michael
Noll.
    p. cm.
Includes bibliographical references and index.
  ISBN 0-7425-2542-2 (cloth) — ISBN 0-7425-2543-0 (pbk.)
  1. Terrorism and mass media. 2. Communication, International. 3.
September 11 Terrorist Attacks, 2001. I. Noll, A. Michael.

P96.T47C75 2003
303.6'25—dc21

                                                    2003011925

♾️™ The paper used in this publication meets the minimum requirements of American
National Standard for Information Sciences—Permanence of Paper for Printed Library
Materials, ANSI/NISO Z39.48-1992.

Contents

Illustrations

Tables

Figures

Preface

A. Michael Noll

THE EVENTS OF SEPTEMBER 11 were totally unexpected and could never have been planned for. Scholars around the globe saw the immediate value of research into the many social aspects of this local, national, and global tragedy that involved many dimensions of communication, technology, and policy at all levels. Communication was essential on that tragic day as people around the world learned of and responded to the unfolding saga. The telephone, cell phones, radio, television, print media, the Internet, and emergency communications were used to express fear, hope, anxiety, curiosity, and every other emotion about the tragedy on that day and in the following weeks.

Communications scholars were presented a unique opportunity to study and illuminate communication in times of crisis, and they responded as documented in this volume. This is perhaps the greatest tribute they—as academic researchers—can make. Humanists, social scientists, and engineers can help the world understand events that challenge our perceptions of the world. They can draw lessons from disaster by critically and systematically exploring these events from their own disciplinary perspectives.

The chapters assembled in this book treat communications broadly, including interpersonal, telecommunications, and mass media. Some of the chapters report on the use of telecommunications, such as wireless, e-mail, and conventional telephone service. For example, AT&T's traffic was 40 percent higher than its past busiest day; wireless calls were made from the doomed airplanes and buildings, with the human voice having a calming influence; e-mail was used to overcome distance and time zones. Other chapters report on the role of the mass media and their use and behavior during the tragedy, applying what has been learned from the behavior of the mass media in past crises to the events of September 11. Interpersonal communication through storytelling played an important role both in conveying information and in coping with the tragedy. Some chapters consider the use of the Internet as a mass medium to obtain information.

This book had its genesis in an edited collection of short papers treating the social and societal aspects of the use of telecommunication and mass media during the tragedy. These short papers were published by Carfax Publishing of the Taylor & Francis Group in the journal *Prometheus* for the first anniversary of the tragedy (*Prometheus*, September 2002). The authors of these short papers then later expanded them for this book, frequently with the inclusion of additional research. A few additional researchers beyond the *Prometheus* symposium also submitted chapters.

A conference on the topic of communications on September 11 was held on October 26, 2002, in New York City with the joint support and sponsorship of the Annenberg School for Communication at the University of Southern California, the Columbia Institute for Tele-Information at Columbia University, and the Media Center at New York Law School. The conference gave the researchers an opportunity to learn personally of the work done by their colleagues so that they could expand on their research and writing.

This book is the continuation to what promises to be a growing effort to understand and learn from the events of September 11. All the contributors hope that the book will contribute to a better understanding of these tragic events and help foster more research on the ways communication, technology, and society interact in often disastrous but heroic ways.

The initial enthusiasm and continuing encouragement of both William H. Dutton (*Prometheus* North American editor) and Donald M. Lamberton (*Prometheus* general editor) are much appreciated, since their vision stimulated the wealth of material that was later gathered for this book. The contributors to this volume are applauded for their efforts and for responding promptly to tight deadlines.

The vision and wisdom of Brenda Hadenfeldt of Rowman & Littlefield is appreciated in recognizing the significance of this collection and in encouraging its timely publication. Arthur Asa Berger wisely suggested her as publisher of this volume.

Michelle T. Gradis, a doctoral candidate at the Annenberg School, assisted in preparation and editing. Thanks go to Taylor & Francis (www.tandf.co.uk) for permission to use much of the material published in *Prometheus*. And last, a substantial portion of the work on this project was supported by a sabbatical from the Annenberg School.

Introduction: A Global Tragedy

A. Michael Noll

WORDS FAIL TO EXPRESS the feelings of horror of the tragic events that occurred on September 11, 2001. Such terms as "terrorist," "tragedy," and
"attacks" are inevitably evaluative and pose real challenges to disinterested academic neutrality. But the enormity of the events of that day were indeed
overwhelming to most people in the United States and the world, and aca-
demics are part of the world rocked by these events. Indeed, researchers are
part of the very world they study. In this case, thousands of people from many
countries lost their lives in the attacks on the Pentagon in Washington, D.C.,
and the World Trade Center in New York City. The total destruction of the
World Trade Center was witnessed live on television as both of the Twin Towers collapsed, plunging Wall Street and financial markets around the world
into a financial crash from which they took months to recover. Years will be
required for New York City to restore the destruction of many square blocks
of Lower Manhattan. Hundreds of firefighters and police were lost at the
World Trade Center.

The memories of September 11 will always be vivid. Live televised images
are forever embedded in our minds of the aircraft crashing into the towers of
the World Trade Center and the ultimate collapse of both towers; of people
fleeing for their lives to escape a crushing wave of debris; and of firefighters
and police grieving over their lost comrades. Phone calls were made to loved
ones from people in the doomed buildings, and wireless calls from the
doomed aircraft. The telephone network was strained as people called family
members and friends seeking comfort and solace in hearing a human voice.
E-mail and the Internet informed colleagues and friends around the world of
the unfolding tragedy.

Television bombarded the world with continuous coverage for days after the tragedy, even though there frequently was little new to report. Over the air broadcast television was wiped out in the New York metropolitan area, except for WCBS, which had a backup transmitter on top of the Empire State Building. Television lost its role as a means of escapism for many. Newspapers and magazines carried photographs of people jumping to their deaths to escape the inferno of the burning buildings. People told stories of the experiences of themselves and friends as a way to cope and relieve their feelings of horror and grief.

Communications and its infrastructure were essential that day. This infrastructure is multifaceted, including many forms of interpersonal communication, such as face-to-face. Mediated interpersonal telecommunication over the telephone, e-mail, and wireless cell phones is also part of this communication infrastructure. The communication infrastructure encompasses a wide variety of mass media, such as radio, television, the print of newspapers and magazines, and information obtained over the Internet. All media played a role on September 11.

On that horrific day, telecommunication infrastructures functioned mostly as designed and facilitated worldwide communication over a variety of modalities. The mass media carried the unfolding tragedy instantly around the globe. Communication technologies of all kinds functioned as the means that most people first heard about the tragedy and then as the means to share feelings and cope with the tragedy. These communication technologies included the conventional broadcast mass media of radio and television, the Internet as a source of news and information, the telephone, wireless cellular service, and e-mail. Emergency communications for the police and firefighters at the World Trade Center area were overwhelmed, however, on September 11.

The real drama was not technology but the social impact of communications—both telecommunications and the media—on people. This is the motivation for this collection of research on the social impacts of crisis communications on September 11.

Crises will occur, and communications will be essential, during and after. Communication systems should be designed and engineered to meet the needs of real users. The research reported in this book illuminates these needs and also describes communication behavior during crises. It thus should be very meaningful to those who design communication systems and are responsible for media coverage.

The Chapters

The themes of the chapters of this book show clearly the central role of communications during the tragedy. Broadcast television and radio were how many people heard about the events of September 11, but person-to-person communication over the telephone and face-to-face was also significant. People told other people about the tragedy and coped with their feelings through storytelling. As conventional telephone lines became clogged, people turned to their cell phones, and sometimes vice versa. Calls from the doomed aircraft and buildings were made on cell phones—a drama that will be forever remembered by those receiving the calls. The new medium of the Internet was important, both for e-mail and also for obtaining information about the unfolding tragedy. The Internet particularly became a major source of news in countries where it took too long for the conventional news media to translate coverage from English.

The chapters in this book can be grouped into various clusters. The first group of chapters focuses on how people learned of the tragedy and their activities in response. The second cluster of chapters treats the use of the telephone, cell phones, and the relatively new medium of the Internet. The third cluster discusses the use of conventional mass media, such as television and print media. The book ends with essays on the effects of media globalization on terrorism and with a final epilogue. Many of the chapters draw lessons from the use and performance of communications on September 11 and give specific advice for the future.

How People Learned of the Tragedy

Telecommunication by the telephone, facsimile, cellular wireless, and e-mail all played roles during the tragedy, as described in first grouping of chapters. Television and radio (over 50 percent) were important ways that people in the United States learned of the tragedy, but conversation (about 40 percent) over the telephone and face-to-face was also important. In Estonia, face-to-face (47 percent) was the single most important way that people learned of the tragedy.

John Carey describes how people used communications during and immediately after the tragedy, particularly television but also multiple sources of information. Carey concludes that media functioned well in meeting extraordinary demands for information and communication, although communications among emergency workers was more problematic.

Everett Rogers reports on his diffusion study of how people in New Mexico first heard about the tragedy and what they immediately did and also incorporates other diffusion studies. The majority of people in New Mexico were at home and television was the dominant mass media channel for conveying initial awareness of the terrorist attacks, with interpersonal channels also of considerable importance. Rogers concludes that, in comparison, the Internet and telephones (including cell phones) played much less important roles in diffusion of this news event.

Elisia L. Cohen, Sandra J. Ball-Rokeach, Joo-Young Jung, and Yong-Chan Kim describe the role of media and interpersonal storytelling in information dissemination and also present a model based on a communication infrastructure approach. They highlight the potential storytelling processes through which urban residents are transformed into members of a broader community as illustrated by their connections to media, and their participation in neighborhood discussions and community organizations after September 11. Their data show that "respondents who reported spending more time talking with others and reading the newspaper were more likely to have taken a broader scope of civic actions than those who did not . . . [but] the amount of time respondents spent watching television and listening to radio after September 11 was not related to their scope of civic actions."

Telecommunications: Telephones, Wireless, and the Internet

Telecommunication over the telephone and wireless cell phones was extremely important during the tragedy. The Internet is a relatively new medium for obtaining information during a crisis and was used during the tragedy, both to obtain information from news sites and also to discuss feelings about the attacks through its use for e-mail and message boards.

Jonathan Liebenau describes the causes of key problems with communication during and shortly after the World Trade Center disaster on 9/11 and assesses the relative importance of different kinds of failures. He shows that some appropriate responses have occurred, particularly in government, but that important lessons are still to be learned about the design of systems. Expectations of telecommunications reliability have gone up just as the financial fortunes of the industry have gone down, creating a challenge in how to reach the expected level of resilience for the future.

Mitchell L. Moss and Anthony Townsend examine the role of digital communications networks during and after the September 11, 2001, attack on the World Trade Center. Digital networks in New York City played a vital role in all three phases of this catastrophe: initial response, interim restoration, and long-term recovery. They conclude that during each of these phases, the digital network infrastructure, while the most fragile of all urban networks, demonstrated remarkable resiliency in serving the citizens of the city and the nation.

William H. Dutton and Frank Nainoa describe how wireless telephones were used from the doomed aircraft and also from the attacked buildings. They perform comparisons across different contexts to provide empirical anchors to more general themes concerning the social dynamics of wireless in the unfolding events of September 11. Events illustrate how the major social role of information and communication technologies like wireless is centered on reconfiguring access—physical and electronic. They conclude that the vivid implications of air phones and mobile cell phones in the crisis could re-define public views on wireless telecommunications and thereby shape policy and regulation in the years ahead.

James E. Katz and Ronald E. Rice categorize the use of telephone and cell phones during the crisis and suggest a broader "syntopian" theoretical per-spective. They explore how ordinary people used telephone technology (land-line, voice answering, mobile phones, PDAs, wireless text) during the tragedy. They document how personal emergency communication was heavily im-bued with emotional meaning, with messages addressing major life problems and values, such as leaving final messages and expressing love and concern, and sometimes requiring extreme efforts.

The Multifaceted Roles of Mass Media

The more traditional mass media were essential during the attacks, partic-ularly the visual imagery of live television. But newspapers and magazines gave more detailed information, without the sensationalism of television. The Internet also became a new medium to obtain timely information.

Jeremy Harris Lipschultz examines the year prior to the September 11 at-tack for evidence that American network television news offered a wider def-inition of terrorism than after the traumatic events. Qualitative content analy-sis, a method for studying the framing of news via language, offered some support for the idea that attack coverage focused the meaning of terrorism on Osama bin Laden and events in the Middle East.

Fiona McNee examines the effect on television coverage and programming during and after the attacks. She discusses the pulling of fictional programs from television and movie screens in the name of public sensitivity and com-pares the ability of fact and fiction to not only provide information to their audience but fulfill more profound needs in a time of crisis. By analyzing an episode of the U.S. television program "The West Wing," she demonstrates fic-tion's potential contribution as a mechanism for recovery rather than a cause for concern.

Joachim W. H. Haes compares the reporting and the formation of interpre-tations of the terror attacks of September 11, 2001, in Germany and in the United States. He shows that while U.S. citizens turned to increased patriot-ism and religion, German commentators stressed the importance of thorough investigation and international cooperation.

Pille Vengerfeldt examines the use of the Internet and newspaper coverage in Estonia for different narratives about the attacks. She determined that people in Estonia first learned about the attacks from face-to-face contacts and also from radio. She discusses the role of the Internet in a country where conventional media is delayed because of the need to translate from English.

Paul Rappoport and James Alleman explore data about the use of the Internet during the tragedy. The data show a dramatic increase in the usage of Internet news sites on September 11. Their analysis shows that this increased usage of Internet news sites seems significant even after the tragedy.

Patrick Martin and Sean Phelan contrast the representation of the attacks on U.S. television and CNN's message board. They conclude that TV discourse about September 11 and history was largely confined to interpretations which colluded with the interests of the political elite and which affirmed America's "moral obligation" to respond militarily to the attacks; and that the message board allowed for the articulation of an "alternative history," which was critically absent from TV. Media theories are used to explain the differences in the representations.

Menachem Blondheim and Tamar Liebes write about the influence of media on the political process that is created by marathon coverage of crises by the media. They also analyze the media coverage of the second anniversary of the tragedy. They conclude that the goal of the media should be "strategies that would diminish the incentives for the ruthless to engage in violence in order to reap the fruits of media coverage."

Media Globalization

James William Carey discusses the role of communications in the formation of Nations and as the stimulus for the creation of conditions conducive to terrorism.

René Jean Ravault discusses the effects of the globalization of U.S. mass entertainment media on fostering the environment for terrorism. He explains how modern telecommunications can enable terrorists to remain isolated in a host country, and also how the images created by U.S. mass entertainment media create expectations and frustrations, unfortunately strong enough to result in tremendous violence.

The many chapters in this book are admirably diverse, and as such they defy placement within research traditions. So rather than attempt to summarize them, Peter Clarke in his epilogue exposes ideas that the authors provoke about communication in crisis. To conclude the epilogue, Clarke reports the results of his study of the corpus of research into terrorism, before and after September 11, 2001, so readers can see how completely this book explores this terrain.

Research Methodologies

The authors who contributed to this volume used many different methodologies of the social sciences to conduct their research. Thus the chapters demonstrate both the variety and the validity of many different methodologies and approaches to the conduct of scholarly research. The methodologies represented by the chapters in this book include survey research, content analysis, secondary data analysis, interpretive and introspective analysis, and firehouse research.

Survey Research

Everett Rogers (with the assistance of Nancy Seidel) conducted a survey using a prepared interview questionnaire, soon after the news event of September 11. A common technique is to contact a sample of respondents by telephone. A newer approach is to gather data via an Internet questionnaire. The usual questions asked in these surveys is whether the respondent has heard of the news event, at what time, via what communication channels, where they obtained further information about the news event, who and how many other people they told about the news event, and what effects the news event had on their behavior (attending a memorial service, etc.).

Elisia Cohen and her colleagues performed telephone surveys. They selected phone numbers from exchanges that fell as much as possible within a census tract defined area, such that we would insure an optimal probability that a respondent reached would be of the targeted desired geographic area. To select the optimal number of telephone exchanges, they restricted the sampling frame so that they would have as many phone exchanges as possible within the targeted area, but as few as possible spilling over into the outside area. The actual questionnaire was administered by a professional survey company whose interviewers were fluent in the major languages spoken by the residents of the area, and sensitive to the social norms of that target community. The overall objective was to create a comfortable exchange between interviewers and respondents.

Jonathan Liebenau conducted numerous interviews with telecommunication industry executives and senior engineers, government officials and senior emergency services workers in New York City, and academic engineers and telecommunications analysts. Although much of the evidence has been reported in the popular or trade press, the author has had unique opportunities to confirm evidence and to learn from participants about the background to events and technologies.

Pille Vengerfeldt first conducted a survey of 156 people in Estonia and from them selected 14 whose level of Internet use was highest. She then conducted dyadic interviews of them so that they could elaborate their views of the Internet and the crisis news.

Content Analysis

Content analysis has been utilized in communication studies for more than fifty years as a way to examine mass media messages. Media content may be studied to verify assumptions about content, to test theories about media messages, to explore *potential* effects on the mass audience, and to offer suggestions about the thoughts of media producers. Content analyses may be quantitative, social science studies, which employ advanced statistics; they may also be qualitative descriptions grounded in the literature of rhetoric, language, and culture.

Fiona McNee obtained a videotaped copy of the television episode as it aired in the United States. She first transcribed the dialogue of the episode, noting significant lighting and nonverbal cues. The text was then analyzed to identify the messages that appeared from its face and the techniques used to convey those messages, drawing on narrative discourse theory and uses and gratifications as a broad framework. She then reviewed popular media sources to identify the messages the product's creator nominated for the purposes of comparison with those identified from the text itself. She also built a temporal context for the creation, broadcast, and receipt of the message/product. Having refined the analysis and determined her own opinion of the product's success at achieving its purpose, she returned to the popular media for an alternative evaluation of its success, both in terms of professional critics and official ratings.

Joachim Haes performed content analyses of public media in Germany and the United States. Basic hypotheses were constructed on the basis of secondary literature, both academic and professional.

Jeremy Harris Lipschultz examined American network television news for the year prior to the attack of September 11 for evidence that a wider definition of terrorism was offered before than after the attack. Qualitative content analysis, a method for studying the framing via language of news, offered some support for the idea that attack coverage focused the meaning of terrorism on Osama bin Laden and events in the Middle East. Further study of earlier news content might reveal that the cultural meaning of terrorism is linked to national interests, governmental relations and international politics.

Patrick Martin and Sean Phelan gathered the largest set of examples of each type of discussion they could find for linguistic analysis (broadcast transcripts from LEXIS-NEXIS) and began archiving contribution to the largest public message board on the web in the week following the attacks (CNN). The size of the samples they collected allowed them to examine large-scale trends in language use and to ask questions about how similar this language is in tone and function to that of the political elite. By "counting" references to historical events they obtained a picture of the kind of "historical map" in which 9/11 was placed by politicians and journalists on TV, and contrast that with the public historical map constituted by discussion on the message board. They were able to see how particular words were used (what context they were given) by examining the way in which certain words carry different meanings due to how they are "collocated" (i.e., how certain terms which relate to history are repeatedly used with a particular adjective or other part of speech).

Pille Vengerfeldt performed content analyses of an online newspaper in Estonia, its online forum, and two chat rooms. Qualitative text analyses were then made to identify content-related categories throughout the different texts. Altogether thirty content categories with fifteen subcategories were identified, but for the clarity of analysis only thirteen of them were analyzed in depth for her chapter. After the content analysis, another qualitative text analysis was made through the different categories in order to identify the differences of discussion in the different channels.

Secondary Data Analysis

The descriptive analyses presented by Paul Rappoport and James Alleman were based on review and assessment of actual Internet transactions data obtained from Plurimus Corporation. Through partnerships with more than fifty Internet service providers (ISPs) across the United States, Plurimus collected the clickstream data from over 500,000 households across the United States. The ISPs were strategically chosen to offer Plurimus adequate coverage geographically, demographically, and across different types of access. Plurimus made use of poststratification adjustment techniques to weight and project its estimates of behavior to the population.

Peter Clarke, in the epilogue to this book, examined key words in *PsycInfo* and *Sociological Abstracts*, two of the most important bibliographic databases in the social sciences. He delimited two slices in time, 1989–2000 and 2001–2003. Within the earlier period, he used "terrorist/terrorists" and "terrorism" as locators, and to find the postattack literature, used "September 11/Sept. 11" as locators. He further refined the searches through the introduction of a dictionary of concepts representing touchstones in the empirical study of communication.

Interpretive and Introspective Analysis

James Katz and Ronald Rice examined an array of published material in news outlets and conducted numerous searches of the World Wide Web. Key words were used to locate sources on the Internet via Google. Interviews were conducted with witnesses, and "snowball" sampling was used in a haphazard manner to identify further informants about the incidents of September 11 and its aftermath. Firsthand experiences of one of the authors, introspection, and Weberian "thought experiments" also provide sources of data. In some cases, e-mails were sent to the authors as part of the ordinary communication that takes place after such an incident. In a few instances, one of the authors contacted people who had placed personal material online in order to follow up with additional questions or seek clarification of what they had written.

Their chapter is an interpretive essay rather than a measurement exercise. Their purpose was to provide contemplative insight.

Menahem Blondheim and Tamar Liebes took a theoretical and methodological approach aimed at shaping a thick description of television's overall performance in the event. They did this through a close reading of the broadcasted media text as the primary unit of analysis. They examined the technological and operational aspects, reflecting the practical options for recording the event, and the potential combinations of visual and verbal, studio and field, live and recorded elements, and their merging into a show fine-tuned to the sensibilities of either local or national, perhaps even globally targeted audiences. They also considered the professional and ethical standards shaping genre, journalistic, and ethical calls, and all the way to dramaturgical/aesthetic decisions in the production process. And finally they attempt to understand the corporate constraints, reflecting commercial, regulatory, and political considerations.

Firehouse Research

When an important but unanticipated event occurs and research about that event requires getting into the field quickly, it is not always possible to design a careful research plan. Rather, researchers have to scramble and use resources that are available to them. This is sometimes called "Firehouse Research." This is what John Carey did. He was in the field shortly after September 11, conducting three studies for commercial clients: a set of focus groups in New York and Los Angeles about TV usage patterns and expectations; an in-home ethnographic study of households with a new digital cable service that included e-mail; and a telephone survey of satellite radio users who reported on their use of radio news. Carey was able to add questions about media use on and after September 11 to each of these studies. However, these measures provided only a partial picture about media use. So, he drew from other available studies conducted by the Pew Internet and American Life Project, the UCLA Center for Communication Policy and Mary Step and her colleagues, as well as published industry data about media traffic and usage patterns. Although not an elegant research design, it helped him capture and assemble much useful data for the analysis presented in his chapter.

Conclusion

The most exciting research is usually stimulated by the problems of the real world, as was the research reported in this book. Researchers seized the opportunity to investigate the events of September 11 from the perspective of their personal interests and past work.

TABLE I.1
Chronology: September 11, 2001

8:43 A.M.	The Federal Aviation Administration notifies military defense command that an airliner has been hijacked.
8:44 A.M.	After it became clear that American Airlines Flight 11 from Boston to Los Angeles had been hijacked and had turned south toward New York City, two F-15 jet fighters were scrambled from Otis Air Force Base on Cape Cod, Massachusetts.
8:45 A.M.	American Airlines Flight 11 out of Boston slams into the north tower of the World Trade Center, tearing a gaping hole in the building and setting it afire.
9:03 A.M.	A second hijacked airliner, United Airlines Flight 175 from Boston, executes a sharp turn and rams the south tower of the World Trade Center. A huge fireball engulfs the upper part of the building.
9:38 A.M.	Two F-16s are scrambled from Langley Air Force Base to intercept hijacked civilian airliners. Presidential orders to the combat jets: if necessary shoot to kill.
9:43 A.M.	American Airlines Flight 77 crashes into the Pentagon. A huge plume is visible for miles.
10:05 A.M.	The south tower of the World Trade Center (WTC 2) collapses, cascading down into the streets. A huge choking cloud begins billowing over the area.
10:10 A.M.	A portion of the Pentagon collapses.
10:10 A.M.	Hijacked United Airlines Flight 93 crashes in Somerset County, Pennsylvania, southeast of Pittsburgh.
10:28 A.M.	The World Trade Center's north tower (WTC 1) collapses top down, releasing a tremendous cloud of debris and smoke.
1:44 P.M.	Guided missile cruisers and aircraft carriers begin emergency departures from Hampton Roads naval bases in Virginia. They are to protect the East Coast from further attack and, by being at sea rather than moored, reduce their vulnerability.

Sources: www.cnn.com/2001/US/09/11/chronology.attack   www.latimes.com/news/nationworld/nation/
    la-091701shoot.story. http://news.bbc.co.uk/hi/english/world/americas/newsid_1620000/1620835.stm.
Note: This table was prepared by James E. Katz and is reproduced here with his permission. All times are
    EDT. Approximately 3,000 people died in the attacks, most at the World Trade Center. At the Pentagon 189
    died, including 64 on American Airlines Flight 77; 44 died on United Airlines Flight 93, which crashed
    outside Pittsburgh. Among those murdered at the World Trade Center were 343 New York City firefighters
    and 70 police officers.

Note

This introduction is an expanded version of the Preface to the Symposium on Communications on September 11, originally published in *Prometheus* 20, no. 3 (September
2002): 195–99.

1

The Functions and Uses of Media during the September 11 Crisis and Its Aftermath

John Carey

Media use during the September 11 crisis provides an opportunity to study the fundamental characteristics of media. The crisis demonstrated the widespread access to multiple media in modern society and the speed at which news can be conveyed, as contrasted with more limited access to media in earlier crises such as the Kennedy assassination.

John Carey describes how people used communications during and immediately after the tragedy, particularly television but also multiple sources of information. After learning about the crisis, Americans overwhelmingly turned to television for more information. However, people also used multiple sources of information. The web and e-mail appear to have played important but secondary roles (to television and the telephone). Carey concludes that media functioned well in meeting extraordinary demands for information and communication, although communication among emergency workers in New York City was more problematic.

A CRISIS, SUCH AS THE TERRORIST ATTACKS on September 11, provides a opportunity to examine fundamental tenets about the functions and use of media in people's lives. Which media do people turn to during a crisis? What capabilities do different media have to meet citizens' informational and emotional needs? This chapter focuses on end users of media: people who used television, radio, telephones, and other media immediately after the terrorist attack on September 11 and in the weeks following. The robustness of different media under circumstances of extraordinary demand are examined, along with the suitability of different media for the types of information and emotional support that people sought during the crisis. This examination can help inform us about the core functions of media in people's lives. In addition, some historical comparisons are drawn, for example, between the use of media on September 11 and after President Kennedy's assassination.

The analysis draws from surveys conducted by the Pew Internet and American Life Project, the UCLA Center for Communication Policy, and Mary Step and her colleagues,[1] as well as published industry data about media traffic and usage patterns. In addition, the author was in the field shortly after September 11 conducting three studies that are relevant to this analysis: a set of focus groups in New York and Los Angeles about TV usage patterns and expectations; an in-home ethnographic study of households with a new digital cable service that included e-mail (some of these households discussed their use of e-mail on September 11); and a telephone survey of satellite radio users who reported on their use of radio news after September 11.

Media Use and Communication Patterns on September 11

September 11 demonstrated the pervasive access to media in modern society and the resulting speed at which news can be conveyed. By one measure, one-third of citizens in the eastern time zone knew about the first plane crashing into One World Trade Center by 9:00 A.M. (the crash occurred at 8:46 A.M. eastern daylight time) and 90 percent knew by 10:30 A.M.[2] More than half of all Americans learned about the terrorist attacks from television, one in four learned about it from another person, one in six from radio, and only 1 percent from the Internet.[3] These patterns varied by time zones. On the East Coast, most people learned about the crash from another person but 22 percent learned about it from television.[4] This suggests that many people turn on television as they wake up and start their day (the first plane hit One World Trade Center at 6:46 Pacific time). Further, it suggests that television is present in many offices, schools, and public locations such as building lobbies and airports: many of those who learned about the crashes on the East Coast would have been at work or at school between 9:00 and 10:00 A.M.

After learning about the crisis, Americans overwhelmingly turned to television for more information: four out of five Americans turned to TV as their main source of information on September 11.[5] Television provided riveting video and sound throughout the day and in the days that followed. Many people reported being "mesmerized" by the television coverage and watched all day and into the night, dropping their everyday routines.[6] However, there are more nuances to the communication patterns on September 11 than to simply note that television was the primary source of news. People used multiple sources of information and often used more than one medium at the same time. In focus groups and in-home ethnographic research conducted by the author shortly after September 11, many people reported making telephone calls or writing e-mail while watching TV. They also watched TV in groups, more so than usual, and talked frequently to others while they were watching. Some people turned on multiple TV sets in the household, each tuned to a different channel so that they could view different perspectives on the crisis. The media composition of many U.S. households supports this form of intensive media consumption. Most households have more than one TV, and approximately one in four U.S. households have a personal computer in the same room with a TV.[7] In addition, people were aware that September 11 would be a constant topic of conversation with others and wanted to be up on the latest news so that they could participate actively in these conversations. In this sense, the crisis led to a close link between media content and interpersonal communication. Some people also reported a "surreal" quality to watching TV on September 11. They knew it was real, but it also had some visual qualities of a disaster movie and they felt awkward in trying to reconcile these two feelings.[8]

Television watching in the weeks after September 11 continued to involve heavy viewing of news programming, as reflected in the ratings for news channels and news programming.[9] However, in the author's research nearly everyone reported wanting regular entertainment programming to return to its normal schedule shortly after September 11. People sought relief and escape from the scary world of terrorist threats that they heard on the news every day. Situation comedies in particular were welcomed. Some predicted that entertainment programming would be impacted by September 11 for months or years, but this was not the case.[10] Apparently television networks and advertisers were more concerned than the public about potentially sensitive content. Television viewing increased for several days after September 11, with more news watching, but it then returned to normal levels of viewing. Entertainment program viewing was only slightly different in October 2002 compared to October 2001.[11] Attendance at movies actually increased in October compared to a year earlier. These patterns do not suggest that people forgot about the crisis quickly. Rather, they used entertainment to relieve the stress that lingered for months after September 11.

People did not turn to radio with the same intensive usage as TV on September 11 and in the next few days. However, this misses two very important ways people used radio: to stay in touch with the latest news while driving and to listen to music to enhance their mood. In a survey of those who listened to a new satellite radio service, people reported that they wanted to have access to news at all times, including while driving.[12] Radio served this function by providing mobile news access outside the home or office.[13] In addition, many of those surveyed indicated that they listened to many radio news channels, including the BBC World News, which was available on their satellite radios, because they provided a different perspective on events than U.S. radio news stations. These radio listeners also reported that radio music helped them relax and enhanced their mood in a time of national crisis. They wanted to stay in touch with what was happening but they also wanted periods of escape and relief from tension, which music provided.

In the weeks following September 11, overall listening to radio news was much higher than normal. National Public Radio reported a 20 percent increase in audience for its news programs during fall 2002 compared to a year earlier.[14] September 11 was a constant topic on radio talk shows, particularly ideological talk shows such as conservative talk show host Rush Limbaugh. This reflects another important function of radio in the United States as compared to television and mainstream newspapers. Radio provides a more direct voice and outlet for explicit political and ideological perspectives on events.[15]

What role did the web play in the mix of media that people employed? This was the first major national crisis in the United States in which the web was available to the public. In examining the use of the web and e-mail on and after September 11, we need to distinguish primary and secondary media sources. The web and e-mail appear to have played important but secondary roles (to television and the telephone) on September 11. In the Pew survey, only 6 percent of respondents characterized the web as their primary news source on September 11. On the day of the attacks, people went to web news sites in record numbers but had trouble, for a couple of hours, in accessing those sites.[16] Later in the morning, they were able to gain access. CNN.com had 11 million unique visitors on September 11, six times the normal number of visitors, and MSNBC.com had more than 9 million visitors, twice its normal traffic.[17] However, in the two months following the attack, visitors continued to access web news sites in numbers two to three times higher than normal.[18] In other words, the web persisted as a source of news about the crisis over time, as television's early advantage in showing video images of the World Trade Center and the Pentagon under attack faded somewhat. Over time, more than 50 million Americans used the web to gather information about the crisis.[19] In addition, much of the increased web volume came from outside the United States, as the international community of web users looked to U.S. news sources for information and perspectives about September 11 and its aftermath.

In addition to seeking news about the crisis, web users sent e-mail to friends and family members about the attack, participated in forums and chat rooms about terrorism, and exchanged instant messages in real time. On September 11, much of the e-mail was sent to check on the safety of friends and family members, to offer or request prayers, and to share emotions.[20] Forums and chat rooms were filled with highly charged expressions of anger and fear. There was also a great deal of international traffic, both e-mails to friends and family in the United States and expressions of sympathy in forums and chat rooms.[21]

Broadband web access has been suggested as an alternative to television for moving video images (i.e., video streaming). This did not materialize on September 11, possibly due in part to the low penetration of broadband web access into homes in September 2001. Approximately 9 million U.S. households had broadband access to the web in September 2001, compared to more than 100 million who had access to television.[22] In addition, video streams put a burden on the servers of news organizations, which were already strained by heavy traffic. Further, the quality of video over the broadband web in 2001 was much lower in quality (often in a thumbnail-size window on a monitor) than regular television video. In the weeks following, there was increased video streaming about the crisis to the desktops of office workers who had greater access to the broadband web (and less access to television) compared to people at home.[23] Overall, September 11 was not a turning point for web video.

Americans also went to government websites in record numbers on and after September 11. The Port Authority of New York and New Jersey had a 7,000 percent increase in traffic on September 11–12. The FBI, CIA, and NYC government websites, as well as the Federal Disaster Relief Agency, experienced much heavier volume.[24] In addition, the web was used extensively for charitable giving. Americans donated over $100 million online for disaster relief in the month following September 11.[25]

There were many reports that people used e-mail as a substitute for telephone calls when they experienced problems in making a telephone call. In the author's in-home ethnographic research several people reported this behavior. One woman told the following story:

> My friend worked in the World Trade Center. I couldn't reach her on her cell phone so I sent an e-mail to her two-way pager. I wrote, "Are you okay? Are you okay? I can't reach you on your cell phone." She answered, "I'm okay. I'll have to walk over the 59th Street bridge to get home, but I'm okay."

It was also reported that many people used e-mail as a substitute for printed greeting cards in the months following September 11, in response to fears about anthrax contamination in the postal system.[26] Presumably some people felt that their greeting cards might be accidentally contaminated by anthrax. Further, it was reported that e-mail greeting cards could more easily be customized to add a message about peace and safety in light of the terrorist attacks.[27]

Conventional telephones were used extensively on and after September 11 to check on the safety of friends and family members, express sympathy, and exchange opinions about the terrorist attacks. Approximately one-third of those who tried to make calls experienced some problems.[28] Many found ingenious ways to use alternate media or human networks to cope with limited access to telephone service. For example, some people in Manhattan who had limited telephone service called friends or relatives in another state and asked them to call friends and relatives informing them that their loved ones in Manhattan were safe.[29]

Cell phones, which like the Internet are a relatively new communication tool for the average person, played a crucial role on and after September 11. First, they provided mobile communication so that people could reach friends and family from locations outside the home and office. Second, they were used for dramatic contacts between office workers trapped in the World Trade Center and loved ones, in some cases to say good-bye, knowing that they would die. Cell phones were also used on the fourth hijacked plane that crashed in Pennsylvania. Passengers on the plane used cell phones and air-to-ground phones to reach friends, from whom they learned the fate of the other hijacked planes. With this information, they decided to fight the terrorists, losing their lives as the plane crashed but preventing a greater tragedy if the plane had gone to its intended target.

An account of communication patterns on and after September 11 must also consider the symbolic and artistic communications that occurred. After September 11, millions of Americans displayed flags on their homes or attached to the windows of cars. A person standing on the street of virtually any American city in the fall of 2001 saw a flag on half or more of the cars passing by. Others purchased and wore hats with emblems of the New York City police and fire departments. In New York City, hundreds of family members of those lost in the World Trade Center posted photographs of their missing loved ones on poles and buildings in Lower Manhattan. Later these communications were collected and displayed as art in New York's Grand Central Station, Union Station in Washington, D.C., and other public buildings. There were many other forms of artistic expression about the tragedy, such as concerts, poems, documentaries, photography exhibits, and plays. Many of these were used to raise money for the victims of September 11. They served as an emotional outlet for citizens and a creative expression about the larger meaning of September 11 for society.[30] In addition, September 11 left a legacy of new words and expressions. The term "9/11" was added to many dictionaries, while expressions such as "Ground Zero" and "let's roll" became part of the everyday lexicon.[31]

Media Availability during the Crisis

How robust were media in meeting the extraordinary demands placed on them? In general, they were remarkably robust under the circumstances, but the crisis also revealed in clear terms the relative strengths and limitations of different media. In New York, the terrorist attacks knocked eight television stations off the air. Thirty years earlier, when cable penetration was less than 10 percent of households, this would have blocked access to television for tens of millions of households. In fall 2001, however, relatively few people received television from over-the-air signals, so the impact was limited. Further, local cable systems received a direct line feed from the stations, so cable transmission of local stations was uninterrupted. In New York and throughout the United States, heavy television viewing put no strain on cable and satellite systems, which have a transmission architecture that can accommodate all subscribers at once. This is a distinct advantage of one-way transmission systems. Major satellite carriers that transmit television signals from mobile on-the-scene trucks to TV networks or from cable networks to local cable systems were able to meet significantly increased demand from television networks and government agencies. This related in part to excess capacity of satellite carriers in fall 2001: a number of events that would have used satellite capacity were cancelled, for example, major sporting events.[32]

Television broadcasters responded to the crisis by dropping regular content and shifting to all-news programming on September 11 and for three days following. Some channels with no news capacity carried news feeds from other channels. The season premiers of most shows and major television events scheduled for broadcast shortly after September 11, such as the Emmy Awards, were postponed. News channels such as CNN and Fox News carried nearly continuous coverage of the terrorist attacks and related events for weeks following September 11. In this way, the public had robust access to news programming on and after September 11.

September 11 was a major test of how well the web could handle massive traffic. Some had predicted that the web would melt until this strain but this was not the case. In the first couple of hours after the attack, primarily from 9:00 to 10:30, major news sites were overloaded and most people could not access them. However, they responded quickly by dropping photographs and graphics that put a strain on their servers under such heavy demand. They also added capacity where possible and borrowed servers from other groups in their organizations. For example, ABC.com borrowed server capacity from its sister website, ESPN.com, assuming correctly that fewer people would be accessing sports information on September 11.[33] The Internet itself handled massive traffic well on September 11. The problem was the strain placed on servers of news websites. The Internet also handled e-mail very well, allowing many people who could not get through on the telephone network to contact family and friends via e-mail.

Government websites also received heavy traffic on September 11. Some were not prepared to respond rapidly to the crisis. Firstgov (www.firstgov.gov), the official government portal, had no notices on day 1 about the terrorist attack or how to reach government agencies such as FEMA that had direct responsibility for providing assistance. By day 2, a number of government websites had responded. For example, Firstgov began to direct people to appropriate agencies for assistance, and the FBI created a tips site to seek leads from anyone who might have information about the attacks. The main problem on day 1 was that most government websites did not anticipate a need to place notices on their websites within minutes or hours of a major event such as the terrorist attacks. This ability to "publish" instantly is a feature on all news sites, but many government agencies did not foresee such a need. Further, many government buildings were closed on September 11 and the personnel who updated the site were locked out of the building. They had not anticipated a need to update the website remotely.

The web as a "network of networks" was able to reroute much traffic on September 11 and maintain relatively good service under extraordinary demand. However, there were some exceptions, which point to limitations in a network of networks. One of the advantages of the web is that components of a particular website (e.g., servers) can be located almost anywhere, as long as the components are connected to the web. On September 11, some Internet service providers (ISPs) in Germany, Italy, and Romania went down and were out of service for several days because key components of their service were physically located in Lower Manhattan and were destroyed in the attack.[34]

Radio shares the same general characteristic of television by transmitting its signal to a virtually unlimited number of receivers within its transmission range. Thus there was no strain on its system. Nearly all of the 12,000 radio stations in the United States responded to the crisis by shifting to all-news coverage on September 11. Many picked up feeds from other stations and retransmitted them, and most dropped commercials.[35] The telephone network held up remarkably well under the demands of September 11, even though some web proponents have tried to paint a bleaker picture, claiming incorrectly that most telephone and cell phone calls to New York were blocked for days.[36] On September 11, the telephone networks carried a record number of long-distance calls.[37] Even in New York City, where two major telephone central offices, ten cell towers, and 300,000 phone lines were destroyed, more than 100 million calls were placed successfully. When people could not get through, many used e-mail as a substitute. In Lower Manhattan, there were severe disruptions to both wired and cellular telephone service. Two-way pagers were reported to have worked well in Lower Manhattan on September 11.[38] Nonetheless, September 11 demonstrates the limits of two-way networked communications such as telephones. They have capacity limits that are strained in a crisis situation.

Damage to the telephone and cell phone networks in Lower Manhattan created significant problems for rescue workers on the scene. Interviews with emergency workers after September 11 revealed that they were often without any communication and had to rely on messengers to communicate among rescue units. This happened when many cell phone towers and radio repeaters were knocked out, and functioning two-way radios were stretched beyond their capacity as hundreds of rescue workers tried to communicate.[39] In addition, there were compatibility problems, as one group of emergency workers was using a system that could not communicate with another group.

Moss and Townsend in this volume discuss the scope of the technical problems and policy implications. They note the uses of available communications by rescue workers, along with some implications for the design of future emergency communication systems. A review of excerpts from transcripts of radio communications on September 11 and published interviews with emergency workers shows that some messages were requests for general information and updates that had been previously sent. This raises three questions. First, could some of this information be conveyed through a one-way communication system rather than two-way radios? Second, could some of the information be carried by a text service rather than voice? Third, could storage of some messages reduce the need for retransmission of the same content? Assessments of future requirements for emergency communications must give prominent consideration to issues such as capacity, compatibility, and resistance to disruption from fires or explosions. It may be useful to ask if some types of messages could be diverted to secure, one-way broadcast services received by any number of emergency workers; further, could text be a substitute for voice in conveying certain types of messages? Storage of voice and text messages might reduce some of the strain on emergency communication systems. Generally, the uses and functions of emergency communications should be assessed along with more technical issues.

Historical Comparisons

The characteristics of media and how they were used on September 11 invites historical comparisons. One issue is speed of communications. On September 11, news about the second plane hitting Two World Trade Center, which alerted news agencies that it was probably a terrorist attack, was conveyed around the world in minutes. In the United States, 90 percent of those on the East Coast knew about the attack less than two hours after it occurred; those in the Midwest and West learned about it as they woke up.[40] By comparison, news of Lincoln's assassination is estimated to have taken two months to travel around the world.[41] There is also a documented case of French and German citizens on a remote island in 1914 who lived together as friends for two weeks, not knowing that their respective countries had begun fighting each other in World War I.[42] By the time of President Kennedy's assassination, modern communications were in place and two-thirds of Americans learned about the shooting within thirty minutes.[43] This spread faster than news of September 11. However, the Kennedy assassination occurred in the middle of the day, when people on both coasts were awake.

September 11 may also be used to explore the issue of accuracy among eyewitnesses to events versus those who receive a mediated report about those events. Much scholarship has focused on the distortions that can be introduced in news coverage through selective attention to some details at a scene or the expectations of reporters and how this can lead them to see what they expect to see. Kurt and Gladys Lang authored a famous study about TV coverage of a 1951 parade with General MacArthur in Chicago. It found that eyewitness accounts differed sharply from media coverage of the events and concluded that the media selectively reported on events at the scene to communicate what they expected to happen rather than what actually happened.[44] Witnesses on the scene were judged to have a more accurate picture of what happened. This perspective has been echoed in much research since then. My interviews with people who were in Lower Manhattan on September 11 suggest that people on the scene—who did not have access to media—had a distorted view of what was happening. They commented that rumors were rampant in Lower Manhattan and they thought that several other locations in the United States had been attacked. In addition, interviews with emergency workers and people who were in the World Trade Center months after September 11 found that there was a great deal of misinformation at the scene and a general lack of understanding about what was going on.[45] While the media are subject to many of the limitations described in the research literature, it is not clear that people at the scene of a chaotic event like the attacks on the World Trade Center and the Pentagon have a better picture of "reality."

The function and use of media following the assassination of President Kennedy were thoroughly researched and provide the most useful comparisons with September 11. There were many similarities between the two events. In both cases, information about the event spread very rapidly. On learning about the event, people relied overwhelmingly on television (in the case of President Kennedy's assassination, radio was also used extensively as a source of news on the day of the shooting). Further, people in 1963 and 2001 reported that they were "mesmerized" by the tragedy and compulsively followed news coverage for days.[46] This was supported by increased news coverage. The major TV networks abandoned regular programming for a few days following both events (four days in 1963; three days in 2001).[47] Important symbols emerged that lasted for decades in the case of President Kennedy's assassination (e.g., pictures of the flag-draped coffin, the open-top limousine in Dallas, and a young widow and her children at the funeral) and are likely to endure for decades in the case of September 11 (e.g., pictures of the Twin Towers with smoke billowing out, firemen raising a flag at Ground Zero and rescue workers covered in soot). From a communication perspective, there was a sharp increase in the flow of information both in 1963 and 2001. There was not just more use of television, but more word-of-mouth communications, more telephone calls, and more use of media generally.[48]

The major difference between 1963 and 2001 was the greater access to a wider range of media by people on September 11 and the availability of round-the-clock news coverage on all-news cable channels for weeks following the attacks on the World Trade Center and the Pentagon. In 1963 there were three broadcast networks, no satellite service, 5 percent penetration of cable in households, five to seven channels available in an average market, one TV per household and no remotes, no cell phones, no computers or e-mail, and, typically, one telephone and one telephone line per household. Further, few offices or schools had a TV (radios were available in many offices and schools). In addition, long-distance telephone costs were significantly higher in 1963, inhibiting high-volume calling patterns to friends and family around the country. By contrast, most people in 2001 had access to eighty or more television channels, e-mail, cell phones, multiple telephones in the household (and lower costs for long distance), and multiple TVs. All of these media were used in high volumes to gain access to a wider range of information sources and communicate with a wider network of people over a longer period of time following the attacks. It remained an intensive event for a longer period of time because of greater media coverage and availability, and, in part, because there was a continuing threat. While there were some rumors about a plot surrounding the Kennedy assassination and the potential for more violence, these rumors dissipated quickly for most citizens. In 2001, however, fears about additional attacks continued over many months.

Discussion

The September 11 attack provides a useful case study for the reexamination of fundamental media characteristics such as one-to-many broadcast (e.g., TV and radio) versus one-to-one communication (e.g., telephone and e-mail), and the communication effects of bandwidth. One-to-many communication systems can handle a virtually unlimited number of users, so they have significant value in a crisis situation when everyone wants access to information. One-to-one communications systems can be strained under high demand. However, they have an important advantage of being interactive and providing personalized communication that supports emotional as well as informational needs in a time of crisis.

One-to-many communication systems are often criticized in the communication research literature as giving too much power to those who control the centralized delivery of information.[49] However, this widely accepted critique may need to be reexamined in light of multichannel cable and satellite services with many different news providers, the wide availability of information sources through other media including the web, increased access to two-way media such as e-mail and cell phones, and in light of the efficiency provided by one-to-many communication systems under conditions of great demand for news.

Television, as a high bandwidth medium, can show vivid moving pictures and sound, which are extremely powerful in the moments and hours immediately after a crisis. Text-based media have less bandwidth but are well suited for reflective analysis of events in the weeks following a crisis. The web is a hybrid medium whose bandwidth varies based on access speeds. On September 11, the web provided a vital complement to the voice telephone network, through e-mail. In the days and weeks following, the web allowed people to exchange views with others through forums and get extensive information about the crisis. The web also emerged as an important archival source of news stories and analysis—available for weeks or months following September 11.[50]

Other media supported people's information and communication needs in different ways: radio provided mobile access to news and mood enhancement through music; cell phones allowed people to stay in touch with friends and relatives while away from home or office; and text-based media such as newspapers and news magazines provided longer form articles with more in-depth information for reflective analysis. In this sense, no single medium meets all of the informational, social, and emotional needs of citizens during a crisis. The media mix on and after September 11 was complementary and in some cases redundant—with one medium filling in when another was unavailable. Redundancy is a characteristic of communication systems that is valued by engineers. It deserves more attention by social scientists and policy makers who are concerned about public access to information and communication in times of a crisis.

An analysis of media use during the September 11 crisis also presents a different perspective from much communication scholarship about the functions and effects of media. Communication scholarship often emphasizes the harmful effects of media, for example, the effects of television violence on children, privacy threats on the web, and telemarketing scams on the telephone network. These are important social issues. Yet there are other pieces to a more comprehensive picture of media in society. Media use and performance on September 11 can fill in some of these pieces. Overall, the media performed well in rapidly informing the public about the terrorist attacks and in continuing to provide information in the days and weeks that followed. Media also met extraordinary demand as hundreds of millions of people worldwide sought information and wanted to communicate with others. In addition, media served important entertainment functions in the weeks following September 11, providing relief from the scary real world of terrorist attacks.

In order to develop a more open perspective about media use and effects, one that can measure positive as well as negative effects and tell us, simply, how media work in society, it may be time to bring back an earlier school of communication research—functional analysis. This approach to media analysis has a long history rooted in the work of Lazarsfeld, Katz, Mendelson, Wright, McQuail, and more recently Kubey and Csikszentmihalyi.[51] It seeks to uncover the functions of media in people's lives and can find positive values in entertainment and relief from the tensions of the everyday world as well as subtle but important functions of media such as keeping people company.

The September 11 crisis also demonstrated the need to understand the interrelationships among media: research may not capture a complete picture of the functions of a medium if it is studied in isolation from other media. Studying the use of television alone on September 11, without understanding the complementary roles of the web and telephones, for example, may miss a larger and more comprehensive picture of what occurred.

The web and cell phones are two relatively new media available to the public during a time of crisis. Each served important roles on and after September 11 and a number of lessons emerged for the future, for example, news websites need to have backup server capacity and may need to strip data-intensive information such as photographs from a site under circumstances of intense demand. The web also brought forward some new problems. One of its great strengths is the dissemination—for all people who want access—of information that previously was too difficult or costly to publish. However, dissemination "for all" includes terrorists. After September 11, a number of U.S. government agencies withdrew information from their websites that might serve terrorism, for example, the Department of Transportation stopped disseminating maps of oil and gas pipelines on its website. How do we balance the need for security with the value of providing broad public access to government data? There is no easy answer.

A second problem associated with the web is its ability to quickly and efficiently spread rumors and false information. There were many examples of malicious rumors and benign but false information spread over the Web. In one case, a Middle Eastern restaurant in Michigan was severely damaged economically by a false rumor that the employees had celebrated when they heard the news about the terrorist attack on the World Trade Center.[52] A less malicious but nonetheless deceptive example was a doctored photograph spread widely on the web that purported to show a tourist standing on the observation deck of the World Trade Center, with a plane in the background about to crash into the building.[53] The roles of cell phones and the web are likely to evolve over time. History demonstrates that we rarely understand the functions and utility of a new medium when it is first introduced. Radio provides a useful historical example. In 1923, shortly after radio was introduced, President Harding died. Many radio stations responded by going off the air—as a mark of respect. A year later, former President Wilson died. This time, there was widespread and continuous radio coverage of the event, including a live broadcast of his funeral.[54] Radio was beginning to learn its role.

Notes

An earlier version of this chapter was originally published as John Carey, "Media Use During a Crisis" in *Prometheus* 20, no. 3 (2002): 201–7.

1. Mary Step, Margaret Finucane, and Cary Horvath, "Emotional Involvement with Media on September 11" (paper submitted to the National Communication Association, February 2002).

2. Step, Finucane, and Horvath, "Emotional Involvement," 12.

3. UCLA Internet Project, press release, February 2002, 2.

4. Step, Finucane, and Horvath, "Emotional Involvement," 12.

5. Pew Internet and American Life Project, "The Commons of the Tragedy," October 2002, 10.

6. Step, Finucane, and Horvath, "Emotional Involvement," 13.

7. Mary Step, Margaret Finucane, and Cary Horvath, *Many Surf and Watch TV at the Same Time* (Westfield, N.J.: Statistical Research, 2002), 2.

8. These comments were made by several participants in focus groups conducted by the author with twenty-four people in New York and twenty-five people in Los Angeles during the week of October 1, 2001.

9. Steven Behrens, "Hunger for News after September 11 Cuts PBS Ratings," *Current*, January 28, 2002, 1.

10. Andy Seiler, "Sea-change in Entertainment?" *USA Today*, December 28, 2001, 9D.

11. Seiler, "Sea-change."

12. The survey was conducted in November and involved one hundred early subscribers to a satellite radio service.

13. For additional commentary about the role of radio in people's lives, see "Radio: The Forgotten Medium," *Media Studies Journal*, Summer 1993, xi–xix.

14. Mike Janssen, "NPR Lands Most Listeners Ever," *Current*, March 25, 2002, 1.

15. Tom Lewes, "Triumph of the Idol: Rush Limbaugh and a Hot Medium," *Media Studies Journal*, Summer 1999, 51–62.

16. Stephen Porter, "Web News Comes of Age," *Video Systems*, January 2002, 40.

17. *Wall Street Journal*, September 24, 2001, R4.

18. Porter, "Web News," 40.

19. Pew Internet and American Life Project, "Commons of the Tragedy," 2.

20. Pew Internet and American Life Project, "How Americans Used the Internet after the Terror Attack," September 15, 2001, 2–3.

21. UCLA Internet Project, press release, 2.

22. Peter Grant and Bruce Orwall, "After Internet's Big Bust, Broadband Shift Went On," *Wall Street Journal Online*, January 8, 2003, 1. www.wsj.com/2003/01/08.html.

23. Melinda Grenier, "Record Number of Office Workers Use Web Broadcasts Last Month," *Wall Street Journal*, October 15, 2001, B8.

24. Pew Internet and American Life Project, "Commons of the Tragedy," 8.

25. Pew Internet and American Life Project, "A Month of Giving," *Wall Street Journal*, October 29, 2001, R4.

26. Thomas Weber, "Anthrax-Laced Letters Boost E-Mail's Allure, but Paper Isn't Dead," *Wall Street Journal*, October 29, 2001, B1.

27. James Barron, "Re: Season's Greetings (Smiley Face Optional)," *New York Times*, December 20, 2001, G1.

28. Pew Internet and American Life Project, "Commons of the Tragedy," 10.

29. Virginia Fields, keynote speech, *Focus on September 11: Lessons in Communication Conference*, New York Law School, October 26, 2002.

30. Anne Midgette, "Responding to Crisis, Art Must Look Beyond It," *New York Times*, March 3, 2002, 2-1.

31. Janny Scott, "Words of 9/11 Go from Coffee Shop to the Dictionaries," *New York Times*, February 24, 2002, A1.

32. Janny Scott, "U.S. Satellite Operators Provide Capacity to Cover Terrorist Attacks," *Satellite Broadband*, December 2001, 38–39.

33. Ken Kerschbaumer, "Internet Slowed but Unbowed," *Broadcasting and Cable*, September 17, 2001, 1.

34. Andy Sullivan, "Internet Performed Well during Sept 11 Attacks: Report," *Reuters Wire Service*, November 20, 2002.

35. Allison Romano, "Radio News: E Pluribus Unum," *Broadcasting and Cable*, September 17, 2001.

36. See Tom Halligan, "Put to the Test," *Internet World*, November 2001, 4.

37. Randy Hayes, "Aftermath of Terrorist Attacks Display Strengths As Well As Vulnerabilities of Telecom/IT Networks," Iowa Telecom User Group, Fall 2001.

38. Brian Fonseca, "A Matter of Minutes," *InfoWorld*, April 1, 2002, 43.

39. Kevin Flyn, "A Focus On Communication Failures," *New York Times*, January 30, 2002, A11.

40. Mary Step et al., *Many Surf and Watch TV*, 12.

41. Tony Schwartz, *The Responsive Chord* (New York: Anchor/Doubleday, 1973), 42.

42. Walter Lippman, *Public Opinion* (New York: Macmillan, 1922).

43. Wilbur Schramm, "Communication in Crisis," in *The Process and Effects of Mass Communication*, ed. Wilbur Schramm and Donald Roberts (Urbana: University of Illinois Press, 1972), 541.

44. Kurt Lang and Gladys Engel Lang, "The Unique Perspective of Television and Its Effect: A Pilot Study," *American Sociological Review* 18 (1953): 3–12.

45. Jim Dwyer, "Accounts from the South Tower," *New York Times on the Web*, May 26, 2002, 1–56. www.nytimes.com/2002/05/26.html.

46. Schramm, "Communication," 551.

47. Wilbur Schramm, "Broadcasting at 50," *Broadcasting*, November 2, 1970, 144.

48. Schramm, "Communication," 530.

49. Denis McQuail, "Mass Communication Research," in *International Encyclopedia of Communication*, ed. Erik Barnouw (New York: Oxford University Press, 1986), 490.

50. Thomas Weber, "Archivists Save Record of Internet's Response to the September 11 Attacks," *Wall Street Journal*, March 11, 2002, B1.

51. Robert Kubey and Mihaly Csikszentmihalyi, *Television and the Quality of Life: How Viewing Shapes Everyday Experience* (Hillsdale, N.J.: Erlbaum, 1990).

52. Jeffrey Zaslow, "How a Rumor Spread by E-Mail Laid Low an Arab's Restaurant," *Wall Street Journal*, March 13, 2002, A1.

53. See www.snopes2.com/rumors/crash/htm.

54. Erik Barnouw, *A Tower in Babel: A History of Broadcasting in the U.S. to 1933* (New York: Oxford University Press, 1966), 146–48.

2

Diffusion of News of the
September 11 Terrorist Attacks

Everett M. Rogers

My stepfather was in the World Trade Center and my uncle was in the Pentagon.

Makes me realize that airport security was a farce.

Oh my God, we are in war!

—Statements made by respondents in our
September 2001 survey in New Mexico.

Everett Rogers describes the diffusion study that he conducted, with Nancy Seidel, of how people in New Mexico first heard about the tragedy and what they immediately did. He also brings together the main findings from various studies of the diffusion of news of the terrorist attacks on the World Trade Center in New York and the Pentagon in Washington, D.C.

Rogers reports that this news event was perceived by the public as highly salient, and the news spread very quickly, with almost all of the adult public hearing within two or three hours. Television was the dominant mass media channel for conveying initial awareness of the terrorist attacks, with interpersonal channels also of considerable importance. In comparison, the Internet and telephones (including cell phones) played much less important roles in diffusion of this news event. Individuals, once informed of the terrorist attacks, gained further information particularly from television. They reacted to the attacks in highly emotional ways, with many people praying or attending a memorial service, contributing money, and donating blood. A strong sense of patriotism was displayed in the aftermath of the attacks.

THE TERRORIST ATTACKS on New York and Washington, D.C., much more than the news events studied in some sixty past studies of news event diffusion, affected audience members emotionally. The terrorist attacks on September 11, 2001, were intended to create terror. My New Mexico survey, along with other research summarized here, suggests that the terrorists were quite successful. The terrorist attacks also brought forth a high degree of American patriotism, with people displaying flags in their homes, at workplaces, and on their vehicles. Once Americans were aware of the terrorist attacks, they were motivated to pray for the victims, give blood, donate funds, and take other actions. The purpose of the present chapter is to synthesize what was learned from several studies of the diffusion of news of the September 11 terrorist attacks.

The September 11 news event was the first to be studied in which cellular telephones and the Internet were widely available to the public (some two-thirds of the adult U.S. public had Internet access at the time, and approximately 50 percent had cell phones). A system overload of telephone calls and the Internet occurred in the early hours after the terrorist attacks on September 11. Cell phones were used to call people in their cars with news of the terrorist attacks, but the data reviewed in the present chapter show that neither telephone calls nor the Internet were particularly important as a channel of communication in diffusing the news event of study.

The September 11 attacks represent a spectacular news event that the public perceived as highly salient, and that diffused rapidly. The mass media devoted hours of news coverage each day, yet most of the public did not become tired of the news, in part because yet newer events continued to occur, such as the bombing of Afghanistan, the threat of anthrax, videotaped speeches by Osama bin Laden, and the landing of U.S. military forces in Afghanistan. Thus the basic news story was of a continuing nature and received very heavy media coverage for months after September 11.

The News Event Diffusion Study in New Mexico

Two days after September 11, 2001, with the assistance of thirty-five communications students at the University of New Mexico, my colleague Nancy Seidel and I began conducting a survey of the diffusion of this news event. Each interviewer contacted three or four people in Albuquerque, using a prepared questionnaire. A total of 127 respondents were interviewed in the following ten days. Although the sample is nonrandom, the interviewers contacted a wide variety of people: respondents include thirty-seven students, seventy-six employed people, three unemployed, three retired people, and eight others. Some seventy-three individuals (57 percent) were male, and fifty-four (43 percent) were female. The average age was twenty-nine years, and the respondents averaged fourteen years of education. The survey participants were fairly characteristic of the adult population of Albuquerque, with the exception of the overrepresentation of university students.

Diffusion is the process through which an innovation is communicated through certain channels over time among the members of a social system (Rogers 2003). An innovation is an idea, practice, or object perceived as new by an individual or other unit of adoption (Rogers 2003). In the present study, the innovation of study is a news event, defined as a newsworthy topic that attracts widespread public attention (Rogers 2000).

Past diffusion research suggests five stages in the innovation-decision process: (1) knowledge, (2) persuasion, (3) decision, (4) implementation, and (5) confirmation (Rogers 2003). "Individuals usually only gain awareness-knowledge of a news event, thus the main dependent variable of study in most news event diffusion studies corresponds only to the knowledge stage" (Rogers 2000, 569). The present news event diffusion study included questions about not only the respondents' sources/channels of awareness-knowledge about the terrorist attacks, but also the sources/channels from which they obtained further information, and also questions about what the respondents first heard, how the news event affected them, and what actions they took in response.

The first news about the terrorist attacks reached Albuquerque at 6:45 A.M., due to a two-hour difference in time zones from the East Coast location of the attacks. The sequence of the September 11 attacks is summarized in table 2.1.

The Rapid Diffusion of News of the Terrorist Attacks

The rate of diffusion is the cumulative percentage of individuals to whom the news event spreads over time. As in past news event diffusion research, the rate of diffusion of news of the September 11 terrorist attacks formed an S-shaped curve (figure 2.1). By noon on Tuesday, September 11 , more than 99 percent of our 127 respondents were aware of the news event, and most were aware of the news event by 9:30 A.M. (Albuquerque time), less than three hours after the first plane crashed into the north tower of the World Trade Center in New York.[1]

The first terrorist attacks on the World Trade Center occurred at 6:45 A.M. (Albuquerque time). The proportion of our 127 respondents knowing of the terrorist attacks increased from 6:00 and 7:00 A.M. to 7 percent. Cumulative diffusion reached 34 percent between 7:00 and 8:00 A.M., which expanded to 70 percent between 8:00 and 9:00 A.M., and then jumped to 92 percent between 9:00 and 10:00 A.M. By noon, 99 percent—120 of the 121 respondents (6 of the 127 did not answer this question)—knew about the news event that Tuesday.

TABLE 2.1
Timeline for the Sequence of the Terrorist Attacks on September 11, 2001

Time (EST)	Events
7:58 A.M.	United Airlines Flight 175, a Boeing 767, takes off from Boston for Los Angeles with 65 passengers on board.
7:59 A.M.	American Airlines Flight 11, a Boeing 767, takes off from Boston for Los Angeles with 92 passengers on board.
8.01 A.M.	United Airlines Flight 93, a Boeing 757, leaves the gate at Newark Airport for San Francisco with 37 passengers on board, but its takeoff is delayed for 30 minutes.
8:10 A.M.	American Airlines Flight 77 takes off from Washington Dulles International Airport for Los Angeles with 64 passengers on board.
8:45 A.M.	AA Flight 11 slams into the north tower of the World Trade Center in New York.
9:06 A.M.	UA Flight 175 slices through the south tower of the World Trade Center; this event is broadcast live by U.S. television networks.
9:35 A.M.	Bridges and tunnels are shut down in New York. The Empire State Building and the Metropolitan Museum of Art are evacuated. New York and Washington airports are closed. The FAA (Federal Aeronautics Administration) orders all commercial planes over the United States to land at the nearest airport.
9:40 A.M.	AA Flight 77 hits the west side of the Pentagon, Washington, D.C., where high-ranking military offices were located.
10:00 A.M.	The south tower collapses, trapping hundreds of rescue workers below, addition to thousands of workers in the building; debris guts the fourth World Trade Center building below.
10:29 A.M.	The north tower collapses.
10:37 A.M.	UA Flight 93 crashes, presumably after its passengers gained control of the plane, in Shanksville, Pennsylvania, 80 miles southeast of Pittsburgh.

The relatively rapid diffusion of this news event was due to its high salience to our respondents, and to its complete dominance of news coverage by the broadcasting media.

The relatively slow diffusion curve in its initial stages may be due to the early hour at which this event occurred (Albuquerque time). Some 6 percent of our respondents woke up to news of the terrorist attack, and 26 percent heard of it approximately forty-five minutes after it occurred. Many respondents were at home, "where the likelihood of being told about the news story by others, and of telling someone else, is more restricted than for individuals who are in a work setting" (Rogers 2000, 568–69). The first individuals to hear about the terrorist attacks were mainly at home, and so the news event spread slowly at first despite its high salience. At this point, calls on cell phones played their most important role, especially to and from people riding in vehicles.

After a slow early growth, the diffusion curve took off around 7:00 A.M. People wanted to share information about the terrorist attacks, and person-to-person communication played a major role in the news event's diffusion. The news

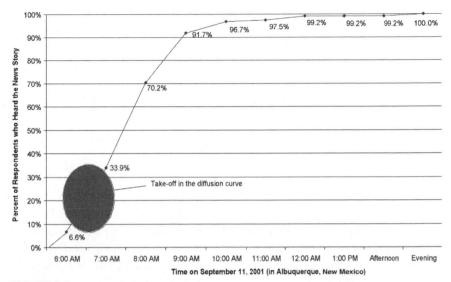

FIGURE 2.1
Time of Day When Respondents First Heard of the Terrorist Attacks on September 11

and pictures were so shocking that people felt they had to share the news, and their feelings, with others. This motivation—to tell others (even complete strangers in some cases) and to discuss the news event with others—was stimulated by the uncertainty resulting from the crisis. Uncertainty is the degree to which a number of alternatives are perceived with respect to the occurrence of an event and the relative probability of these alternatives. The terrorist attacks led individuals to seek further information about the severity of the event (How many people were killed?), who was responsible (Was it bin Laden?), the safety of airline travel, and so forth. Information is a difference in matter-energy that affects uncertainty in a situation where a choice exists among a set of alternatives.

The rapid diffusion of news of the terrorist attacks among the New Mexico respondents was also reflected in the several other studies of the diffusion of this news. Whether the respondents were adults in the United States or in Germany, and whether the respondents were college students or adults, news of the terrorist attacks spread very quickly, in large part due to its relatively high perceived salience. Salience is defined as the degree to which a news event is perceived as important by an individual or individuals (Rogers 2000). For example, 73 percent of Hoffner and colleagues' (2002) East Coast college students knew of the event within one hour of its occurrence, and 70 percent of Emmer and colleagues' (2002) 1,460 German adults knew of the terrorist attacks within one hour (the attacks occurred in midafternoon, German time). Almost complete diffusion of this news event was achieved relatively rapidly, within three hours in New Mexico (Rogers and Seidel 2002), and within two hours for 314 Michigan adults (Greenberg et al. 2002).

The local time of day when the terrorist attacks occurred (8:45 A.M. eastern standard time in New York and Washington) was an important factor in the relative speed of diffusion. In Albuquerque, New Mexico, this event occurred at 6:45 A.M., a time when many people were still asleep or were awakening and traveling to work (Rogers and Seidel 2002). In Germany, the first terrorist attack was at 2:45 P.M., when most people were at work or at home.

Channels of Communication

Tuesday is a weekday, so many people went to work or school on the day of the terrorist attacks. Mayer and others (1990, 114) stated that "people tend to hear of the occurrence of a major news event from another person when the event takes place during a weekday, but from the media when the event takes place on a weekend." Table 2.2 shows that television (32 percent) and radio (27 percent) played a major role in how people first heard about the September 11 news event in Albuquerque, New Mexico. Broadcasting channels are able to respond quickly to a fast-breaking news story (Rogers 2000, 564). Television was the most frequently named communication channel in four of the seven studies summarized in table 2.2. Interpersonal channels were most frequently named in three of the seven studies.

Person-to-person communication (26 percent) and telephone (14 percent) were important in diffusing news of the terrorist attacks in New Mexico. Newspapers were reported by none of the Albuquerque respondents as a source/channel for first hearing about the news event, perhaps because the September 11 morning editions were already distributed before the terrorist attacks occurred. The *Albuquerque Tribune,* the city's afternoon newspaper, was the first to publish the news locally at 10:00 A.M. By that time, 97 percent of the New Mexico respondents already knew about the terrorist attacks.

Many Americans turn on their television set when they wake up to obtain the latest news. Radio (27 percent) was frequently named as a source/channel in New Mexico because many people woke up to a radio alarm clock or were in their cars on the way to work when they heard the news. The relatively high frequency of person-to-person communication (26 percent) indicates the news event was so salient that people told complete strangers about it, as well as their family members, friends, and work associates. Basil and Brown (1994, 316) stated, "When a story is personally relevant to people, a person is more likely to pass the news on to others." Mayer and others (1990, 114) pointed out that "news of an important event quickly diffuses throughout the populace by word-of-mouth, while people discover the occurrence of a less important event through the media."

TABLE 2.2
Communication Channels for First Hearing about the September 11 Terrorist Attacks

Research Study/Sample	Television (%)	Interpersonal Channels (%)	Radio (%)	Telephone (%)	Other or No Answer (%)	Totals (%)
1. Brown et al. (2002): 734 Internet respondents	24	54	20	0	2	100
2. Emmer et al. (2002): 1,460 German adults	46	23	29	0	2	100
3. Greenberg et al. (2002): 314 U.S. adults	33	50	15	0	2	100
4. Jones and Rainee (2002): 2,039 U.S. adults	44	16	22	15	3	100
5. Rogers and Seidel (2002): 127 adults	32	26	27	14	2	101
6. Ruggiero and Glascock (2002): 320 students	28	33	24	15	1	101
7. Cohen et al. (2002): 190 adults	40	34	20	0	6	100
Totals	34	33	22	6	5	100

Table 2.2 shows that the telephone also played an important role in diffusing news of the terrorist attacks in New Mexico and at two of the other six study locations. Some 14–15 percent of the respondents mentioned the telephone as their source/channel for first hearing of the news event. However, the percentage of audience members reporting telephones (including cell phones) as their first source/channel about the September 11 news event (14 percent) is not as high as in the Indian study (25 percent) by Singhal and others (1999). The Internet played only a minor role in providing news about the terrorist attacks, 1–2 percent or less, depending on the study (see table 2.2). Some respondents reported that they resorted to e-mail when they could not reach a person by telephone. Soon after the terrorist attacks occurred, news websites were flooded by information seekers.

Which source/channel provided the most accurate news? Television and radio broadcast almost every item of information they obtained during the first hour or two of the terrorist attacks, even information coming via telephone calls from members of the public. As a result, certain information was broadcast that later proved to be incorrect. This bogus information was then passed along to others by interpersonal channels and by telephone. People who learned of the news event from interpersonal channels often sought additional information via the mass media, especially television.

We asked our New Mexico respondents what they first heard about the terrorist attacks of September 11, 2001. People stated: "A small plane hit one of the World Trade Towers." "The World Trade Center and the Pentagon have been dive-bombed." "A bomb went off in New York's World Trade Center." "We are under attack; it was the Palestinians." "The Pentagon blew up." These responses indicate that incorrect information about the news event diffused. Most of our New Mexico survey respondents knew that the World Trade Towers had been hit (68 percent), but fewer mentioned the Pentagon (16 percent). In other words, the basic information about the terrorist attacks got through to the public.

Most New Mexico respondents recalled where they were when they first heard about the September 11 news event. Some 68 percent of the respondents were at home. Many students and other younger people were at home and were told by their family members about the terrorist attacks. Nearly 13 percent of the respondents were at work or at a university; 12 percent were in their car, where they possibly heard the news on their radio or received a call on their cell phone.

Some 116 of the 127 New Mexico respondents (91 percent), after first hearing of the terrorist attacks on September 11, searched for further information. Television played the major role in providing further information, increasing from first hearing (32 percent) to further information (52 percent). The terrorist attacks were visually powerful, and the television networks broadcast images of the burning World Trade Towers, Ground Zero, and the Pentagon. Coverage of the terrorist attacks filled television broadcasts all day on September 11 and dominated television news thereafter.

Interpersonal Network Diffusion

Few previous news diffusion studies asked questions about interpersonal network diffusion. Singhal and others (1999) studied the important role of interpersonal diffusion networks for a highly salient news event in India. A network comprises the communication links that connect people through a process of information exchange.

The news diffusion process is shaped by each individual's interpersonal communication network, and "how the previous person in the diffusion chain judges the news" (Basil and Brown 1994, 316). When people in a network think that the news is not very salient, the interpersonal diffusion process can slow or stop.

Some 88 of the 127 New Mexico respondents (69 percent) told someone else about the terrorist attacks. These 88 people reached, in total, 418 other people, an average of 4.8 people. Some 80 percent of the 88 respondents told between one to four people; two respondents reported that they each informed over 50 people about the terrorist attacks! Some 41 respondents informed 87 other people by telephone, an average of 2.1 people. As already explained, the rate of news diffusion took off in New Mexico shortly after 7:00 A.M. when enough individuals knew about the terrorist attacks and began spreading this news to others.

Time of Hearing by Communication Channel and Location

The diffusion of a news event depends on (1) situational factors, such as being at home or at work, (2) salience, how important the news is to the respondent, and (3) time, such as the time of day or the day of the week when the news event happened (Rogers 2000, 572).

Mayer and others (1990, 114) proposed that "the length of time between the event's occurrence and discovery of the event is correlated with how people hear of the event." These scholars found that the early half of the people who obtained information about a news event did so mainly through the mass media, while many of those who heard about a news event later were informed through interpersonal channels. For the sample of New Mexico respondents, the average time of first hearing about the terrorist attacks from mass media channels was 8:38 A.M., while that for first hearing from interpersonal channels was 10:03 A.M., about an hour and a half later. Mayer and others (1990) found important differences in the time at which people first heard of the 1986 *Challenger* disaster on the basis of whether they were at home or at work. Mayer and others (1990, 114) argued that "people at work tend to discover the occurrence of a major event from another person, while those who are at home or elsewhere discover the occurrence of the event from the media." However, we found no relationship between the location of the New Mexico respondents (at work or at home) and the role of interpersonal channels versus mass media channels in first hearing of the terrorist attacks. Perhaps this news event was so salient that its diffusion swamped the usual differences in channels by location at work or home.

Effects of the News

Of the 127 New Mexico respondents, 75 people (59 percent) said they were personally affected by the terrorist attacks of September 11, 2001. Our respondents made the following statements:

"I am depressed, sad, upset and angry."
"I now live in a country that is going to war."
"I no longer want to move to New York."
"Reaffirmed my patriotism."
"My grandson is in the service and on full alert."
"I am in the military and ready to fly."
"My uncle almost died, but he was late to work."

Some respondents knew someone who was flying on September 11 or was in New York or Washington (13 percent). Many respondents said that they became more conscious of life, and more thankful that they still had their loved ones. Other respondents reported they felt less safe (19 percent) or said that the terrorist attacks were an attack on the freedom of the United States (5 percent), the first step to a never ending uncertainty in everyday life. An increase in patriotism (reported by 6 percent) occurred as many felt the terrorist attacks were directed at all American people. Many New Mexico respondents were depressed, scared, nervous, and said they could not sleep (37 percent). A few expressed anger against people of the Muslim religion. One respondent stated that "this terrorist attack puts a lot of things in perspective."

Parallel evidence of the emotional impacts of this news event is provided by other studies. For example, 44 percent of 314 Michigan adults reported that they cried during the first day or two after the terrorist attacks, and one-third worried about flying on commercial aircraft (Greenberg et al. 2002). The proportion of respondents saying they had trouble sleeping ranged from 6 percent to 62 percent in various surveys, and the percentage of adults experiencing nightmares about September 11 ranged from 8 percent to 18 percent (Snyder and Park 2002).

Respondents' reactions are somewhat comparable to those of the public after Princess Diana's death in 1997; Rogers (2000, 568) stated that there was a "widespread outpouring of grief" and explained it as due to parasocial interaction, defined as the degree to which audience individuals perceive that they have a personal relationship with a media personality. Millions of people attended a memorial service for Princess Diana, viewed her funeral on television, or brought flowers or candles to Buckingham Palace.

Among our Albuquerque respondents we observed a high degree of patriotism. Many felt closely connected to the people who died in the World Trade Towers and the Pentagon. They perceived a parasocial relationship with the victims. Respondents stated: "Because I'm a U.S. citizen" and "I'm an American."

Some 86 percent of the 127 New Mexico respondents took action as a result of the terrorist attacks. Some 67 percent said that they prayed for the victims. Some 21 percent participated in memorial events,[2] 16 percent contributed money, and 8 percent contributed blood. Some 37 percent of the respondents displayed a U.S. flag on their home or vehicle. Similar actions were reported by respondents in other studies: Cohen and others (2002) reported that 73 percent of their respondents purchased or displayed an American flag; 31 percent attended a memorial service, 66 percent contributed money, and 20 percent donated blood. Other people spoke with Muslim friends, volunteered to help in New York, or gave lessons or talks about the terrorist attacks to a class or at a meeting.

Discussion

Rogers (2000) suggested that the news event diffusion research tradition, under way for over four decades, could be rejuvenated by pursuing an additional set of questions (to those studied in the earlier research), such as how individuals give meaning to the news event and how their perceptions affect what actions they take, including how many other people they tell about the news event and who these people are. Essentially, these new leads to research amount to taking a social constructionist approach to understanding how audience individuals make sense of a news event of study, thus moving beyond studying variables related to awareness-knowledge of the news event, the most common dependent variable in earlier news event diffusion research.

Fortunately, news events are for communication scholars what *Drosophilia melanogasters* (fruit flies) are for geneticists. A new generation comes along very quickly (Rogers 2000). News event diffusion studies represent a type of "firehouse research" in which investigators gather data under great time pressure (De Fleur 1987; Deutschmann and Danielson 1960; Rogers 2000). Our sample of Albuquerque respondents was modest in size and nonrandom in nature. These shortcomings were necessitated by the speed of gathering survey data in quick-response research. Similar difficulties faced the other news event diffusion investigations summarized in this chapter (e.g., Greenberg 2002; Brown et al. 2002).

The present investigation differs from previous news event diffusion studies in several important ways. We investigated the emotional impacts of the terrorist attacks and the actions that people took as a result of hearing about the news event. We followed the leads suggested by Mayer and others (1990) in studying location, time of day, day of the week, and other situational variables that might affect news event diffusion patterns. We found that television and interpersonal communication channels played particularly important roles in diffusing news of the terrorist attacks, in a variety of studies. Relatively newer media like cell phones and the Internet were relatively unimportant. We conclude that many interesting research questions are available for study in future news event diffusion research.

Notes

An earlier version of this chapter was originally published as Everett M. Rogers and Nancy Seidel, "Diffusion of News of the Terrorist Attacks of September 11, 2001" in *Prometheus* 20, no. 3 (2002): 209–19.

1. The results of our survey are comparable to a study conducted by Professor Arvind Singhal and others (1999) in September 1995, in New Delhi, India. People believed that religious statues were drinking milk. Cows are considered sacred by Hindus, and milk is also perceived as sacred (Rogers 2000, 571). Although this news event happened at 4:00 A.M., the news spread very rapidly (Singhal et al. 1999). Almost 90 percent of the 199 respondents heard about the news by 11:00 A.M. Some 99 percent of the respondents gained initial knowledge via interpersonal channels, one-fourth by telephone, and three-fourths through face-to-face interaction.

2. Miller (1987) found that "6 million Americans (6 percent of the population) participated in a memorial service for the seven astronauts who were killed [in the *Challenger* explosion]. And even more Americans, 16 percent, viewed a television memorial service."

References

Basil, Michael D., and Brown, William J. 1994. Interpersonal communication in news diffusion: A study of Magic Johnson's announcement. *Journalism Quarterly* 71, no. 2: 305–20.

Brown, W. J., Bocarnea, M., and Basil, M. 2002. Fear, grief, and sympathy responses to the attacks. In *Communication and Terrorism: Public and Media Responses to 9/11*. Edited by B. S. Greenberg. Creskill, N.J.: Hampton.

Cohen, E. L., Ball-Rokeach, S. J., Jung, J.-Y., and Kim, Y.-C. 2002. Civic action after September 11: Exploring the role of multi-level storytelling. *Prometheus* 20: 221–28.

De Fleur, Melvin L. 1987. The growth and decline of research on the diffusion of news. *Communication Research* 14: 109–30.

Deutschmann, Paul J., and Danielson, Wayne A. 1960. Diffusion of knowledge of the major news story. *Journalism Quarterly* 37: 345–55.

Emmer, M., Kuhlmann, C., Vowe, G., and Wolling, J. 2002. Der 11. September: Informationsverbreitung, Medienwahl, Anschluss-kommunikation (September 11: Diffusion of innovations, media choice, and communication). *Media Perspektiven* 4: 166–69.

Gantz, Walter, Krendl, Kathleen A., and Robertson, S. R. 1986. Diffusion of a proximate news event. *Journalism Quarterly* 63: 282–87.

Greenberg, B. S., ed. 2002. *Communication and Terrorism: Public and Media Responses to 9/11*. Creskill, N.J.: Hampton.

Greenberg, B. S., and Hofschire, L. 2002. Summary and discussion. In *Communication and Terrorism: Public and Media Responses to 9/11*. Edited by B. S. Greenberg. Creskill, N.J.: Hampton.

Greenberg, B. S., Hofschire, L., and Lachlan, K. 2002. Diffusion, media use, and interpersonal communication behavior. In *Communication and Terrorism: Public and Media Responses to 9/11*. Edited by B. S. Greenberg. Creskill, N.J.: Hampton.

Hoffner, C., Fujioka, Y., Ibrahim, A., and Ye, J. 2002. Emotion and coping with terror. In *Communication and Terrorism: Public and Media Responses to 9/11*. Edited by B. S. Greenberg. Creskill, N.J.: Hampton.

Jones, S., and Rainie, L. 2002. Internet use and the terror attacks. In *Communication and Terrorism: Public and Media Responses to 9/11*. Edited by B. S. Greenberg. Creskill, N.J.: Hampton.

Mayer, M. E., Gudykunst, W. B., Perrill, N. K., and Merrill, B. D. 1990. A comparison of competing models of the news diffusion process. *Western Journal of Speech Communication* 54: 113–23.

Miller, Jon D. 1987. *The Impact of the Challenger Accident on Public Attitudes toward the Space Program*. DeKalb: Northern Illinois University, Public Opinion Laboratory. Report to the National Science Foundation.

Noelle-Neuman, E. Public responses in Germany. 2002. In *Communication and Terrorism: Public and Media Responses to 9/11*. Edited by B. S. Greenberg. Creskill, N.J.: Hampton.

Rogers, Everett M. 2003. *Diffusion of innovations*. 5th ed. New York: Free Press.

———. 2000. Reflections on news event diffusion research. *Journalism and Mass Communication Quarterly* 77, no. 3: 561–76.

Rogers, E. M., and Seidel, N. 2002. Diffusion of news of the terrorist attacks of September 11, 2001. *Prometheus* 20: 209–19.

Ruggiero, T., and Glascock, J. 2002. Tracking media use and gratifications. In *Communication and Terrorism: Public and Media Responses to 9/11*. Edited by B. S. Greenberg. Creskill, N.J.: Hampton.

Singhal, Arvind, Rogers, Everett M., and Mahajan, Meenakshi. 1999. The gods are drinking milk! Word-of-mouth diffusion of a major news event in India. *Asian Journal of Communication* 9: 86–107.

Snyder, L. B., and Park, C. C. 2002. National studies of stress reactions and media exposure to the attacks. In *Communication and Terrorism: Public and Media Responses to 9/11.* Edited by B. S. Greenberg. Creskill, N.J.: Hampton.

Stempel, G. H., III, and Hargrove, T. 2002. Media sources of information and attitudes about terrorism. In *Communication and Terrorism: Public and Media Responses to 9/11.* Edited by B. S. Greenberg. Creskill, N.J.: Hampton.

Step, M. M., Finucane, M. D., and Horvath, C. W. 2002. Emotional involvement in the attacks. In *Communication and Terrorism: Public and Media Responses to 9/11.* Edited by B. S. Greenberg. Creskill, N.J.: Hampton.

3

Civic Actions after September 11: A Communication Infrastructure Perspective

*Elisia L. Cohen, Sandra J. Ball-Rokeach,
Joo-Young Jung, and Yong-Chan Kim*

Many people first heard of the tragedy through interpersonal communication and coped with their feelings through storytelling, and some still do years after the tragedy. Elisia L. Cohen, Sandra J. Ball-Rokeach, Joo-Young Jung, and Yong-Chan Kim describe the role of media and interpersonal storytelling in information dissemination and describe a communication infrastructure approach to help understand participation in civil society after September 11.

Elisia Cohen and her colleagues analyze survey data collected during August and September 2001 by their project, Metamorphosis: Transforming the Ties That Bind. These data highlight the potential storytelling processes through which urban residents are transformed into members of a broader community as illustrated by their connections to media, as well as their participation in neighborhood discussions and community organizations after September 11. Their data show that "respondents who reported spending more time talking with others and reading the newspaper were more likely to have taken a broader scope of civic actions than those who did not . . . [but] the amount of time respondents spent watching television and listening to radio after September 11 was not related to their scope of civic actions."

Prior to September 11, we began an eighth wave of computer-assisted random-digit telephone interviews for our large research project called Metamorphosis: Transforming the Ties That Bind (for project details, see www.metamorph.org). The 2001 study was designed to select residents of an area in Los Angeles County for participation in a forty-minute telephone survey administered in the respondents' language of choice. The survey was launched on August 30, 2001, but it was interrupted on September 11.

Facing such a crucial turning event, we added several questions that would assess people's communication and civic-minded behaviors on and after September 11.

Our post–September 11 research inquiry has three distinct goals. The first goal of the study is to contextualize individuals' connections to television, radio, newspapers, and the Internet both before and after September 11.[1] Our research project takes a "communication infrastructure" approach to understanding the complex communication contexts in which people live. By communication infrastructure, we mean a storytelling system set within a communication action context in a residential community that affords residents the opportunity to reflect on and tell stories about their daily lives. The mission of our research is to examine the dynamic role of storytellers in the communication infrastructure to investigate communication across all levels of analysis: interpersonal, intrapersonal, mass and local media forms, and organizations. After September 11 the mission of our research turned to examine the dynamic storytelling system (of interpersonal, community organizational, local media, and mainstream media ties) in people's everyday lives to highlight how the communication infrastructure can be mobilized to advantage civic engagement after national crisis.

At the broadest macrolevel, we are concerned with mainstream commercial media, which engage in storytelling production and dissemination. At the lowest microlevel, storytelling resources flow through interpersonal storytelling networks, and are often reinforced by meso-level local media and grassroots organizations when they promote community storytelling. Although we are interested in pursuing a comprehensive and multileveled analysis of storytelling,[2] given the nature of our data collected after September 11, we are only able to examine people's mainstream media connections, organizational participation, and interpersonal storytelling processes to illustrate their potential influence on civic engagement in residential locales of Los Angeles County.

Our second goal is to understand how individuals' communication behaviors after September 11 are influenced by their embeddedness in the communication infrastructure. Several studies conducted based on media system dependency theory,[3] from which communication infrastructure theory was developed, have found the central role of mass media in the modern society as a source of information. One of the most important propositions of this line of prior research is that when people face ambiguous situations, their dependency on the mass media will increase.[4] Given the centrality of mass media as an information source in the modern society, these studies proposed that risk perception leads to more intense media system dependency relations.

For example, Hirschburg, Dillman, and Ball-Rokeach studied how people connect to various communication forms right after the eruption of Mount

St. Helens in Washington.[5] People in the affected area faced an ambiguous situation when they were uncertain of the effects of ashes on their property and what they could do to protect their houses and farms. Few experts had answers to relieve their uncertainty. In such an ambiguous situation, Hirschburg and colleagues found that people went to mass media to seek information about the situation rather than rely on interpersonal communication. Given the centrality of the mass media as information system or resource in modern society, these studies suggest that ambiguous and threatening social environments should lead individuals and groups to more intense media system dependency relations.

Our third goal is to examine the potential for a well-integrated communication infrastructure to become a resource during crisis, as expressed in the interpersonal conversations among neighbors, the shared orientation of media and organizations, and its influence on individuals' civic actions in response to September 11. Our previous research emphasized how mutual engagement by residents, local media, and community organizations in a storytelling network may construct a sense of imagined community, consistent with other urban researchers' observations of residents' collective capacity for social action or collective efficacy in orientation to specific tasks.[6] Latent capacities for civil society building were found at the community level of analysis by examining the dynamic role of local public media and commercial media, grassroots organizations, and interpersonal conversations in community building. This research supports a conversation model of democracy to show how interpersonal storytelling processes mediate mainstream media influence, which in turn effectively influences the level of participation in civic actions.[7]

Our research adds insight into the communication contexts activating civic engagement after crisis. In the case of September 11 narratives, news reports from both national storytellers (CNN) and local storytellers (e.g., *Korea Times*) contained local referents of significance: two planes flying toward Los Angeles crashed, with many Los Angelinos presumed among the dead and missing. We know anecdotally, and from personal experience, how the stories told in interpersonal conversations reinforced local concerns about terror plots to bomb Los Angeles International Airport (LAX), as well as topics distant to the residential community about September 11.

Exploring the nature of storytelling after September 11 can highlight the level of latent tendencies in individuals to engage in civil society in response to crises. The influence of interpersonal networks, organizational participation, and media connections on people's civic actions are important to consider, as such civic actions (e.g., donating blood, attending a memorial service, displaying an American flag) are crude indicators of how people participated as members of a broader community after September 11. To this end, we explore how people's connectedness to mass media and interpersonal communication changed due to the September 11 tragedy. We would expect that the ambiguity and threat wrought by September 11 turned an established multilevel storytelling network to larger issues of community, thereby increasing civic engagement.

Data

A total of 332 households participated in a telephone survey assessing a range of communication, media, social, and political behaviors. The unique aspects of the survey methods employed in the Metamorphosis Project originated with our decision to respect intact communities—to maintain the geographic boundaries of real communities and to sample from within those boundaries. Specifically, survey interviews were prepared and executed to identify the communication infrastructure of an urban residential environment. This means that our sampling procedures are somewhat complex. A geographic statistical analysis is performed to establish which phone exchanges fell as much as possible within the residential community's census tract–defined boundaries. The survey participants are then selected by random digit dialing using these phone exchanges (for overall research methodology, see www.metamorph.org). This technique helps ensure an optimal "hit rate" for enrolling participants from our target community. In our work, we often target specific ethnic groups or geo-ethnic communities, including many new immigrant communities often left out of survey research because they do not feel comfortable speaking English. In order to reach the diverse populations of the incorporated residential community on the cusp of Los Angeles, the survey was administered in the language of respondents' choice (English, Spanish, and Armenian).[8] Another unique feature is that we include the full range of mediated and interpersonal communication modalities that people use in tandem in their everyday lives.

There was another unique feature of this particular research effort. We took advantage of our being in the field collecting telephone survey data when September 11 occurred. Data collection began on August 30, 2001, and was stopped due to the events of September 11 after 141 participants had completed interviews. The survey resumed on September 21, ten days after September 11, with additional items added to account for changes in people's communication behaviors and social responses after the tragedies. A total of 191 respondents participated in the survey conducted after September 11. We had sufficient numbers of respondents in hand that we could make preevent and postevent comparisons. Survey researchers often long for occasions that allow us to examine the effects of a naturally occurring event on variables that are particularly germane to our larger research interests. Our overall design allowed us to examine the effects of 9/11 on a "real community" with respect to residents' communication and participation behaviors.

In our sample, 42 percent of the survey respondents were male, while 58 percent were female.[9] The ethnic breakdown of the sample was 56 percent white, 18 percent Armenian, 17 percent Hispanic, 8 percent Asian, 2 percent African American, and 1 percent Native American. The median income reported was between $45,000 and $60,000, with a majority of respondents having attended at least some college or technical school. Clearly our sample may be biased toward higher education, more female, and a higher income. Common sense also suggests that our sample overrepresents people who are interested in community issues. There are no significant differences between the samples before and after September 11 in terms of age, income, gender, or educational level.[10]

Findings

How Individuals Connected to Media before and after September 11

We asked our respondents how they first learned about the September 11 incidents (see table 3.1). Of those surveyed after September 11, 33.7 percent found out about the attack from a conversation with a family member, friend, neighbor, or stranger. Forty percent of our sample found out about the attack from television, 19.5 percent from radio, and 4.7 percent from another source.

We then asked respondents if their media habits were influenced by the September 11 incidents (see table 3.2). A majority of respondents (62.4 percent) reported spending more time watching television since September 11. Individuals reported spending increased time with newspapers and radio, and engaging in interpersonal conversation as well. Thirty-eight percent of the sample after September 11 reported that they spent more time reading newspapers, nearly a third of respondents (31.7 percent) reported spending more time talking with their neighbors, and 29.8 percent reported spending more time listening to radio. Nearly one-quarter of respondents (24.1 percent) reported

TABLE 3.1
How Respondents First Learned of the
September 11 Tragedies

Television	40.0%
Conversation	33.7%
Radio	19.5%
Other	4.7%
Don't know	2.1%
Total	100.0% (n = 191)

TABLE 3.2
Respondents Reporting Increased
Attention to Media after September 11

Media	(n = 191)
Television	62.4%
Newspapers	38.5%
Talking with neighbors	31.7%
Radio	29.8%
Internet	24.1%

spending more time on the Internet after September 11. Overall, 25.4 percent of survey respondents increased the amount of time spent with one medium, 29.2 percent with two media, 19.2 percent with three media, 6.9 percent with four media, and 5.4 percent with five media. More than two-thirds of our respondents spent more time with more types of media (e.g., they spent more time with TV *and* more time on the Internet) than before 9/11. These findings are consistent with previous research, which suggests that the importance of mass media as an information resource, compared to smaller-scale targeted media or interpersonal communication, increases in ambiguous situations.[11]

Civic Actions after September 11

After September 11, Americans were enlisted to take a wide variety of civic actions. We examined the degree to which respondents (n = 191) took the following civic-minded actions in response to September 11: talk about it with neighbors, talk about it with strangers, call to check on the welfare of a person you know who might have been injured, buy or display an American flag, post a message on an Internet public message forum, contribute money to a relief fund, write a letter to the editor or call in to a radio talk show, attend a memorial service for the victims, attend a candlelight vigil, or donate blood. In response to the September 11 incidents, 67.9 percent reported that they talked about it with their neighbors, and 48.4 percent reported that they talked about it with strangers. Only 5.3 percent wrote a letter to the editor or called in to a radio talk show, and the same percentage (5.3 percent) posted a message on an Internet public message forum.

A large minority of our sample (41.1 percent) called to check on the welfare of a person they knew who might have been injured. Almost a third (31.1 percent) reported attending a memorial service for the victims, and 18.4 percent reported attending a candlelight vigil. A majority of respondents reported contributing money to a relief fund (65.8 percent) or buying or displaying an American flag (73.2 percent). Twenty percent of our respondents reported donating blood.

We summated the number of affirmative responses to our ten civic action items (above) to create a scope variable that reflects the breadth of respondents' civic-minded responses to September 11 (range = 0 to 10; $M = 3.9$; $SD = 1.84$). Given the range of civic-minded behaviors taken in response to the September 11 tragedies, we turn to investigate to what extent the communication infrastructure acted as an emergent resource for these respondents during a time of uncertainty.

The Role of Residential Belonging

Both subjective and objective dimensions of individuals' belonging to residential communities were assessed to measure their sense of community attachment and involvement in the samples both before and after September 11.[12] Following our previous research, an eight-item belonging index (Cronbach's alpha = .78) estimated the degree to which residents expressed attachment and involvement with their neighbors.[13] The belonging index estimates both subjective assessments of attachment (e.g., the level of respondents' interest in knowing what their neighbors are like) and objective measures of involvement (e.g., the number of neighbors the respondent knows well enough to keep watch on their house or apartment). There was no significant difference in belonging between the samples before and after September 11.[14] We divided the sample after September 11 into "high" and "low" belonging groups (split at the median, $Md = 23.000$; $M = 23.869$; $SD = 9.413$). We examined whether these two groups differed in terms of their levels of participation in community-related activities after September 11. We found that "high belongers" were significantly more likely to engage in civic actions in response to September 11 than "low belongers" (see table 3.3).

TABLE 3.3
Storytelling Individuals' Civic Actions after September 11

	Civic Actions		
	Low (Mean)	High (Mean)	
Level of neighborhood belonging	3.620	4.268	$F(1, 189) = 5.919$*
Intensity of participation in neighborhood discussion	3.613	4.304	$F(1, 189) = 6.696$**
Membership in neighborhood organizations	3.489	4.302	$F(1, 189) = 9.673$**

*Statistically significant at the .05 level.
**Statistically significant at the .01 level.

The Role of Neighborhood Conversations and Organizational Participation

Two important factors in individuals' civic involvement after September 11 were the intensity of individuals' participation in interpersonal discussions about their residential community and their participation in community organizations. Put simply, the more deeply embedded people were in the established communication infrastructure of their community (indicated by links to community organizations and participation in neighborhood discussions), the more likely they were to take civic actions in response to September 11. Intensity of interpersonal discussion about the residential community was measured by asking the respondent to indicate, on a scale ranging from 1 (never) to 10 (all the time), "How often do you have discussions with other people about things happening in your neighborhood?" We divided the sample into "high" and "low" neighborhood discussion groups (split at the mean, n = 330; $M = 5.02$, $SD = 2.79$). There was a significant difference between the two groups in terms of the number of civic actions taken in response to the September 11 tragedy (see table 3.3). Respondents who frequently had discussions with other people about things happening in their neighborhood, those who were in the "high" neighborhood discussion group, took a broader scope of civic-minded responses to the September 11 tragedy than those who did not.

We also asked individuals whether or not they belonged to five different types of community organizations: (1) sport or recreational, (2) cultural, ethnic, or religious, (3) neighborhood or homeowner, (4) political or educational, or (5) any other organizations or groups. Individuals who belonged to community organizations were more likely to take a broader scope of civic actions than those who did not (see table 3.3).

The Relative Importance of Different Storytellers on Civic Actions after September 11

The civic actions (or inaction) of individuals can be understood in terms of their participation in storytelling (in this case, about September 11). Furthermore, the extent of their participation in storytelling can be understood as a consequence of how deeply embedded they are in the communication infrastructure by virtue of their connections to their neighbors, to community organizations, and to media that provoke them toward storytelling behavior.

Our data show that respondents who reported spending more time talking with others and reading the newspaper were more likely to have taken a broader scope of civic actions than those who did not (see table 3.4). The amount of time respondents spent watching television and listening to radio after September 11 was not related to their scope of civic actions (see table

TABLE 3.4
Correlation between Media Connections and Civic Actions after September 11

	Civic Actions (n=191)
Talking with neighbors after September 11	$r = .286$**
Reading the newspapers after September 11	$r = .161$*
Watching television after September 11	$r = -.079$ (n.s.)
Listening to radio after September 11	$r = .035$ (n.s.)

*Statistically significant at the .05 level.
**Statistically significant at the .01 level.
n.s.: Statistically nonsignificant

3.4). These preliminary data are consistent with research linking newspapers and interpersonal conversations as crucial resources for "political talk," opinion formation, and civic engagement in deliberative democracy.[15]

Discussion

The findings we have reported here are suggestive of a storytelling model of civic participation in a crisis. The storytelling model of civic participation shows that when a well-integrated storytelling system focuses on a national referent, such as the September 11 tragedy, mainstream media, local media, community organizations, and interpersonal networks work to stimulate one another toward stories that focus attention toward opportunities and possibilities for civic engagement. Previous research we have reported suggests that this same basic model applies in noncrisis periods.[16] There are important differences between crisis and noncrisis periods, however, that make a difference in the speed and scope of civic activation. In the case of September 11, for example, it is likely that people's personal and collective experiences of both ambiguity and threat intensified dramatically, no matter how they learned of the events of the day. The more that people were implicated in the events directly, or felt that they might become implicated in the hours and days following September 11, the more we would expect to find them activated toward civic participation by the storytelling system. For a variety of reasons (e.g., two of the planes were scheduled to arrive in L.A.), many residents of Los Angeles considered that they might be next.

Our position is that a parsimonious way to understand the process of civic activation after September 11 is to see it as an outcome of (1) the extent to which residents were embedded in a storytelling system before September 11 and (2) the extent to which they were embedded in the storytelling system that arose after September 11. There is considerable overlap in the storytelling systems before and after September 11, the major difference being the importance of mainstream as opposed to community (locally or ethnically oriented) media after September 11. As we have shown, residents whose engagement in their residential area storytelling system (connections between residents, community organizations, and media) created relatively high levels of belonging were more likely to take civic actions responsive to September 11. We interpret this as a generalization effect; that is, residents oriented to civic participation in their neighborhoods (as evidenced by their involvement and their attachment to their neighborhoods) expanded (or redirected) their activities to a national need.

Of course, there appears to have been escalation in the level of civic participation that cannot be explained by the state of affairs before September 11. In other words, we surmise that residents who were less civically engaged before September 11 became more engaged due to their increased connectedness to key storytellers—mainstream newspapers, community organizations, and their neighbors. In this case, we observe activation of a latent potential for civic engagement.

Of the two processes—generalization and activation of latent potential—we expect that the former will be more stable over the long term. Residents who were embedded in their residential storytelling networks before September 11 are more likely than the newly active to sustain their level of civic participation after September 11 because they are grounded in a storytelling communication infrastructure fabric. Moreover, the storytelling referent of mainstream national media had to shift as time went on from an extremely heavy focus on September 11 to consider other stories. Thus the after–September 11 storytelling system and residents' connections to it are necessarily less stable than the storytelling system established before September 11.

Final Thoughts

One of the most interesting observations that we did not highlight in our earlier *Prometheus* article was the stability of people's "belonging" to their residential community before and after September 11. Had our study been conducted in New York, as opposed to Los Angeles, it is likely that there would have been a difference due to the tragedy's local level influence on New York City neighborhoods.[17] However, as a result of our ongoing inquiry, our research provides a unique communication infrastructure framework for interpreting individuals' willingness to participate in community level civic activities in response to September 11, and explaining the degree and impetus for individual civic commitments after September 11.

The preliminary data we present from our Los Angeles pre– and post–September 11 survey research indicated that the roots of individual belonging to community were not deepened by the crisis. Those individuals who were "high belongers" were more likely to be activated during the crisis to take civic actions than those who were not. Individuals who engaged in civic actions after September 11, but expressed a low level of involvement and attachment to their neighborhood, may have experienced an intensification of their connections to communication infrastructure resources during the crisis. Although individuals were "activated" to engaging civically, interpersonal and media storytellers after September 11 directed individuals toward commemoration (to donate or to memorialize the victims) and consumerism (as President Bush called on Americans to return to work and shopping activities), rather than toward sustainable civic institution building (toward volunteer activities, or directed social action).

The validity of these interpretations cannot be assessed until there is follow-up research to track people's communication and civic participation behaviors. However, our subsequent research, testing a communication infrastructure model, supports the conclusion that those who evidenced high levels of belonging and were embedded in the communication infrastructure that arose after the September 11 crisis engaged in a broader scope of civic-minded behavior.[18] One important long-term variable to consider in exploring the activation and maintenance of civic engagement, which will continue to be measured in our future research, is the role of "belonging."

We would expect a similar pattern to arise in noncrisis situations as well. Our previous research shows that above home ownership, many predictors to belonging are individuals' embeddedness in a broader storytelling network, with strong ties to participation in neighborhood discussions, connections to local storytelling media, and linkages to grassroots community organizations.[19] In contrast to arguments that civic actions activated after national tragedy arose from the pressing need to restore and recreate civic connections, we are among those researchers who believe that individuals' enduring civic-minded responses to September 11 have more significant linkages to civic society and point to their roots in communication infrastructure, which may be mobilized toward a broader course of action. Our future research will examine how "high belongers" with deep ties to their community storytelling system evidence a greater likelihood to engage in traditional measures of political and civic action.

Clearly this research was valuable in providing confirmatory evidence to show that the challenge to communication and community after September 11 remains much the same as it was before September 11: How can communication scholars work to improve individuals' objective and subjective measures of belonging to their residential neighborhoods? Our mission in conducting ongoing communication research is to diagnose these problems of building and sustaining urban communities to address these concerns.

Notes

An earlier version of this chapter was originally published as Elisia L. Cohen, Sandra Ball-Rokeach, Joo-Young Jung, and Yong-Chan Kim, "Civic Actions after September 11: Exploring the Role of Multi-level Storytelling" in *Prometheus* 20, no. 3 (2002): 221–28.

This research was funded by grants from the Annenberg School for Communication, the Annenberg Center for Communication, and First Five L.A. The authors also thank Mary Wilson and Elizabeth Gutierrez-Hoyt, who contributed to the discussion of Metamorphosis survey procedures.

1. Yong-Chan Kim, Sandra J. Ball-Rokeach, Elisia L. Cohen, and Joo-Young Jung, "Metamorphosis of civic actions post September 11: From local storytelling networks to national action," in *Communication and Terrorism*, ed. B. Greenberg (Cresskill, N.J.: Hampton, 2002), 289–304; Sandra J. Ball-Rokeach, "A theory of media power and a theory of media use: Different stories, questions, and ways of thinking," *Mass Communication and Society* 1 (1998): 5–40.

2. Sandra Ball-Rokeach, Yong-Chan Kim, and Sorin Matei, "Storytelling neighborhood: Paths to belonging in diverse residential environments," *Communication Research* 28, no. 4 (2001): 394–99; Kim et al., "Metamorphosis," 289–301.

3. Sandra J. Ball-Rokeach, "The origins of individual media system dependency: A sociological framework," *Communication Research* 12 (1985): 485–510; Ball-Rokeach, "Theory of media power," 5–40.

4. Ball-Rokeach, "Origins," 485–510; Ball-Rokeach, "Theory of media power," 5-40; Peter L. Hirschburg, Don A. Dillman, and Sandra J. Ball-Rokeach, "Media system dependency theory: Responses to Mt. St. Helens," in *Media, Audience, and Social Structure*, ed. Sandra J. Ball-Rokeach and Muriel G. Cantor (Beverly Hills, Calif.: Sage, 1986), 117–26; William E. Loges, "Canaries in the coal mine: Perceptions of threat and media system dependency relations," *Communication Research* 21, no. 1 (1994): 5–23.

5. Hirschburg et al., "Media system dependency theory," 117–26.

6. Jeffrey Morenoff, Robert J. Sampson, and Stephen Raudenbush, "Neighborhood inequality, collective efficacy, and the spatial dynamics of homicide," *Criminology* 39, no. 3 (2001): 517–60.

7. Robert O. Wyatt, Elihu Katz, and Joohan Kim, "Bridging the spheres: Political and personal conversation in public and private spaces," *Journal of Communication* 50, no. 1 (2000): 71–92; Kim et al., "Metamorphosis," 289–301.

8. A survey research firm was employed using trained bilingual interviews (the survey was translated and back translated in each language) programmed for computer assisted telephone interview (CATI) administration. These unusual multilingual data collection procedures afford inclusion of non–English speaking new immigrants often excluded from survey research.

9. Our survey response rate was 54 percent when calculated by dividing the number of completed interviews by the number of theoretically eligible phone numbers. Eligible phone numbers were calculated by examining the total number of study phone numbers excluding phone numbers for which eligibility could not be determined, inappropriate/duplicate phone numbers, nonqualified household phone numbers (e.g., outside study area), and the estimated number of initial refusals not likely to qualify for our study.

10. The responses after September 11 include slightly more Armenian respondents (23 percent) than the sample before September 11 (11 percent), due to the number of Armenian-speaking households identified for callback. However, there were no other significant differences in the ethnic breakdown of the samples before and after September 11.

11. For a review, see Ball-Rokeach, "Origins of individual media system dependency," 485–510; Ball-Rokeach, "Theory of media power," 5–40; Hirschburg et al., "Media system dependency theory," 117–26; Loges, "Canaries in the coal mine," 5–23.

12. Ball-Rokeach et al., "Storytelling neighborhood," 405–6.

13. Ball-Rokeach et al., "Storytelling neighborhood," 406.

14. F (1, 330) = .434, p = n.s.

15. Wyatt, Katz, and Kim, "Bridging the spheres," 71–92; Joohan Kim, Robert O. Wyatt, and Elihu Katz, "News, talk, opinion, participation: The part played by conversation in deliberative democracy," *Political Communication* 16 (1999): 361–85.

16. See Ball-Rokeach et al., "Storytelling neighborhood," 405–6; Sorin Matei and Sandra J. Ball-Rokeach, "Real and virtual social ties: Connections in the everyday lives of seven ethnic neighborhoods," *American Behavioral Scientist* 45, no. 3 (1991): 550–64.

17. As the chapters in this book indicate, telecommunication failures, such as the inability of individuals to sustain telephone and cell phone conversations, may have pushed people more toward telephone and radio than in a city more distant from the tragedies, such as Los Angeles.

18. Kim et al., "Metamorphosis," 389-404.

19. Matei and Ball-Rokeach "Real and virtual social ties," 550–64.

4

Communication during the World Trade Center Disaster: Causes of Failure, Lessons, Recommendations

Jonathan Liebenau

Jonathan Liebenau describes the causes of key problems with communication during and shortly after the World Trade Center disaster on September 11 and assesses the relative importance of different kinds of failures. He shows that some appropriate responses have occurred, particularly in government, but that important lessons are still to be learned about the design of systems. Expectations of telecommunications reliability have gone up just as the financial fortunes of the industry have gone down, creating a challenge in how to reach the expected level of resilience for the future.

THE DESTRUCTION OF the World Trade Center, more than any other historical event, brought to public attention the many different critical roles that communications play when disaster strikes. For months afterward, the media dwelled on people's use of mobile phones from the burning buildings and hijacked airplanes, the utility of the Internet in helping people learn of their fate and whereabouts, and the problems that emergency service workers had with their communications equipment. Even on that day the public was cautioned not to contribute to the telecommunications congestion of what immediately became the heaviest use of the network ever.

In the aftermath, the telecommunications industry, already impoverished by the bursting of the investment bubble, was subjected to intense scrutiny by the federal government and damaging criticism from major customers. The government too has been subject to intense scrutiny and many of the assumptions of the preceding years about regulation and competition, and about the strengths that the National Information Infrastructure would provide, were called into question when the network was revealed to be inadequate to handle this national emergency. That frailty was not first noted on September 11. There was a politicized response to problems of the telecommunications system after Hurricane Andrew (1992) and the Northridge earthquake (1994) (and indeed to many of the twenty-four other incidents since 1989 that caused the mobilization of the National Coordinating Center for Telecommunications of the Department of Defense's National Communications System). In this chapter I show that a detailed understanding of the causes of failings points to a more subtle analysis of public expectations, corporate capabilities, and policy implications.

Our perception of the effectiveness of various forms of communication during and shortly after the destruction of the World Trade Center has been affected by factors such as the media coverage about communications failures and by the millions of personal experiences of trying to get through to telephones on those days. These events revealed our expectations about how resilient communication networks ought to be. In recent months we have had access to more careful studies about what worked and what did not during the disaster, and in November 2002 came the revelation that firefighters in one of the towers had radio links throughout the rescue effort, even very high up in the building.

In this chapter we will consider which forms of communication worked and which didn't, on and immediately after September 11. Although the extent of the destruction was unprecedented and the communication traffic at an all-time peak, nevertheless most systems behaved in a manner consistent with what we might have expected. Not that such a scenario had been anticipated. Indeed, the combination of the particular kinds of destruction and the character of the congestion have much to teach us about the resilience of communication networks.

Seven main forms of communication were affected: plain old telephone service (POTS), cell phones, pagers, local area networks, the Internet, emergency services, and television and radio broadcasting. Their efficacy can be summarized as follows:

- Overall, conventional telephone service withstood unprecedented congestion well, outside the damaged zone.
- Cell phone (wireless services) fared worse.
- Messaging devices and pagers worked well.
- Corporate local area networks generally failed but the recently popular wireless local areas network devices (especially WiFi devices) were not much in use at the time.
- The Internet worked, but damage to some service providers caused unanticipated problems in far-flung places, and congestion affected certain services, especially CNN and other news providers.

- Emergency services suffered from robustness and interoperability problems.
- Broadcast television stations other than WCBS were out of service when the transmitting towers were destroyed, but cable services continued and radio broadcasting was able to maintain continuity after circumventing the destruction of many key antennas.

The Physical Causes of Failure

Some elements of the telecommunication infrastructure suffered considerable damage and yet survived in a workable state, operating on backup power supplies until batteries failed late in the day and generators ran out of fuel. Other elements of infrastructure, in particular fiber SONET rings that were thought to be available after parts were cut at the site of destruction, were found to have been improperly installed, maintained, or designed.

The major causes of public communications failure can be summarized as follows:

- Destroyed towers and antennas
- Cut cables
- Damaged switches
- Flooded equipment rooms

Each form of damage had different effects on the performance of the telecommunications system. The most direct was the destruction of the Twin Towers, which held numerous antennas, including most of the cell phone towers serving that part of downtown. Although cell phones in the area could connect with other towers outside the zone of destruction, the overloading of these towers by redirected traffic radically reduced their reliability. Furthermore, the massive load of calls from cell phones during the tragedy created unprecedented local congestion, the appearance of which was compounded by the fact that people from all over the world were frustrated trying to reach cell phone users in the area. The destroyed antennas were compensated for by "cells on wheels"—temporary antennas mounted on vans that were moved in by Verizon and AT&T and eventually were used to handle cell phone traffic in Lower Manhattan.

The effect of cut cables was immediate. Cables passed through the Verizon switching center at 140 West Street that served much of Lower Manhattan but also served as the node for numerous routes that reached a few customers well into midtown Manhattan. Regular telephone service was cut to the Wall Street area, the Lower East Side, and Chinatown, in addition to the extensive downtown office areas around the World Trade Center site. Some of the cable layouts were designed as optical fiber SONET rings in which a cut triggers an immediate rerouting of traffic without discernable interruption. However, the large number of cables that came together at 140 West Street, as well as the fact that some SONET rings were not optimally designed or had not been properly maintained, meant that some failures occurred that might have been avoided.

Central switches, on the other hand, performed remarkably well. Designed to withstand shocks from being dropped during installation, they turned out to be more rugged than expected and continued to operate until they suffered water damage from firemen's efforts to control the main blazes, or power ran out when backup batteries drained after about twelve hours. Battery power was needed when the backup power generator that was first relied on was destroyed in the collapse of Seven World Trade Center. It was flooded equipment rooms, in addition to the destruction of the outside walls and much key internal equipment, that finally silenced telephone equipment at 140 West Street.

Emergency services were plagued by a variety of communications problems, some of them anticipated, some surprising, and some perhaps aggravated by the scale, confusion, and drama of the events. In the aftermath much attention was given to problems with the firefighters' radios. In contrast to police equipment, fire department radios are intended to function mainly for two-way communication between a firefighter at work and the incident manager. The equipment was not capable of communicating with police or other emergency services radios and was generally not used to connect groups of firefighters as opposed to individual firefighters. This design reflects the traditional method of communication among firefighters at the scene of an emergency. This inherent design characteristic was most responsible for the lack of flexibility that was needed at the World Trade Center disaster site. Firefighters would have benefited from more communication among themselves and with the police and other emergency workers. They also would have benefited from access to better data and as the rescue efforts and firefighting activities stretched on the lack of capability to transmit, for example, the special maps generated by the Phoenix Unit geographical information system office of the Fire Department of New York.

Another problem that is still being analyzed is the extent to which the metal frame of the buildings, the encased architecture of the stairwells, and other physical features interfered with radio transmission. The World Trade Center Towers had transmission repeaters built into the structures, and evidently the built-in equipment in one of them continued to work to the moment of destruction. It is not clear why the other did not work; the system of repeaters may have failed, or possibly the radio handsets or other equipment.

Responses

A heartening aspect of this disaster is how people responded. In the days after the damage to the telecommunications infrastructure, coordinated efforts came to play an unexpectedly significant role. Most surprisingly, these coordination activities took place despite the poor performance of many of the formal coordinating mechanisms.

What did work well was the swift rollout of mobile cellular antennas, the now well-known COWS—cells on wheels—that both replaced the destroyed antennas and provided the special access that emergency workers and rubble-clearing crews needed. The COWS, delivered by Verizon and AT&T, worked despite no clear deployment plan, perhaps a tribute to the good intentions of particular managers. The Mutual Aid and Restoration Consortium, the body of the City of New York that was explicitly reestablished to bring the relevant managers together to coordinate just these elements of the response, should have been able to function in this emergency. However, MARC had fallen into disuse shortly after it was established in 1991. It had been invoked only once, during the bombing of the World Trade Center in 1993, when it functioned appropriately. But in the intervening years the drills necessary to maintain a state of readiness, and even the contact names and telephone numbers of those responsible for implementing their company's contribution to mutual aid, had fallen into abeyance.

A much better demonstration of how mutuality could respond to the emergency had less to do with reestablishing telecommunications services and more to do with assisting emergency workers. In an impressive show of technical imagination about what could and could not be accomplished by trying to locate the sources of cell phone signals, and an even more impressive display of coordinating ability, an ad hoc group, the wireless emergency response team (WERT), was formed within a day of the disaster. It brought together engineers to contribute ideas, techniques, and analyses to reassess the characteristics of cell phones from a variety of viewpoints and coordinated the deployment of "signal sniffing" equipment on site in an effort to locate any buried cell phones. Beyond that, WERT activated a nationwide network of signal analysts who, from as far away as Seattle, were able to contribute to monitoring all telephone calls coming from the site. Although no buried survivors were rescued, these methods contributed in many technical ways to the reconsideration of what characteristics of mobile telephones could be used to locate people. They did this, for example, by reassessing the signal propagation characteristics of rubble to determine how far it could be penetrated and with what became of the signal characteristics. They also worked on honing location analysis using "signal sniffing" equipment. One tangible contribution at the time was in altering the instructions that 911 telephone operators used to guide their procedures for calls coming from cell phones. Whereas normal procedure was to extend the length of calls to maximize the opportunity to locate callers, with signal sniffing equipment available, the caller could be told to speak briefly and preserve battery life. Perhaps the most interesting result generated by WERT was not the technical developments in signal sniffing but the managerial achievements in coordinating and sustaining a rigorous work schedule under emergency conditions. That it was accomplished outside any formal cooperation agreements and without reference to commercial constraints is remarkable.

Two other supplements to the damaged telecommunications infrastructure had not been anticipated in most contingency plans. One was the distribution of cell phones, free of charge, to all emergency workers, including site clearance workers. This was undertaken by both Verizon and AT&T and they were able to organize the distribution process quickly and relatively free of hassle. The other was the installation of trailers with cell-operated pay phones, also set to work for three minutes free of charge. This was intended mainly for local residents, including the severely affected and densely populated Chinatown neighborhoods. However, the telephones were also available for anybody in the area to use and they did a little to compensate the local population for the long time it took for residential services to be restored.

Some other initiatives taken to restore service were technically and managerially well-known, but had never been deployed under emergency conditions, despite knowledge that they would be feasible, for example, efforts to wheel out free space optics and portable microwave connections that would allow for critical links, such as those between Lower Manhattan and nearby Jersey City, to carry traffic. AT&T set up at least three such links, and in a few months an entirely new focused microwave technology for the 70GHz band was deployed on a demonstration basis in the Wall Street area under the initiative of a major real estate owner and a specialist equipment manufacturer. Other responses included the quick rigging of voice-over IP equipment at New York University and Columbia University, mainly to assist university community members to reach families and friends.

Direct Results over the Following Year

The national mood of healing and then anger contributed to the attitude that formed when attention was turned in public and political circles to the effects of the terrorist attack on communication. Although there was a consensus that the actual attack had more to do with destroying major national symbols and killing large numbers of people, many commentators pointed out that it was also an attack on critical infrastructure. Nobody suggested that the communication system per se was the target (indeed, they pointed out that destroying some other key buildings could have created even more damage), but the communications problems that followed were the subject of immediate concern in the popular press. *New York Times* articles appeared from the next day onward.

Two organizations that had long existed for the purpose of responding to communications disasters had fallen into abeyance and were dramatically changed by the events of September 11, the New York City Mutual Aid and Restoration Consortium (MARC) and the FCC-coordinated Network Reliability and Interoperability Council (NRIC). MARC had been formed in the early 1990s with the realization that the increasing number of network operators in the competitive environment following the breakup of the Bell system needed some means to coordinate responses to problems that either affected numerous service providers or that drastically damaged one of the large providers. The Mayor's Office and other groups recognized that the ability of the financial services industry to operate in Manhattan relied on telecommunications, and, despite long odds, catastrophic failure constituted a "trillion dollar gamble."

Brought together in 1991–1992, MARC was called on only once, when the World Trade Center was bombed in 1993, to restore services interrupted when cables were cut by the underground blast. With some goodwill the coordinating mechanisms of MARC, the contact lists and know-how necessary to muster the aid and restoration techniques, were maintained for a few years following that first use, but by the end of the decade MARC was useless for two reasons. First, interest had dissipated because the system was not used. Lacking a regular schedule of drills, exercises, or scenario-building activities, there was no community of interest during that period. The contact list of participants was outdated: people moved positions, retired, or lost their jobs, and replacements were often not named and rarely asked to participate in drills that would show them how they might act to solve problems.

Second, the new environment of competition, especially following the 1996 Telecommunications Act, fostered a greater sense among participants that they were in a cutthroat business where customer loyalty and bottom-line profits were the new rules of business. The cooperative legacy that survived to that point among seasoned telecommunications executives and engineers was severely strained. Schemes of cooperation and mutual aid did not loom large in the late 1990s.

With an appropriate sense of urgency, MARC-II was established with slightly revised terms of operation and a strong sense that the highly successful cooperation that emerged regarding September 11 was unique. For the next disaster, especially one not caused by a world-shatteringly dramatic act of terrorism, real coordination mechanisms need to be in place. Although there is still sufficient goodwill within the industry, poor financial conditions have constrained companies that may not feel able to allocate resources to contingency planning. It may be necessary for the city government to apply pressure to ensure cooperation, perhaps in the form of its consumer power as a major user of communications services.

On the national level the National Reliability and Interoperability Council, previously an overlooked industry cooperation body coordinated by the FCC, has found a new sense of purpose since September 11, 2001. The stated goal of its sixth council is to "assure homeland security, optimal reliability, interoperability, and interconnectivity of, and accessibility to, the public telecommunications networks." This has brought it into the center of a nexus of activity that includes organizations such as the Alliance for Telecommunications Industry Solutions, the National Infrastructure Protection Center of the Department of Justice, and numerous other organizations, many now presumably to be coordinated by the Department of Homeland Security.

One further development has been a renewed interest in ensuring that the technologies, facilities, and procedures are soon in place to apply "Enhanced 911" emergency calling. This was initially intended to ensure that technology to locate the source of emergency calls from mobile phones is in place in 911 call centers. But the renewed focus on emergency services has extended the expectations of the public and of government so that other new technologies, such as wireless local area network systems, might also be taken into consideration.

Conclusion

Communication networks are astonishingly resilient. Expectations regarding them have been realistic; we readily accept their limitations and frailties. Nevertheless, we always recognize the need for greater resilience, and we expect our systems to live up to the high demands of large-scale, data-driven commerce, of national and personal security systems, and of our love affair with being constantly on the phone or online.

In this chapter we have considered the limitations of resilience in a variety of ways. One is statutory and related to the expectations of licensing authorities (the FCC, state commissions, national governments, or international authorities), another is commercial and measured by the premium that businesses are willing to pay to feel that their communication is secure. But limitations are most dramatically noted when events, especially tragic events, reveal frailties. When Hurricane Andrew wreaked havoc in Florida in 1992, the frailties of the communication networks were regarded as scandalous. When the Baltimore Tunnel fire of 1999 cut the main East Coast cable, it was blamed for huge financial losses and massive inconvenience. And when the World Trade Center was destroyed, the troubles of the local, regional, and national communication networks were an immediate issue of concern. In the aftermath of those events, our current concern for the strategic significance of networks for homeland security has been heightened.

Military communications have long been built with resilience foremost in mind, but their remit and capacity was limited and, perhaps most significantly, their specifications bore little resemblance to commercial systems. As commercial networks have grown, government resilient systems have utilized expensive redundancy rather than try to be conceptually different. At the same time, the increased competitiveness of the telephone system since the 1980s has pushed resilience to the back to the queue as price cutting, profitability, and operational efficiency have risen to the fore. In more recent times financial failures in the whole telecommunications industry have directly affected the resilience of individual networks as well as the national and worldwide networks.

5

Response, Restoration, and Recovery: September 11 and New York City's Digital Networks

Mitchell L. Moss and Anthony Townsend

This chapter examines the role of digital communications networks during and after the September 11, 2001, attack on the World Trade Center. Digital networks in New York City played a vital role in all three phases of this catastrophe: initial response, interim restoration, and long-term recovery. Mitchell L. Moss and Anthony Townsend conclude that during each of these phases, the digital network infrastructure, while the most fragile of all urban networks, demonstrated remarkable resiliency in serving the citizens of the city and the nation.

L OWER MANHATTAN HAS BEEN the world's leading telecommunications hub ever since the invention of the telegraph. This area, located from Canal Street south to the tip of Manhattan Island, has historically been the site of the nation's leading stock exchanges, banks, law firms, and financial service firms as well as the epicenter for the municipal government of New York City, an entity with a current annual budget of approximately $40 billion. Telecommunications technologies evolved symbiotically with the financial services industry, providing the means for firms and individuals to communicate easily and inexpensively within the city or across the globe. As a result, there is more fiber optic cable strung beneath the streets of Manhattan than on the entire continent of Africa. The two main telephone switches in the financial district each house more lines than many European nations. The ether above is saturated through an endless variety of wireless transmissions, including those that emanated from the more than 1,500 antenna structures mounted atop the World Trade Center north tower.

The September 11, 2001, terrorist attacks sparked the largest telecommunications event in human history. The attack has focused attention on the scale and pervasiveness of the digital network infrastructure in large cities. Admittedly, transportation, water, and power networks are essential to the proper functioning of a modern metropolis, but during a catastrophe, communications networks play a critical role by informing the public about the precise character of an attack and the steps necessary to respond to it.

Methodology

Data for this chapter was obtained through the use of multiple methodological techniques. Telephone traffic use patterns were obtained from leading private carriers, and Internet traffic data was obtained from public records and reports. Interviews were conducted with public officials from the City of New York's Office of Emergency Management, Department of Design and Construction, New York Police Department, and the Fire Department of New York. In addition, interviews with representatives of Verizon, AT&T, and Con Edison were conducted to obtain detailed information about the facilities damaged or destroyed on September 11, and the priorities for rebuilding. The authors also conducted fieldwork in the days and weeks after September 11 to observe the efforts to rebuild the telecommunications and power networks in Lower Manhattan.

Response

Almost as soon as the first plane struck Two World Trade Center at 8:48 A.M. on September 11, 2001, telecommunications systems throughout the world began experiencing what would soon become the biggest surge of use in history. New York City's role as a media capital—it is the headquarters of the nation's major broadcast television and radio networks as well as leading magazine and book publishers—was undoubtedly a factor in selecting the World Trade Center as a terrorist target, both in 1993 and again in 2001. As others have noted, it was almost certain that video cameras would inadvertently capture the attacks live for transmission around the world.[1]

Even before emergency workers responded to the high-rise fire caused by the impact of the first plane, television networks and news websites were pumping images of this urban catastrophe across the globe. While most people prefer the richness and immediacy of broadcast media such as radio and television over the Internet, popular news websites were swamped with requests for images and streaming video.[2] Traffic to the CNN website doubled every seven minutes between 9:00 and 10:00 A.M. on September 11, until its servers were no longer able to keep up with demand and crashed. Even after stripping it down to the so-called end of the world page, CNN could not keep up with an estimated 2 million page requests per minute.

The Telephone Network under Strain

Tens of millions of Americans reached for their telephone as news of the plane crashes began to spread; record call volumes were sustained throughout the day and during much of the week. On September 11 alone, AT&T connected some 431 million calls, 20 percent more than normal. Based on AT&T's long-distance market share, it is likely that over 1 billion long-distance calls were connected nationwide on September 11, 2001. Approximately double that number of calls were attempted, but AT&T's experience with previous local-ized disasters such as earthquakes and hurricanes had helped prepare the company for crises. Giving priority to the needs of affected people, AT&T blocked incoming calls to keep outgoing lines from New York and Washington open. Local telephone systems were swamped as well, with Verizon reporting over 250 million local phone calls in the New York region in the week of September 11–18. Phone traffic in and around New York City was at double the normal levels, an unprecedented level.

Government Response

Millions of people around the world watched as both towers of the World Trade Center burned. Millions also tried to contact friends and family members who lived, worked, or were enrolled in the numerous colleges and universities located in Manhattan. Many of those who worked in the World Trade Center or nearby buildings tried to call their family members to let them know they were safe or were in perilous circumstances. At the same time, the Fire Department of New York was sending hundreds of firefighters into the burning towers to rescue people while the New York Police Department, along with state and federal emergency workers, was evacuating Lower Manhattan for the second time in a decade and cordoning off what had quickly been transformed from disaster area to crime scene after the impact of the second plane at 9:03 A.M.

The failure of the mobile wireless emergency communications devices provided to the brave men and women of the Fire Department of New York is a most tragic part of this story. The breakdowns fell into two main categories. First, the repeater systems for fire and police radios (installed inside the World Trade Center towers after the 1993 terrorist bombing) failed when power was cut after the planes' impact. Few can forget the voices of firefighters captured on documentary footage as they desperately try to understand the weak voices coming through their radios. A report prepared by McKinsey & Co. found that problems with the radio system put many of the fire companies out of touch as they ascended the stairs into the Twin Towers. As a result, at least 120 firefighters did not receive the order to evacuate and were killed in the second collapse.[3]

Even when radio equipment worked well, many first responders were hindered due to the lack of interoperable radios. Supporting firefighters arriving from New Jersey were unable to communicate by radio with their New York City counterparts, since each used a different communications frequency. Other problems, caused by psychological factors rather than technological ones, also strained the capacity of emergency radio channels. The system used by the Emergency Medical Service in New York City was flooded with unnecessary transmissions from panicked operators, causing congestion that interfered with important messages.

The sheer number and variety of first responders further contributed to the breakdown of communications. Dozens of local, state, and federal authorities responded to the attack. Since few law enforcement agencies share compatible communications technologies, however, many rely on public networks like the cellular telephone system for interagency communications. Throughout the day, congestion plagued the public cellular systems as historic call volumes combined with oversubscribed networks. During the morning of September 11, fewer than one in twenty mobile calls were connected in New York City. Since no system was in place to prioritize calls for emergency workers, response was confused and uncoordinated throughout much of the day.

The Financial Industry Response

While law enforcement and local government responded haphazardly due to a lack of effective communications, the financial services industry responded rapidly and decisively to the attack and resulting destruction. This quick and capable response was the result of disaster preparations and recovery plans that were formulated after the 1993 World Trade Center bombing.

One of the most severely affected firms, Lehman Brothers, responded almost instantly. Lehman CTO Bob Schwartz was able to activate the company's disaster recovery plan just after 9:00 A.M. by sending a message from his portable BlackBerry® communicator while descending the stairwell in One World Trade Center. While Lehman's Manhattan data center was destroyed in the collapse of the towers, operations were seamlessly transferred to a twin backup center in New Jersey. The firm was ready for trading at backup facilities in New Jersey the next day, five days before the stock markets were ready to reopen.[4]

While Lehman Brothers was one of the most severely affected firms, it was not alone. By noon on September 11, every major bank in New York City had activated some form of disaster recovery plan. By September 12, nearly fifty firms located in and around the World Trade Center had declared disasters and called on their disaster recovery contractors—firms such as SunGard and Comdisco—to retrieve sensitive data from off-site backups. Many firms, such as Lehman Brothers, were able to switch over instantaneously to backup systems in other locations—notably in midtown Manhattan, New Jersey, and downtown Brooklyn.[5] Cantor-Fitzgerald, which lost some seven hundred employees when the World Trade Center collapsed, was up and running when the bond market reopened on Thursday morning, forty-seven hours later. This was possible because the firm had duplicate data centers in New Jersey and London.[6]

National Trends

Outside New York City, September 11 was marked by abrupt shifts in telecommunications use. As the afternoon wore on, telephone traffic began to subside and many turned to the Internet for more detailed information. Around 4:00 P.M., a surge of users rushed to AOL and other online services, flooding the Internet with short e-mails and instant messages. Presumably, once closest contacts had been reached by telephone, people were broadcasting their whereabouts and status through blanket mailings to their entire address book. AOL reported an astonishing 1.2 billion instant messages per day throughout September, far higher than ever before.

Across the Internet, there were similar patterns. At Columbia University in New York City, e-mail use surged 40 percent to nearly a million messages per day. The AP photo archive on AOL, which had only received 30,000 requests daily before the attacks, received over a million daily afterward. Content distribution networks like Akamai observed a three- to fourfold increase in streaming media demand. Ironically, the insatiable demand for Internet pornography could not be deterred—"World Trade Center" still ranked just seventh among keyword searches on AOL, behind "Nostradamus" (ranked number one) and five pornographic terms!

As rapidly as Internet use surged on September 11, it diminished as President Bush addressed the nation that evening on live television concerning the terrorist attacks on the Pentagon and World Trade Center. As with other major television events such as the Super Bowl, AOL and other ISPs recorded record low usage during the president's speech. Millions logged off the Internet and gathered around television sets to watch the president explain what the terrorist attack meant for the nation and its future.

Restoration

The second phase of telecommunications activity began in earnest on September 12 as the extent of damage to the city's digital network infrastructure became clear. Direct physical damage to the city's telecommunications infrastructure was extensive. The facilities destroyed included:

- 3.5 million local phone lines served by Verizon from 140 West Street central office, directly across from the World Trade Center, which was severely damaged by falling debris, smoke, and water that flooded the basement vaults.
- AT&T lost the large central office it operated in the basement of the World Trade Center. Remarkably, however, the equipment was undamaged during the building collapse and continued to operate until it lost battery power at 4:00 P.M. on September 11. This switch served some 20,000 T1 lines and over 1,200 T3 lines in the World Trade Center area.
- Fifteen hundred antennas atop Two World Trade Center, including most major TV and radio broadcasters in the New York metropolitan area.
- At least fifteen cellular telephone antenna sites were lost, severely constraining local wireless capacity in and around Ground Zero. Many other cell sites were left intact, but their landline connections into the grid were knocked out by the damage at 140 West Street.

Rebuilding the local phone system cost Verizon some $1.4 billion, took more than twelve months, and involved some 3,000 technicians and engineers. AT&T spent an undisclosed amount in the "hundreds of millions" to replace facilities that were lost in the attacks.

Meanwhile, the surviving digital networks were called on to help revive the city's morale and ensure the continuing operation of the financial markets—the lifeblood of the city and a crucial linchpin of the national and global economy. While digital networks proved to be fragile on September 11, the sheer diversity of overlapping systems and the self-healing properties of increasing integration made them remarkably resilient. This telecommunications resiliency allowed New York City to manage the recovery effort and restore economic activity in parts of Lower Manhattan that had been devastated by the attack.

The Internet

Not surprisingly, the Internet was one of the few telecommunications networks not seriously disrupted by the terrorist attacks. Designed around Cold War ideas for attack-proofing communications networks and built by a broad range of competing firms, the Internet's present architecture is a dense web of overlapping, redundant, and interconnected networks. According to Matrix.net, the leading analysts of traffic patterns on the Internet, network disruptions caused by the September 11 attacks were few and highly localized in the New York region.[7]

The ability of the Internet to withstand damage stems from its reliance on two protocols for routing traffic around damaged areas. The first, TCP/IP, has a packetized nature, meaning that data doesn't care how it gets to its destination. The second, a less well-known cousin of TCP/IP is BGP, or the border gateway protocol. Because it is fairly common for a packet to transit several networks between its origin and destination, a system needs to be in place to determine the shortest path along each multinetwork journey. This is complicated by the fact that each network has multiple entry and exit points in multiple cities. BGP provides a way for each network to "advertise" its shortest routes, while revealing nothing about its internal structure (which is a competitive secret). The advantage of BGP is that it provides for dynamic reassignment of routes, which comes in handy during a disaster like September 11. While it does take time (and often some human intervention) for networks to adjust, BGP is remarkably effective at keeping localized disruptions from propagating throughout the network. This is in contrast to other tightly coupled networks like the air transport system, in which localized problems tend to propagate quickly throughout the network (e.g., your flight from Los Angeles to New York is delayed because of bad weather in the Midwest).

These protocols helped the Internet in the United States remain remarkably resilient in the face of two fundamental challenges posed by the September 11 attack. The first challenge was the surge in traffic caused by a major media event. Globally this surge was barely noticed and most major ISPs reported a 5 percent increase in data traffic across the board, which was easily handled by existing capacity. However, in the New York metropolitan region, late-night Internet activity caused significant congestion from about 9:00 P.M. on September 11 until early the next morning. The congestion in the New York area Internet lasted several days, according to John Quarterman of Matrix.net.

The second challenge was dealing with the physical damage and outages of Internet routing equipment. Intermittent power problems at two major Internet switching stations in New York produced some routing problems for U.S.–European Internet connections. However, BGP was able to quickly and effectively route around these problems. Many carriers such as Sprint and Qwest offered each other capacity on transatlantic lines to deal with these outages.

Restoring Telephone Service

Despite the extensive damage to Lower Manhattan's telecommunications networks, and the resulting service disruptions that continued to ripple throughout these systems in the days following the attacks, restoring telecommunications and reopening the financial markets was of utmost urgency. Furthermore, with transportation systems disrupted and firms displaced from destroyed buildings, digital networks were called on to provide flexibility for employers and employees as they tried to rebuild economic activity in New York City.

The New York Stock Exchange (NYSE), located a few blocks south of the World Trade Center, was physically undamaged but was forced to close on September 11. The NYSE reopened just six days after the attacks, largely through the enormous efforts of Verizon and Con Edison, which mobilized hundreds of technicians and workers in the hours and days after the attack. By the start of trading on the Monday morning following the attacks, some 14,000 of the NYSE's 15,000 lines were back in service. The market depends on its member firms, and Verizon also managed to restore service to many of the financial companies that had been served out of 140 West Street, with as many as 2 million of the 3.5 million lost lines back up by the start of trading on Monday morning, September 17.[8]

To accomplish this feat, Verizon worked almost exclusively on restoring service to the exchange and the largest financial firms for the first week after the disaster. Some 3,000 technicians and managers descended on Lower Manhattan and Verizon trucks were parked over nearly every manhole south of Canal Street. Eighteen new SONET rings were installed; one urban legend claims that Verizon employees managed to maneuver past the Secret Service perimeter around Ground Zero to retrieve vital equipment from 140 West Street that was used to restore service to the NYSE. Lines were laid on the street surface throughout the financial district and covered with asphalt, in semipermanent installations that were reburied underground weeks or even months later.

Other telecommunications companies rushed in to help restore services as well. AT&T's Network Disaster Recovery team was in place by midnight on September 12, less than forty-eight hours after the attacks.[9]

Restoring Wireless Networks

Wireless carriers responded even more quickly, drawing on lessons learned in previous urban disasters like the 1994 Northridge earthquake in Los Angeles. Using trailer-mounted mobile cell sites, various carriers quickly restored service to locations where antenna installations had been destroyed, such as Ground Zero. Other cell sites, whose landline connections had been lost due to the damage of wired networks near the World Trade Center, were linked back to the grid using temporary point-to-point microwave links. These "wireless backhauls" patched into receivers along the Brooklyn waterfront and on tall buildings in midtown to reconnect the stranded cell sites to the citywide phone grid.

Even the network of a bankrupt wireless company played an important role in facilitating the rescue and recovery at Ground Zero. Metricom, a wireless data provider that had failed during the summer of 2001, had deployed a medium-speed (128kbps) wireless data network throughout much of Manhattan. Metricom's financial problems forced it to shut down its network on August 8 and lay off much of its staff. It had entered bankruptcy proceedings at the time of the September 11 attacks. With the massive amount of evidence collection and rescue-related communications needed at Ground Zero, officials at New York City's Department of Information Technology and Telecommunications saw an opportunity and petitioned the bankruptcy court to release some of the company's Lower Manhattan assets.[10] Within two weeks, between 500 and 1,000 rescue workers were using the network to log evidence, communicate, and access death certificate records.

While digital networks were healing, both by themselves and with the help of technical crews working around the clock, the city's social and economic networks were also recovering from the shock of September 11. However, portions of Lower Manhattan, such as Chinatown, which had suffered a loss of telephone service after the September 11 attacks, were especially slow to regain full telecommunications service since priority had been given to restoring the telecommunications systems in the financial district in Lower Manhattan.

Telecommuting

More than 13 million square feet of Class A office space was destroyed at the World Trade Center, and an additional 13 million square feet in the surrounding area was seriously damaged. Major office complexes such as the World Financial Center were forced to close in order to assess the damage they had sustained and make the necessary repairs. Furthermore, many of the transportation systems that brought workers to Lower Manhattan were either destroyed or damaged, or were restricted to emergency rescue and recovery vehicles. As a result, many office employees in Lower Manhattan were forced to work from home or in temporary office settings throughout the region. Telecommuting played an important role in allowing the region to cope with the physical destruction of mass transit links, and the restrictions on river crossings like the Holland and Brooklyn-Battery tunnels.

In the early 1980s, when the rise of the personal computer created the possibility of mass telecommuting, many futurists envisioned a highly decentralized society that still provided access to the benefits of urban civilization. Alvin Toffler suggested the "electronic cottage." Telework, or telecommuting, could eliminate travel caused by the spatial separation of home and work. Throughout the 1980s and 1990s, telecommuting made gains as both personal computers and high-speed data communications got cheaper and were widely deployed in homes around the United States, Europe, and Asia. Contrary to the wholesale decentralization envision by futurists, however, home-based telecommuting remains a limited phenomenon. In fact, the knowledge-based workers most prone to telecommuting are the same workers whom employers want to keep in close proximity to management and teammates in order to maximize productivity.

Ironically, the financial service firms based in Lower Manhattan relied on advanced communications technology and New York City's density of talent to bring highly skilled teams together in face-to-face settings with each other and with clients. Partly as a result of this paradox, telecommuting never really caught on as it was originally envisioned—as a replacement for the traditional office worker's commute. Yet it has fulfilled what is arguably a far more important role, as a backup technology following natural disasters and civil emergencies. For example, Dow-Jones, the publisher of the *Wall Street Journal*, was forced to move its operations out of the World Financial Center after September 11. Many *Wall Street Journal* editors were relocated to a New Jersey facility, but the reporters were encouraged to work from home in the days and weeks following the September 11 attack. In addition, approximately 3,000 Lehman Brothers employees telecommuted on a daily basis during the second half of September while temporary offices were being procured.

Prior to September 11, natural disasters had provided the main impetus for the use of telecommuting as a component in disaster planning. The 1994 Northridge earthquake in Los Angeles is the archetypical example because it destroyed so much transportation infrastructure. Yet it also coincided with the widespread arrival of two essential tools for telecommuting—personal computers and modems.

Telecommuting during emergencies is not limited to the United States alone. In 1998 Auckland, New Zealand, experienced a cascading power failure that compromised all four of the central business district's redundant power arteries caused a month-long blackout between February and March. Although the entire central business district was darkened—even the New Zealand Stock Exchange has to shut down and switch to a backup center—it was widely reported that business as usual went on with workers setting up shop at home, pubs, and coffee shops relying on mobile phones, laptops, and modems to digitally reconstruct their social and professional networks.

Relocating Displaced Firms

The destruction of the World Trade Center illustrated the vulnerability of high-rise office buildings. However, until corporations find a substitute for bringing workers together in one place, firms must house their workers in an office building. In the wake of September 11, the need for a quick return to the markets, the scale of destruction, and the limited supply of readily available space forced many firms to use digital network technologies to help find creative solutions.

Perhaps the most widely used strategy was the activation of backup sites by many financial firms. Backup "hot sites" tend to be located in the same region as primary sites for both human and technological reasons. First, at least some of the workers who are expected to staff backup sites would be those displaced from the main work site. Second, there are limits to how far digital network infrastructure can be stretched to decentralize corporate information systems. In the financial services sector, especially, the amount of data that needs to be archived and stored at remote disaster recovery facilities stretches the capabilities of even the highest-speed networks. The precise timing required by these ultra–high capacity networks limits the distance across which such systems can function. For example, IBM's ESCON protocol used by mainframes to talk to remote mass storage devices is limited to about twenty miles.

Recovery

Digital networks are critical to the long-term recovery of the New York region from the September 11 attacks. Furthermore, a number of precautions to "harden" digital network infrastructure need to be considered. In the long run, one of the major outcomes of September 11 may be to firmly place the planning, provisioning, and preparedness of digital network infrastructure solidly on the agenda of urban planners and policy makers. Several key issues and strategies have emerged from the September 11 attack on the World Trade Center.

Redundancy through Wireless Alternatives

The destruction of large concentrations of wired network infrastructure around the World Trade Center site had devastating consequences on telecommunications services in Lower Manhattan and the entire New York region. One strategy that was widely used to quickly restore communications links was the deployment of temporary point-to-point wireless links. Microwave links were widely used to connect rooftop sites to uplinks in midtown Manhattan, New Jersey, and Brooklyn. Laser-based optical networks were deployed by AT&T to provide high-bandwidth backbone links to New Jersey.

A report by the Lower Manhattan Telecommunications Users Working Group recommends the development of a rooftop wireless network in Lower Manhattan to provide a fallback in future disasters. At an estimated cost of less than $1 million, a six-node rooftop mesh network could serve over 2,000 buildings in the financial district.

Interoperability

The Fire Department of New York is revamping its radio system, spending some $14 million to upgrade its two-way radio system. The new system will eventually be interoperable with the city's Office of Emergency Management as well as the New York Police Department.

Terrorism and Urban Decentralization

Many urban observers have argued that office activities will be increasingly decentralized as a result of the September 11 attack, as firms seek to spread risk and reduce the number of large targets they must insure. As Lehman Brothers managing director David Shulman stated in 2002, it is "the impact of imposing a terrorism tax on the economy that is undoing many of the agglomeration economies now extant in the economy. Put bluntly, the gains associated with the clustering of functions within a firm and of firms in similar industries are being offset by the risk of terrorism."[11]

Preliminary evidence from New York City suggests that there has been little to support this point of view. According to calculations by New York University's Real Estate Institute, some 80 percent of displaced demand from the World Trade Center and surrounding buildings was accommodated in existing office space throughout the five boroughs. The remaining 20 percent, mostly in the urban New Jersey waterfront just across from Lower Manhattan, have not committed to long-term leases. Put simply, the "terrorism tax" does not appear to be strong enough to overcome the advantages of agglomeration in a large business cluster like the financial district. In fact, some of the most affected firms have made even more substantial commitments to New York City. Lehman Brothers, while relocating out of Lower Manhattan, purchased a 1 million square foot office building in midtown.

The Internet Needs Power: The Web of Urban Networks

For their resiliency, digital networks remain highly dependent on older, less flexible infrastructure systems for food and shelter. Much of Lower Manhattan's telecommunications would have remained online if Con Edison had been able to maintain the electricity grid. The lack of physical access to Manhattan also means that many telecommunications networks must share the same physical conduits into the Manhattan central business district—the Lincoln, Holland, and Brooklyn-Battery tunnels. Should these transportation arteries be compromised by a terrorist plot (one was uncovered by federal investigators in the mid-1990s), Manhattan might be cut off from Europe or lose much of its ability to talk to the rest of the United States.

Targeting Digital Networks

While the Internet's performance was highly regarded by many, it must be remembered that the Internet was not targeted by the September 11 attacks. The Nimda virus (later determined to be unrelated to 9/11), which struck some 85,000 Internet servers a week later on September 18, caused enormous network congestion in cities worldwide at an estimated economic cost of $1.2 billion—placing it on the scale of the World Trade Center attack.

The Internet appears vulnerable to physical attack as well, especially in dense urban areas. It is unclear how meshed the Internet architecture actually is, particularly at the global scale.[12] The New York metropolitan area is the world's largest single international bandwidth hub, according to market analyst Telegeography, with gigabytes per second. Yet the three main Internet interconnection points in the region lie within miles of each other along the west side of Lower Manhattan. There has been speculation that taking out three carrier hotels in Manhattan (111 8th Avenue, 25 Broadway, and 60 Hudson Street) would effectively separate the U.S. Internet from Europe for several days or more.

Telecommuting as a Backup in Emergencies

Postdisaster telecommuting experiences had long-term impacts on the evolution of the Los Angeles region. The Northridge earthquake led many firms that had previously ignored telecommuting to reconsider its possibilities for reducing long-distance commuting, which in turn had long-term benefits for the region. As one observer put it: "the January 1994 earthquake provided the jolt that many California companies needed to try new, innovative work methods to change their corporate cultures. Now the broader use of flextime, telecommuting, compressed work-weeks, vanpools and carpools are subtly changing the corporate culture for the better."[13] Pacific Bell's telecommuting information hotline, set up in the quake's wake, fielded some 2,000 calls from small businesses seeking to use telecommuting as a solution to managing transportation problems.

The long-term impacts of the Northridge earthquake on the Los Angeles region have been to accelerate the decentralization of the region's already highly dispersed commercial infrastructure. Telecommuting's role in coping with the disaster has reinforced telecommuting as an integral part of the region's ongoing battle to provide mobility and accessibility. Perhaps the most telling observation of the technological response to the quake appeared in *PC World*, where one group of editors wrote, "It took an earthquake to make Los Angelinos avoid their cars and consider telecommuting . . . [but] government officials pledged to open freeways by year's end, so it remains to be seen whether Angelinos abandon their sacred autos for modems."[14]

Conclusion: Lessons Learned

This chapter highlights the importance of telecommunications systems during a catastrophe and the need to develop strategies for strengthening urban digital networks to cope with future disasters and catastrophes. Telecommunications systems are essential for informing the citizenry about a catastrophe and are also critical to the deployment of first responders. The September 11, 2001, attack on the World Trade Center demonstrated the need for redundancy in our digital networks. Most important, wireless communications systems must be improved for use in high-rise buildings.

Notes

1. S. Graham, "In a Moment: On Global Mobilities and the Terrorized City," article circulated by e-mail, September 2001.

2. According to a Pew Research Center study, only 1 percent of people surveyed first found out about the attacks via the Internet, compared to 44 percent by television and 15 percent by telephone.

3. "9/11 Exposed Deadly Flaws in Rescue Plan," *New York Times*, July 7, 2002.

4. "Lehman Brothers' Network Survives," NetworkWorldFusion, (www.nwfusion.com), November 26, 2001.

5. "Businesses Start the Recovery Process," NetworkWorldFusion, September 12, 2001.

6. "Cantor-Fitzgerald: 47 Hours," *Baseline*, October 29, 2001. www.baselinemag.com/article2/0,3959,36807,00.asp.

7. Ironically, these disruptions were caused by power failures at two network exchange points in Lower Manhattan in the week following the attacks, illustrating the interdependency of urban technological infrastructures (see Graham and Marvin book splintering urbanism).

8. Shawn Young and Deborah Solomon, "Verizon Effectively Rebuilds Network for NYSE," *Wall Street Journal*.

9. "AT&T Network Disaster Recovery Team—Deployments." www.att.com/ndr/deployment.html.

10. "Ricochet Rebounds at Ground Zero," Cnet News, October 1, 2001. news.com.com/2100-1033-273743.html?tag=bplst.

11. "Real Estate Strategy, Post 09/11/01: In Part, a Whole New Ballgame," Site Selection, September 24, 2001.

12. Consider the case of South Africa. All of its largest connections to the global Internet backbone are routed through New York City. As a result of the Internet outages in New York City, South Africa lost about 50 percent of its international Internet capacity for a week.

13. Gail Dutton, "Can California Change Its Corporate Culture?" *Management Review*, June 1994, 49–54.

14. "Temblor Telecommuters," *PC World*, April 1994, 63–64.

6

The Social Dynamics of Wireless on September 11: Reconfiguring Access

William H. Dutton and Frank Nainoa

William H. Dutton and Frank Nainoa describe the use of wireless telecommunication media within the different locations directly affected by the hijackings on September 11. Comparisons across these different contexts provide empirical anchors to more general themes concerning the social dynamics of wireless in the unfolding events of this day. Events illustrate how the major social role of information and communication technologies like wireless is centered on reconfiguring access— physical and electronic. The vivid implications of air phones and mobile cell phones in this crisis could redefine public views on wireless telecommunications and thereby shape policy and regulation in the years ahead.

The Power of the Untethered Human Voice

A MAJOR THEME EMERGING from news coverage of the events of September 11 was the power of the untethered human voice, enabled by wireless telecommunication media. These anecdotal accounts of wireless mobile cell phone and air phone[1] calls by hijacked airline passengers and the occupants of the World Trade Center were important elements of stories about the hijacked planes and rescue efforts. This news coverage was so thorough that it created the opportunity for a comprehensive analysis of this unique case of the use of wireless telephones, which also addresses and illuminates more general questions about the social role of electronic communication.

Wireless media supported flexible and spontaneous networks of communication on September 11. In critical cases, they circumvented and undermined more formal hierarchical systems of communication. This reinforces a theoretical argument about the bias of new information and communication technologies (ICTs) in facilitating one-to-one and many-to-many networks of communication, in contrast to more controlled forms characteristic of hierarchical networks. The hijackers themselves were a network that employed the cell phone to coordinate their attack. Passengers on hijacked planes were able to get information from outside the official channels of communication, which evaded the hijackers rapidly enough to enable a spontaneous network to form and overtake the hijackers on one plane. On the ground, World Trade Center occupants used cell phones to network with individuals outside the buildings to obtain information counteracting unsafe official announcements.

The use of wireless media by both heroes and villains highlights the broader double-edged nature of communication. Similarly, the same technology that was used to help search for victims at Ground Zero could be used for unwarranted surveillance in other contexts. The ability of digital "e-technologies" to reshape access to information and people to alter outcomes in sometimes dramatic ways was a poignant motif in the September 11 story. The role of ICTs in reshaping access, or "tele-access," took the form of instrumental changes in behavior as well as conveying love, sorrow, and other deep social emotional values in final "communions."[2]

After describing our approach, we set the scene by detailing key wireless events at the heart of the analysis. This is followed by a discussion of themes that emerge from examining these cases and a concluding section that explores some significant implications of this experience for society at large.

Approach

Analytically, it is useful to view the unique events of September 11 as a set of embedded case studies of how wireless media were used in each of the four separate hijacked planes, in the three different structures that were struck and in the underground rubble of the World Trade Center.[3] We therefore collected online, print, and other news coverage about the use of wireless media in these incidents.[4]

There are notable limitations to our approach. First, there are inconsistencies across media reports. For instance, without better records, it is not possible to be precise about the exact times and sequences of many events, including wireless calls. Second, incorrect information can be consistently reported as journalists pick up each other's news reports. Unintentionally, the words of a journalist or family member paraphrasing a call can be taken as the exact words of a victim. Finally, journalistic reports are neither random nor comprehensive, raising issues about the bias of any sample represented in coverage. For example, dozens of books, documentaries, and websites have been developed on the basis of these events with a particular focus on some of the most heroic events, such as the passengers on United Flight 93 and the firefighters at the World Trade Center.

Given these concerns, we have taken the details that might be problematic into account in drawing conclusions. Moreover, the broad sweep of wireless interactions, not just the details, is indicative of general patterns and themes that have a foundation in communication theory and practice, which provide added support to our conclusions.[5] Moreover, as new evidence has become available to the public, through court cases and family members, there has been more confirmation of the general patterns of use described in this chapter.[6]

The Social Dynamics of Wireless Calls on September 11

Each plane and crash site for which we have records presents a unique set of circumstances that help us understand the social dynamics of wireless calls made in parallel sequences as events unfolded.

Aboard the Hijacked Planes

The first plane to crash into the World Trade Center in New York City was American Airlines Flight 11, which left Boston's Logan Airport at 7:59 A.M. Two critical calls are reported from this plane (box 6.1). The first, made before takeoff, was by Mohamed Atta, a hijacker on AA 11, who called an accomplice on United Airlines Flight 175. While no content was recorded from this call, which lasted less than a minute, investigators assumed that this was one go-ahead signal between the hijackers. The second call was from flight attendant Madeline Sweeney to the American Airlines Operations Center. Sweeney was composed enough to provide details of the stabbing of two other flight attendants, the death of a passenger, and the storming of the cockpit by the hijackers, whom she described as appearing "Middle Eastern." When asked by an American Airlines ground manager at Logan Airport in Boston to give her location, she reported seeing water and buildings just before hitting the north tower of the World Trade Center. Her last words were: "Oh my God!"

The second plane to hit the World Trade Center, United Airlines Flight 175, took off at approximately the same time as AA 11 (box 6.2). A passenger, Peter Hanson, used a cell phone to reach his father, telling him that the plane had been hijacked and that the hijackers were stabbing flight attendants and forcing the crew to open the cockpit door.

Ten to twenty minutes after AA 11 and UAL 175 took off, American Airlines Flight 77 departed Dulles Airport in Washington, D.C., for Los Angeles (box

---

Box 6.1. American Airlines Flight 11 (AA 11) Chronology

5:45	Mohamed Atta passes through security checkpoint in Portland, Maine, en route to Logan Airport in Boston, where he boards AA Flight 11.
7:45	Atta calls Marwan Al-Shehhi, aboard United Airlines Flight 175 on a cell phone and talks for less than 60 seconds.
7:59	AA 11, a Boeing 767, departs Logan for Los Angeles International Airport with 92 people aboard.
About 8:15	AA 11 is hijacked.
8:40	Federal Aviation Administration alerted North American Aerospace Defense Command (NORAD) that AA 11 had been hijacked.
About 8:45	Flight attendant Madeline Sweeney calls AA Operations Center, alerting them to hijacking, ending her call with: "I see water and buildings. Oh My God! Oh My God!"
8:48	AA 11 flies into the 90th floor of WTC north tower in New York City.
10:29	WTC north tower collapses.
17:20	Number 7 WTC, a 47-story building adjacent to the Twin Towers, collapses.

6.3). After the hijack, journalist Barbara Olson made two cell phone calls from the rear of the plane to her husband, U.S. Solicitor General Theodore Olson. During the first, she had time to describe the hijacking and how the passengers were separated into groups, with the pilot and some crew forced to the back of the plane. Olson believed the hijackers were armed only with knives and cardboard-box cutters. When she contacted her husband again, she gave him more information and he told her of two planes crashing into the World Trade Center. When Olson asked him what she should do, he advised her to hang up and call back later as he was concerned she would be discovered. Minutes later, AA 77 crashed into the west side of the Pentagon.

Box 6.2. United Airlines Flight 175 (UAL 175) Chronology

7:45	Marwan Al-Shehhi, aboard United Airlines Flight 175, receives cell phone call from Atta, possibly giving a go-ahead or coordinating their actions.
7:58	UA 175, a Boeing 767, departs Boston for Los Angeles with 65 people.
8:43	FAA notifies North American Aerospace Defense Command (NORAD) that UAL 175 had been hijacked.
About 8:45	Passenger Peter Burton Hanson uses a cell phone to call his father, saying the "plane [was] hijacked, flight attendants stabbed, hijackers in cockpit."
9:05	UA 175 plows through the WTC south tower.
9:10	Andrew Card whispers news of attacks to President George Bush, who was reading to children in a Florida classroom.
9:40	FAA orders nationwide air traffic system to shut down, stopping all flights at U.S. airports.
10:05	WTC south tower collapses.

Box 6.3. American Airlines Flight 77 (AA 77) Chronology

8:10 or 8:20	AA 77 departs Washington, D.C., Dulles Airport for Los Angeles with 64 people.
About 9:25	Passenger Barbara Olson, a journalist, makes first cell phone call to her husband, U.S. Solicitor General Theodore Olson, telling him of the hijacking. Signal is lost.
About 9:30–9:35	Barbara Olson reaches her husband a second time. Her husband ends call to prevent her from being discovered and harmed.
9:40	AA 77 crashes into the west side of the Pentagon, outside Washington, D.C., in Arlington, Virginia.
9:45	The White House and the Capitol are evacuated.

The last flight to depart, and crash, was United Airlines Flight 93. It left the gate at Newark International Airport approximately the same time as the other flights, but its departure was delayed about thirty minutes until 8:40. It was still climbing toward cruising altitude when AA 11 hit the north tower of the World Trade Center. At least nine wireless phone calls were made from UAL 93.[7] One reason for this relatively high number was that one or more hijackers told UAL 93 passengers to call their families and "say good-bye" (box 6.4).

Box 6.4. United Airlines Flight 93 (UAL 93) Chronology

8:01	UAL 93, a Boeing 757, leaves gate at Newark, bound for San Francisco.
8:41	UAL 93 departs, after delay, with 45 people. Only 37 of 182 seats occupied.
8:46	UAL 93 climbing to cruising altitude when AA 11 hits WTC north tower.
9:35	UAL 93 is hijacked, with hijackers soon telling passengers to call their families to "say good-bye." Passenger Thomas Burnett makes four calls to his wife, providing information for authorities and telling of plan for passengers to attack hijackers. Flight attendant CeeCee Lyles calls her husband and tells him she loves him and their four boys. Passenger Tony Garcia calls his wife. She heard only "Dorothy" through static. Passenger Lauren Gandcolas calls home about hijacking, saying: "They are being kind. I love you." Passenger Jeremy Glick provides information about hijackers during a 20-minute call with his wife, Lyz, who contacts authorities at his request. Passenger Mark Bingham calls his mother, leaving a message on her answering machine that describes hijacking.
9:58	Male passenger calls 911 from locked bathroom, reaching emergency dispatcher in Pennsylvania, saying, "We are being hijacked. We are being hijacked!" Passenger Elizabeth Wainio calls her stepmother, saying, "They're going to storm the cockpit." Passenger Todd Beamer is unable to use his credit card in air phone but is connected to Verizon/GTE Airfone supervisor. He provides her with information, says the Lord's Prayer with her, and leaves line open as he and other passengers attack hijackers. She hears: "Are you ready guys? Let's roll."
10:03	UA 93 crashes in Shanksville, Pennsylvania, 80 miles SE of Pittsburgh.

Many callers from UAL 93 did say good-bye. But a significant number also provided information to families and authorities, as well as receiving relevant news. An unidentified passenger locked himself in a lavatory and called 911, the U.S. emergency number, to report the hijacking in progress. Another passenger, Thomas Burnett, reached his wife on four separate calls. He told her of the hijacking, the knifing of a passenger, and the hijackers' bomb threat. Mrs. Burnett called the FBI after the first call. When Burnett called his wife back, he told her that the hijackers were talking about crashing the plane—and she was able to tell him about the planes hitting the World Trade Center. During a third call, they concluded there was probably not a bomb on the plane. On the fourth and final call, Mrs. Burnett learned that her husband and other passengers planned an action against the hijackers, who were positioned near the pilot's cabin.

Flight attendant CeeCee Lyles, a former police officer, reached her husband by phone. He could hear screaming in the background while she expressed her love for him and her children. Passenger Jeremy Glick contacted his wife, Lyz, and in-laws on his cell phone, saying that three men, one with a red box strapped to his waist, had hijacked the plane. He asked about the truth of another passenger's report that planes had crashed into the World Trade Center. He told his wife to call authorities, adding that "the men voted" to attack the terrorists.

When another passenger, Todd Beamer, was unable to use his credit card for an air phone call from UAL 93, he was directed to the telephone company's air phone supervisor. Beamer gave her information about the hijacking and asked her to recite the Lord's Prayer with him. He left the phone line open as he and other passengers stormed the hijackers, saying, "Let's roll." A few moments later voices were heard saying, "Get out of here. Get out of here," on a radio transmission from the cockpit; then there were sounds of a struggle, followed by silence. UAL 93 had crashed in an open field about eighty miles southeast of Pittsburgh, Pennsylvania.

Calls in the Targeted Structures and from the Rubble of the World Trade Center

Once AA 11 crashed into the ninetieth floor of the World Trade Center north tower, the use of landline and wireless telecommunications increased dramatically, and communication infrastructures in the immediate vicinity of the crash began to be overwhelmed. When the towers collapsed, as many as ten local cellular sites were knocked out. Some cell phones were picked up by nearby sites, but wireless phone use was generally unreliable. For instance, John Labriola, who escaped from the seventy-first floor of the north tower, said: "People were constantly checking their cell phones . . . but no one's calls could get out." Similarly, Jennifer Daly was late getting to work at the World Trade Center when the north tower was hit. She ran from the scene. Checking her cell phone, she found twenty-seven missed calls from worried friends and family. Difficulties were not limited to the telecommunication infrastructure. Broker Robert Matos on the fifty-fifth floor of the south tower was shaking so much after seeing ten people jump to their deaths that he could not dial his cell phone.

An example of how crucial information was passed to occupants of the towers by wireless calls that did get through was the way a cell phone call received in World Trade Center's south tower helped save the lives of the recipient of the call and a nearby colleague because they were alerted to the fact that a plane had caused the damage to the north tower. This led the pair to ignore announcements that the south tower was now safe and that they should return to their building.[8] Other victims may seem to have put their lives at risk by stopping at pay phones in the midst of the chaos of Ground Zero at the World Trade Center to call family or friends.[9]

Later, in the rubble of the north and south towers, at least one victim and two police officers were reported to have used their cell phones to direct rescuers to their location. The mere possession of a cell phone created the potential to locate survivors. The Federal Emergency Management Agency (FEMA) sent the Wireless Emergency Response Team (WERT) to the World Trade Center. WERT has electronic equipment to pinpoint cellular and pager devices that are turned on by tracking the source of their signal.

The Social Roles of Wireless: General Patterns and Themes

Analysis of the details of calls across these varied contexts of key September 11 events surfaces a number of more general themes concerning the use and impact of wireless media.

A Multimedia Ecology

Much discussion of the media on September 11 has examined the relative impact of different modes of communication, such as whether television was more important than the Internet. The use of wireless phones on the aircraft and at the crash sites on September 11 suggests more complementarity than competition among the media. The most apparent complementarity was the degree to which phone calls with loved ones depended on television as a source of information that could be fed to the planes or the World Trade Center. Wireless phones were effective in part because they were supported by interpersonal and broadcast communications. Discussion of the impact of wireless phones, TV, or the Internet must be tempered by this ecology of interdependence across multiple media.

The Double-Edged Sword of Communication

In supporting networks, wireless media can be employed by hijackers and the hijacked, victims and criminals. Wireless phones helped save lives on September 11, as much as they were employed to kill and maim. Not only did the hijackers use cell phones to give the go-ahead to the plot, but a series of telephoned bomb threats to the control centers monitoring the hijacked flights were apparently orchestrated to confuse controllers and weaken their ability to understand and respond to the rapidly unfolding events.[10]

Similarly, the technology of wireless enables rescuers to track victims, yet the same technology can be used for unwarranted surveillance. This was emphasized in the aftermath of September 11 by heightened discussion of privacy concerns raised about wireless and enhanced 911 services that enable tracking of wireless 911 calls. In these ways, the uses of wireless reflect earlier observations about the telephone having what Ithiel de Sola Pool called "inherently dual effects" in that the "telephone is an agent of effective action in many directions."[11] Understanding this feature of the social implications of communication media can lead analysis to more subtle types of effects, such as in reshaping physical and electronic access to information, people, services, and technologies—what has been called the "shaping of tele-access."[12]

The Instrumental Value of Wireless: Reconfiguring Access to Information

Wireless media on the planes and in the buildings played a critical role in getting information from the inside to the outside and vice versa. Cell phone calls from the planes informed authorities of the hijacking as it was in progress. Families were able to inform passengers of events they were watching on TV. Occupants in the World Trade Center towers were able to get information on the big picture from friends and associates outside the towers. A few individuals buried in the rubble of the World Trade Center were able to direct rescuers to their locations using cell phones. These events show how ICTs can reshape not only access to information in ways that reconfigure who knows what and when, but also electronic and physical access to people—changing who is in, and who is out, of any network of communication.

Social Emotional Values: Reshaping Access to People

The instrumental value of wireless in performing various surveillance functions—getting and giving information—was emphasized by news coverage. However, the manner in which individuals made social connections using wireless to give and receive emotional support was as important as exchanges of instrumental information, and possibly more prevalent. A striking feature of reported calls is the degree to which so many carried relatively little or no instrumental information exchange. Instead, people wanted to say good-bye, reassure, say their last words, or convey their love to their family.[13] Phones were used in a final "communion" or intimate action of coming together. In doing so, wireless appeared to play a major calming influence that reduced the level of panic. The social and emotional support gained by access to people helped passengers shore their courage, such as suggested by Todd Beamer's conversation and the value he saw in leaving the line open as he and others marshaled the action with "let's roll."

Networks versus Hierarchies

In reconfiguring access to information and people, wireless media supported the formation of flexible and spontaneous networks of communication on September 11, while they circumvented and undermined more formal hierarchical systems of communication. This reinforces a theoretical argument about the bias of new ICTs in facilitating one-to-one and many-to-many networks of communication, in contrast to more controlled one-to-many, center-to-periphery forms more characteristic of hierarchical networks.[14]

The hijackers themselves were grouped in more or less loosely coupled networks and employed the cell phone to coordinate their attack. The passengers aboard more than one plane were able to get information from outside the official channels of communications aboard the aircraft and also circumvent the hijackers in time to enable a spontaneous network to form on at least one plane to overtake the hijackers of UAL 93. In the World Trade Center, occupants were able to network with individuals outside the buildings to obtain information that was useful in convincing them to evacuate even in the face of official announcements that it was safe to return.

The Limits of Technological Determinism

An important exception to this pattern is the Pentagon, where military culture and security systems appeared to erect an effective barrier to the formation of unintended networks of communication with outsiders. We found no reports of any calls into or out of the Pentagon. If this is indeed the case, it underscores the point that new ICTs might bias communication, such as in favoring networks over hierarchies, but they are not deterministic, since they are facilitated and constrained by their social and institutional settings. Military protocols and security systems were effective in maintaining official channels of command and control.

More generally, many hierarchical networks prevailed on September 11. Ad hoc networks were not the rule. For instance, the fire services appeared to follow their traditional chains of command even though this may have contributed to a lack of coordination and information exchange during this crisis at the World Trade Center.[15] In this sense, wireless communications might have enabled the formation of these ad hoc networks but did not determine this organizational form. There are major social, technical, and institutional constraints on the role of wireless in supporting ad hoc network forms of organization that were effective on September 11—for better or worse.

Long-Term Social and Policy Implications

The circumstances of September 11 were unique. However, the prominence of wireless media in the ways chronicled above could have long-range implications on the meanings people attribute to different communication media—and therefore on journalistic coverage of events as well as on policy and practice.

The Very Meaning of Wireless

Since the late 1990s, pagers, cell phones, and other wireless media have diffused widely within most industrialized nations. But in the months preceding September 11, phone shipments had slumped worldwide. In the aftermath of September 11, the wireless industry experienced a major boost. Stocks rose. More phones were sold. More minutes were billed. People and the press began to talk about the cell phone as a "lifeline" in case of emergency, for example, with some schools in the United States giving cell phones to teachers and lifting bans on students having cell phones on their campuses.[16] To some degree, this emergency role was a factor in the early diffusion of cell phones. But the rapid expansion of colorful covers, sharp designs, and ubiquitous use enabled notions of fashion, conviviality, and easy contact ability to define the cell phone more as a necessary everyday social and business aid. September 11 resurrected more instrumental definitions of wireless phones.[17] However, this impact has receded over time as sales leveled and advertising shifted to more entertaining roles of wireless, such as in sending video images.

Journalistic Coverage: Wireless as Enabler versus Savior

Media coverage of September 11, particularly in the United States, tended to focus attention on wireless technology, particularly the role of cell phones and air phones in the unfolding tragedy. Moreover, the coverage was disproportionately focused on the positive role that wireless played in the events, as illustrated by the focus of media attention on UA 93 and the takeover by the passengers.

This case study shows how wireless media enabled passengers to gain access to critical information and share a last communion with their loved ones. It was also apparent that wireless enabled the hijackers to coordinate their attack, that many—probably most—wireless calls failed, and that many victims, such as those in the World Trade Center, placed their lives in jeopardy by stopping to call home rather than evacuate the buildings. This is one aspect of an overly deterministic view of technology as an actor versus an enabler. Some individuals—victims and terrorists—used wireless media to enhance their communicative power, others did not. Journalistic coverage needs to look behind claims about the technology, which itself has no inherent impact, to understand how individuals use this medium to reconfigure access in strategic or tragic ways.

Reshaping Policy and Practice

A significant impact on telecommunication policy and practice could be made if the cell phone continues to be perceived as a more central and safety-critical medium for communication. There is support for such a view outside of September 11, but the maintenance of this perception is not a certainty.[18] Telecommunications has played an important role in earlier disasters, such as earthquakes, without having a lasting effect. However, no previous disaster has brought such attention to wireless technology, which rapidly became a highly visible element in public debate.[19] For instance, the words of Todd Beamer's wireless conversation were incorporated in President George W. Bush's 2002 State of the Union Address, when he implored Americans to embrace "a new ethic and a new creed: 'Let's roll.'" They have also become the title of one of many books about September 11 and UA Flight 93.[20]

Reflecting the double-edged nature of communication technologies, including wireless, the events of September 11 have apparent implications for the use of this medium by other terrorists. More than a year after September 11, on October 22, 2002, the leader of armed Chechens who held hundreds of theatergoers hostage in Moscow stood on the stage and told the hostages with cell phones to call home and say good-bye—mimicking the September 11 hijackers.[21] Yet wireless media played a valuable role in the Chechen crisis as well by providing Russian authorities with information about the location and actions of rebels holding hostages in the theater.

Public officials have argued that a higher priority should be placed on developing more reliable, universal, and standard forms of wireless connectivity in light of September 11.[22] This new significance assigned to wireless could support the allocation of more spectrum space to wireless and ensure more universal coverage. Clearly, present systems were unable to handle reliably the congestion and other special requirements of wireless media on September

11. This experience will raise the priority given to designing and building the infrastructures to support wireless communication in times of crisis, when the instrumental and social emotional values of connecting with another human voice arise once again.

Notes

The authors thank a London-based colleague and journalist, Malcolm Peltu, for his comments.

This chapter expands on an article published originally as William H. Dutton and Frank Nainoa, "Say Goodbye . . . Let's Roll: The Social Dynamics of Wireless Networks on September 11," *Prometheus* 20, no. 3 (2002): 237–45, and presented at Focus on September 11: Lessons in Communication, a conference held at the New York Law School, October 26, 2002.

1. Cell phone networks are a combination of wireless radio signals and hard-wired landlines that connect by radio frequency to cell sites with the equipment to receive and transmit radio signals within the circular footprint of its geographical area. The mobility of cell phone use is maintained seamlessly by automatic transference of calls between adjacent sites. Air phones on board planes work with similar principles, but the ground stations are further apart and designed specifically for air-to-ground signaling.

2. This theme of reconfiguring access, or tele-access, is further developed in W. Dutton, *Society on the Line: Information Politics in the Digital Age* (New York: Oxford University Press, 1999).

3. Embedded case study designs are discussed by R. K. Yin, *Case Study Research: Design and Methods,* 2d ed. (Thousand Oaks, Calif.: Sage, 1994).

4. Using electronic search engines, we located over thirty articles that dealt explicitly with the use of cell phones, air phones, and other wireless networks on September 11. Sources included stories by major news outlets, such as the Associated Press, BBC News, CNN, *Newsweek, New York Times,* and Reuters, as well as more local, trade, and online news media, such as the ABC News.com, Akron.com, the *Baltimore Sun,* the *Cincinnati Enquirer, Computerworld,* CTIA's World of Wireless, EQE Publications, and the Yankee Group.

5. Over the months following September 11, the unveiling of additional material and official records has confirmed the basic details of the account provided in this chapter.

6. For example, see Ricardo Alonso-Zaldivar, "Flight 93 Families Hear Tape of Jet's Last Moments," *Los Angeles Times,* March 26, 2002. The tapes played from the cockpit tape of United Flight 93 corroborate many aspects of the hostage takeover of the cockpit, even if they open up new questions about the final minutes before it crashed.

7. A particularly detailed account of events on this flight on which we draw is K. Breslau, "The Final Moments of United Flight 93," NEWSWEEK Web Exclusive, September 22, 2001. www.msnbc.com/news.flight93.org/newsweek-0922.html.

8. There are a number of similar accounts of individuals outside the World Trade Center observing developments and informing those within the structure to evacuate.

9. This is recounted by a police training officer in a story by Jerry Schwartz, "Response to Terror: A Narrow Escape from Darkness into the Light," *Los Angeles Times,* December 16, 2001.

10. We do not know if wireless or landline calls were used for some or all of these threats.

11. I. de Sola Pool, introduction to I. de Sola Pool, ed., *The Social Impact of the Telephone* (Cambridge: MIT Press, 1977), 4.

12. Dutton, *Society on the Line,* chap. 1.

13. In the days and weeks following September 11, the Internet was used in very similar ways, to make emotional connections rather than obtain or give information. See Center for Communication Policy, "Post-September 11," special press release, February 7, 2002. Los Angeles: UCLA Center for Communication Policy. Available at ccp.ucla.edu/pages/NewsTopics.asp?Id=2.

14. This argument is comprehensively developed by M. Castells, *The Rise of the Network Society,* 2d ed. (Oxford: Blackwell, 2000); and J. Arquilla and D. Ronfeldt, *Networks and Netwars: The Future of Terror, Crime, and Militancy* (Santa Monica: RAND, 2001).

15. John J. Goldman, "N.Y. Faulted for Disaster Plan on 9/11," *Los Angeles Times,* August 20, 2002.

16. M. Brown, "Area Schools May Rethink Ban on Cellphones," *Tampa Tribune,* January 16, 2002.

17. This general point is argued, for example, by the Yankee Group, *What Changes for Wireless: Taking Stock of the Industry after September 11,* October 4, 2001.

18. For example, research on the role of another wireless technology—pagers—in the aftermath of a blackout suggested that they play a far more central role than often attributed by the press. See W. H. Dutton, A. Elberse, T. Hong, and S. Matei, "Beepless in America: The Social Impact of the Galaxy IV Pager Blackout," in S. Lax, ed., *Access Denied in the Information Age* (London: Palgrave, 2001), 9–32.

19. In some respects, this case is comparable to the *Challenger* disaster, which riveted attention over a sustained period of time on the management of the National Aeronautic and Space Administration.

20. Lisa Beamer with Ken Abraham, *Let's Roll: Ordinary People, Extraordinary Courage* (Wheaton, Ill.: Good New Publishers, 2002).

21. Mark Franchetti, "Holiday Family Relive Their Moscow Terror Siege Ordeal," *Sunday Times,* November 24, 2002, 10–11.

22. For example, see the speech by N. J. Victory, assistant secretary of communications and information, U.S. Department of Commerce, to the Latin American Wireless Industry Association on November 26, 2001. Available at www.ntia.doc.gov/ntiahome/speeches/2001/alacel_112601.htm.

7

The Telephone as a Medium of Faith, Hope, Terror, and Redemption: America, September 11

James E. Katz and Ronald E. Rice

James E. Katz and Ronald E. Rice categorize the use of telephone and cell phones during the crisis and suggest a broader "syntopian" theoretical perspective. They explore how ordinary people used telephone technology (landline, voice answering, mobile phones, PDAs, wireless text) during the tragedy. They document how personal emergency communication was heavily imbued with emotional meaning, with messages addressing major life problems and values, such as leaving final messages and expressing love and concern, and sometimes requiring extreme efforts.

A S WE HAVE POINTED OUT elsewhere,[1] people view themselves in social situations as humans struggling to meet personal needs and handle social structural exigencies, not as mere operators of one particular type of communication tool. In our enthusiasm to focus on what is new and possibly different, we overlook the fact that these technologies are part of a built environment in and through which people pursue human and social activities. People enjoy using these tools with usually little curiosity about the nature and workings of the tools themselves. This is true no less of the automobile and the range than of the computer and mobile phone. Although we do focus on technology, we seek to show that technology is valued by humans for what it can achieve in terms of enduring social needs and individual inclination rather than for any attribute or feature of the technologies themselves.

Using this framework as a departure point, we will explore some of the ways the telephone, both mobile and fixed, as well as associated technologies such as two-way pagers and other digital interactive electronics, were used on and after September 11. It would be difficult to overestimate the role of the telephone in modern life despite its near invisibility to scholars of communication.[2] The effects of September 11 on telephone service were felt beyond the New York and Washington areas. Telephone outages occurred as far away as in parts of the Midwest. Wireless communication played a huge role in the response to the tragedy, since it appears that typically one-third of 911 calls originate from cellular phones.[3]

Propositions about September 11 Telephone Use Based on a Syntopian Perspective

We have organized our analysis around eight propositions, which we later explain using a syntopian perspective.

The Telephone Allows Intense Immediacy

Conventional landline telephones

Since the landline phones in the World Trade Center were so robust, people in the building could communicate with those outside until the buildings themselves collapsed. Shortly after the attack began, someone who answered the phone on the trading floor of broker Cantor Fitzgerald, whose offices were near the top of One World Trade Center, was asked what was going on. He said, "We are fucking dying!"[4] John Lugano nearly lost one brother in the attack and days later was still searching for another. Lugano said that he called his brother Sean, twenty-eight, a bond trader at Keefe, Bruyette & Woods, immediately after the first plane rammed the north tower. "I'm okay," Sean said from the south tower. "My floor is ten floors below . . . I'm just watching it." When the second plane hit Sean's building, John again called him at his desk and told him to leave. Sean protested that he was told to stay put, but John said, "Seanny, just get out of there." "Hopefully he listened," John said. Describing Sean's love of rugby—he was former All-American scrumhalf—and physical vigor, Lugano said, "The kid's a tough, tough kid and he's not somebody that ever gives up." Lugano aggressively circulated a flyer throughout Lower Manhattan and made many postings on the Internet in his search for his brother. Sean did not make it out.

A mix of landline and mobile phones

Due to mobile and landline phones, Rick Rescorla was able to stay deeply involved with his wife, Susan, and friends even as the situation at the World Trade Center was rapidly evolving. The telephone enabled them to share extremely tense moments and extend mutual encouragement during the attack. Susan was at home on the morning of September 11, talking to one of her daughters by phone. Susan then heard her call waiting tone and put her daughter on hold to take the other call. The other caller turned out to be another daughter who was calling from Manhattan, where she lived. "Put on the TV!" Rushing to the TV, Susan saw smoke pouring from the north tower. She hung up the phone and called Rick, whose office was on the seventy-third floor of the south tower, Two World Trade Center. Rick oversaw security for Morgan Stanley and had not even been scheduled for work that day. Susan's call was taken by Rick's coworker, Barbara Williams, who told her not to worry. Although the attack was on the other building, Rick was "out there with the bullhorn now."

Even as Rick was shepherding Morgan Stanley people out, a few refused to heed Rick's call to evacuate immediately after the initial attack on One World Trade Center, including Morgan Stanley managing director Bob Sloss. He was the only employee who did not evacuate the sixty-sixth floor after the first plane hit, pausing instead to make full use of the still functioning telephones. He made calls to his family and several underlings, even taking a call from a *Bloomberg News* reporter.

Meanwhile, Rick called his old army buddy in Florida, Dan Hill. They talked briefly about the attack. Rick said he was going to evacuate the Morgan Stanley people, even though the Port Authority was insisting they not do so. They told him to order people to stay at their desks, Rick fumed. "Everything above where that plane hit is going to collapse, and it's going to take the whole building with it. I'm getting my people . . . out of here," Rick said. After hanging up, Dan resumed his TV watching but within minutes saw another plane swing into view, execute a sharp left turn, and plunge into the south tower. Susan, watching TV in Morristown, saw the maneuver too. She again phoned her husband's office, this time frantically. There was no answer.

At the same time, Bob Sloss reevaluated his decision to stay behind. When the second plane hit, his office walls cracked. Realizing the danger, he began clambering down the stairwells. When he got to the tenth floor, he found Rick Rescorla, sweating through his suit in the heat, telling people they were almost out but making no move to leave himself. Rick had even broken into a patriotic song to give his people heart.[5] At about this time Rick called Susan. When she heard his voice, she burst into tears and could not talk. "Stop crying," he told her. "I have to get these people out safely. If something should happen to me, I want you to know I've never been happier. You made my life." Then he said he had to go.

Rick soon was back on his mobile phone, this time getting in touch with Dan Hill. Rick said he was taking some of his security men and making a final sweep, to make sure no one was left behind, injured, or lost. Then, he said reassuringly, he would evacuate himself. "Call Susan and calm her down," he instructed Mr. Hill. "She's panicking." Rick then began singing "God Bless America" and ended his phone conversation. Dan quickly called Susan. She herself had just been on the phone seeking reassurance from a family friend in England. Hearing her sobbing loudly, Dan had tried to comfort her. As he was speaking, Susan suddenly gave out a profound shriek of anguish. In Florida, Hill turned to his own television to see the south tower cascading down on itself.[6]

Contact and Reassurance Communication with Primary Social Group Members

Synchronous communication of the end of one's life and the permanence of love

Although wanting to know that others were safe was an extremely important reason for communications during the attack, letting others know they were loved by their special someone was the highest priority, and people tried to accomplish this by any communication means possible. Many messages of love and concern were sent out across landline, mobile phones, pagers, and the Internet that day. Declarations were not frilly, fancy, or creative. They were terse and conventional—and extraordinarily meaningful.

This directness is seen in a September 11 incident related by "RLMF," who worked near the World Trade Center. Her husband, though a New York City firefighter, was supposed to be on vacation that day. She heard about the first crash from her boss. As people gathered before the office windows to watch, the second plane struck. She recalled, "I saw the fireball. I heard the sirens. And that's when it hit me: My husband is a New York City fireman." Her panic was allayed somewhat because she knew he was off duty that week, but then she also remembered he was in the city for a meeting. "How on earth do I get in touch with him?" she wondered. Then what she describes as a miracle happened. The phone rings. "He is calling me from a pay phone twenty blocks away. He tells me, 'I'm on my way to the firehouse. I have to help.'" But RLMF pleads with him, "Don't go. You're on vacation. You could be killed." He tells her, "You know I have to. I can't leave my brothers alone out there; they will need all the help they can get." RLMF starts to cry but her husband interrupts her. "Say it." "Say what?" RLMF asks. "I can't go until you say it, like you always do." RLMF: "I squeak out the words that I say to him every time I leave him, 'Be good, Behave, Be careful—I love you always.'" Abruptly the line went dead.[7]

Bob Lynch, of Cranford, New Jersey, who helped supervise the elevators at the World Trade Center, called his wife, Elisabeth, right after the first plane hit. She recalls, "He was in the (outdoor) plaza. He told me he loved me, that he was okay." Lynch then reentered the burning building to help others escape; he perished.[8] The telephone also allowed a mother and daughter to share their last minutes together. In the case of Olabisi Shadie Layeni-Yee, the situation on September 11 was doubly poignant. Layeni-Yee worked at the World Trade Center in 1993, when it was bombed by terrorists. Her mother had watched that event unfold on television but had no idea what was going on with her daughter. Hours dragged by as the event was covered live on local TV. Finally she got a call from her daughter. "Mom, I'm fine;" she had been helping a pregnant woman walk down from the seventy-ninth floor. On September 11, things were different. On that morning, the mother's phone rang. It was her daughter. She urged her mother to turn on the TV and quickly told her the situation, concluding with the words, "If worse comes to worst, I'm just calling to say good-bye to all of you." Then she told her mother that the lights were going out and the floor was buckling. The mother turned around quickly toward the TV screen; it was a long shot of the tower collapsing.[9]

Answering machines and enduring immediacy

The telephone answering machine and voice messaging allowed some to receive a message that they would otherwise have missed, and has continued to give enduring meaning and a sense of emotional immediacy to the lives and relationships that were destroyed that day. When disaster struck that day, executive Melissa Hughes, who was working on the 101st floor of One World Trade Center, tried to reach her husband but only got his answering machine. (Hughes shared the recording with the news media, which then posted it on the web.) Against a background of pandemonium one can hear Melissa, gasping for breath and sobbing, "A bomb—or an airplane—has hit the building—I just wanted you to know—that I love you—always."

Lauren Grandcolas, aboard the hijacked plane above Pennsylvania, used her mobile phone to speak with her husband, Jack. Making a quick cell phone call before the plane crashed, she said, "We have been hijacked. They are being kind. I love you." A week or so after September 11, a reporter called the Grandcolas family. The reporter was nonplussed to hear the bright greeting: "Hi! Lauren and Jack aren't available. Leave us a message. Thanks!" No, she is not available, thought the reporter, she is spread over a scorched hill in Pennsylvania. Her voice, though, was still at home, welcoming callers. The reporter tried the number of another victim. There a telephone answering machine picked up his call. The pleasant-sounding woman's voice explained that Ian and Christine couldn't take the call, please leave a message. The reporter commented that Christine would never be able to take the call, as she too was killed by the hijackers. Trying back later, he reached Christine's husband, Ian Pescaia. He said he had not intentionally left the message on the machine. He explained to the reporter, "I haven't had a chance to go get another tape . . . It's just the only tape. And I didn't want to erase it."[10] As one columnist said, "When all that's left of your loved one is a voice on the answering machine, how can you hit delete?"[11]

Shared last words and thoughts

Last words: We who are about to die love you. Clearly many messages dispatched by pager, e-mail, and voice mail were eventually received. Probably many more were never received. There has already been serious probing of incompletely crushed and melted computer drives extracted from the World Trade Center rubble.[12] Although to date these efforts have been directed at looking for evidence of criminal intent, there is doubtless a large volume of personal messages and information as well.

Lee Hanson's son Peter, his wife, Sue Kim Hanson, and their two-year-old daughter Christine were killed September 11 when their flight, United Flight 175, crashed into the World Trade Center. Peter, thirty-two, used his cell phone to call his parents in Easton, Connecticut, moments before his plane hit the south tower. "The fact that he called me—he could have called any number of people," Mr. Hanson said. "I take a lot of comfort in that. He thought enough to do that."[13]

But even without the mobile phone, a constant in human affairs seems to be that at the end of life, getting and giving reassurance is important. Primo Levi, when he recounted his experience in the Nazi death camps, noted that the last wish of those who were about to be put to death was simply to get a word through to their family. That was all they wanted, he said, and would try any means possible to smuggle word in or out. Just confirmation that the family might be okay and that the condemned loved them, Levi recalled.[14]

Communication Technologies Used to Seek Information, Reassurance, and Establish Contact

Adam Mayblum was in the north tower, which was struck by the first airplane. His office, located below the point of impact, lurched back and forth ten or more feet. Light fixtures and the ceiling collapsed and smoke began billowing through holes in the ceiling. No one dreamed an airplane had struck their building; rather, many thought a bomb had gone off. He thought the worst was over. Like many others in an emergency situation, his thoughts turned to his family. He found that the phones were working. He relates, "My wife had taken our nine-month-old for his checkup. I called my nanny at home and told her to page my wife, tell her that a bomb went off, I was okay and on my way out. We were moving down very orderly in staircase A. Very slowly. No panic. At least not overt panic. My legs could not stop shaking. My heart was pounding. Some nervous jokes and laughter. We checked our cell phones. Surprisingly, there was a very good signal, but the Sprint network was jammed. I heard that the BlackBerry two-way email devices worked perfectly. On the phones, one out of twenty dial attempts got through. I knew I could not reach my wife so

I called my parents. I told them what happened and that we were all okay and on the way down. Soon, my sister-in-law reached me. I told her we were fine and moving down. I believe that was about the sixty-fifth floor. We were bored and nervous. I called my friend Angel in San Francisco. I knew he would be watching. He was amazed I was on the phone. He told me to get out, that there was another plane on its way. I did not know what he was talking about. By now, the second plane had struck tower 2. We were so deep into the middle of our building that we did not hear or feel anything. We had no idea what was really going on. We kept making way for the wounded to go down ahead of us."[15] Note that Mayblum and those around him, though in the bowels of the World Trade Center in New York, only got the first inkling of what had happened through talking by mobile phone to someone in San Francisco.

Magdalen Powers commented that what affected her most deeply was not the "screaming horror" of the World Trade Center collapse. Rather, when she went to back to her job at a New York City hospital, people would dial her office searching for their missing loved ones. "It's the helplessness and utter inadequacy I feel when I transfer them to the person with the list—the person I know probably won't be able to help them either." Callers would tell her that they had tried every other hospital. "I just try, as much as I can, to sound kind, sound compassionate, sound calm, and let them hope just a few seconds more."

A former U.S. Air Force servicewoman in Nevada, two time zones behind New York, recalls getting a call at 7 A.M. "The phone rang. I slowly pull my growing, pregnant body out of bed and to the phone. Who would be calling me this early? An old air force buddy is on the other line. His voice is slightly quivering. 'Wendy, turn on the news, America is being attacked.' . . . Suddenly, I feel my whole body shudder as I wonder where my daughter is at this moment. Anna is only three years old. She's spending the summer with her dad at the air force base that he is stationed at. I begin to panic with the possibility that the base could be a potential target. I immediately grab the phone again and call down there. No answer . . . I want her off that base. I want her home. I thought about making the four-hour drive to go pick my daughter up . . . but at nearly six months pregnant, I am in no condition to make the drive alone. Finally, the phone rings again. A familiar voice on the other line. It's my ex-husband's girlfriend reassuring me that Anna is okay. She was at day care."[16]

Transmission of Both Information and Affect Are Highly Important, and Users May Be Extraordinarily Sensitive to Nuances

Telephoning facts and feelings

Tom Burnett, aboard the doomed United Airlines flight above Pennsylvania, used his mobile phone to alert both his family and the authorities. When he reached his family, who lived in a suburb of San Francisco, his wife, Deena, was in the middle of making breakfast for their three girls. The call took her aback, and Tom sounded odd, she thought. She asked, "Are you okay?" "No," was his reply. Speaking in a quick, low voice he said, "I'm on a plane, it's United Flight 93, and we've been hijacked. They've knifed a guy, and there's a bomb on board. Call the authorities, Deena." Then he hung up.[17]

Cherri Simmons, who lives in Salt Lake City, shows how important and nuanced telephone communication can be. She wrote in an online commentary that she was sleeping late on her day off work when was she was awakened by the phone. She said, "It was my daughter-in-law telling me to turn on the TV. Just as I turned the set on and awoke my husband, we both watched in horror at the gaping hole and smoke in the first tower and then watched the crash of the second tower. I ran to the phone to call all my eight grown children. I felt desperate to hear the sound of their voices. I called them for reassurance, and it took me by surprise how devastated they were."[18]

BlackBerry® allows text to transcend voice

The BlackBerry® and other handheld wireless e-mail devices, like two-way pagers, served as lifelines to friends and loved ones and workmates, and as a way to stay in contact with the office. Lawyer Christopher Karras was at a meeting in an office near the World Trade Center when they heard and felt the first crash. Rushing to the windows, they saw hundreds of people scurrying below. Like others in the room, Karras said his first impulse was to tell his family he was okay. He reached for his BlackBerry wireless e-mail unit. "I don't even remember picking up a landline," said Mr. Karras. He typed a brief message to his wife in Minneapolis and his assistant in Philadelphia. The message dated 8:58 A.M., September 11, said, "We are three blocks from the crash. Heard the plane go by and hit. All here OK."[19]

People without hearing were able to use their mobile technology for text-based communication to reassure friends around the world in the midst of the horror. Susan Zupnik and Carl Andreasen, thirty-seven, both deaf employees of the Port Authority, were breakfasting in a cafeteria on the forty-third floor of the north tower. "Suddenly, my face was thrown against a window," Zupnik told a reporter. She then saw debris falling down outside the windows. People were screaming around her, but she could hear nothing. "I threw my bagel on the floor and ran out," she says. Zupnik had an AOL mobile communicator, a device she purchased only months earlier that allows her to send and receive text messages. She keyed in a message to a friend, an administrator at the New Jersey Institute of Technology, that something was wrong. Then she received a news bulletin over her pager—a plane had hit the World Trade Center. As she slowly made her way down the stairs, the communicator buzzed constantly. Friends from all over the world—in California and Maryland and Ireland and South Africa and England—were asking whether she was safe. "I'm on the twenty-sixth floor," she punched on the tiny keyboard to answer one concerned note and continued her escape.[20]

Use of Telecommunication Technology Leaves Important Residues that Reveal Complex Communicative Interactions

Using telecommunication technologies inevitably leaves residues because the modern telecommunications infrastructure involves many computers, with associated store-and-forward capacities and with complex abilities to track message flow for both billing and system optimization purposes. After the fact, these residues can be used to reconstruct communication interactions and messages. For example, numerous pictures were made of some of the hijackers using ATM machines, going through airport security, and entering newsstands.

News outlets carried hopeful stories that perhaps someone with a mobile phone could call for help from under the rubble. Perhaps, it was thought, even if the individual were unconscious, the mobile phone could still generate signals that would enable rescue. A man caught under the rubble used his mobile phone to contact his family in Pennsylvania for help. An emergency coordinator from Allegheny County said that the family member had "received a call from him saying he was still trapped under the World Trade Center. He gave specific directions and said he was there along with two New York City sergeants." Unfortunately reports of this nature were later shown to be spurious.[21] One journalist who traveled to Ground Zero on September 11 said that according to firefighters, neither the raucous noises of rescue nor the rare silences were the most moving sounds. Rather, the eeriest sound of all was mobile phones and pagers ringing underneath the debris as loved ones frantically tried to find and contact those missing.[22]

New Social Relationships and Arrangements Emerge around the Use and Nonuse of New Media

When confronted by disaster, people usually band together, overcoming preexisting social barriers. In studies of telephone service breakdowns, people share their limited resources and turn to neighbors; friendships and community spirit develops.[23]

Unsurprisingly, parallel instances arose during September 11. A young man relates how he and a previously unknown neighbor befriended each other as they stood on their Manhattan tenement roof watching events unfold. "After exchanging a few scant phrases of disbelief (after all, what could one say?), he invited me down through his window to use his phone. (Like most New York-ers, mine was nearly useless for most of the day.) I called my mother back in Michigan."[24] Bill Singer, an attorney who was escaping Ground Zero by foot, noted scores of individuals milling about, sobbing. "They often held cell phones. They cried that they couldn't reach their husband, their brother, their father, their sister, their mother, their friends. And strangers would simply walk up to them, put their arms around them, comfort them."[25]

Users Can Be Highly Creative in Developing Ad Hoc Solutions and Crossing Media Boundaries

People are primarily concerned about the goals and processes of communi-cation, not the technology. Thus people were creative in their use of available telecommunication technology to solve their immediate needs. When their first communication channel was blocked, they tried the next available alter-native. If the plausible alternatives failed, they would begin cobbling together their own patchwork and fallback systems to get messages to loved ones, no matter how. For example, they would use one technology to get a message dis-patched via another if necessary, as illustrated by this e-mail message:

From: Jennie Diluvio
Sent: Tues, September 11, 2001 10:03 AM
To: [several e-mail addresses]
Subject: OH MY GOD. . . . .
THE TOWER IS DOWN!!!!!!!!!!!!!!!
Drew, call mom and dad. I don't know if they remember I'm not there . . .

One mother was vacationing at the Habitat in Bonaire, when a friend ran to her group and said, "They're bombing America." A few moments of watch-ing TV in the open-air bar panicked her, as her daughter might have skipped school and gone shopping at Pentagon City. "Running for a telephone proved to be a futile proposition. There were simply no lines available. Instead, I bought a forty-five-minute Internet card and stuck myself at the Internet kiosk in the lobby at Habitat. While I was frantically e-mailing, the first tower of the World Trade Center imploded onto hundreds of rescue workers . . . . Within ten minutes I got the answer I was waiting for from my ex-husband. Morgan and everyone else I knew was fine. That information was priceless."[26]

People also used telephone communication for command-and-control pur-poses as victims sought to influence their fate. Amazingly, there was consider-able coordination between passengers on the aircraft and their loved ones on the ground. The case of Mrs. Alice Hoglan is instructive in this regard. Even though Hoglan's efforts did not bear fruit, they highlight impressive courage and presence of mind that people involved in the tragedy brought to bear on the situation. Hoglan had been phoned by her son, Mark Bingham, who was a passenger on the doomed UAL plane, while the hijacking was in progress. She called him back at 9:54 A.M. and left two messages on his cell phone's voice mail. She urged him and the other passengers to rush the cockpit because the flight appeared to be a suicide mission. Her son apparently never got the messages. Nonetheless, the messages, later retrieved from the phone company, are instructive as to what Mrs. Hoglan was trying to accomplish: "Mark, apparently it's terrorists and they're hell-bent on crashing the aircraft. So, if you can, try to take over the aircraft. There doesn't seem to be much plan to land the aircraft normally, so I guess your best bet would be to try to take it over if you can, or tell the other passengers. There is one flight that they say is headed toward San Francisco. It might be yours. So, if you can, group some people and perhaps do the best you can to get control of it. I love you, sweetie. Good luck. Good-bye."[27]

Emergency Can Create an Opportunity for the Misuse of Communication Technologies

The telephone, mobile phone, and Internet enabled many things to take place that otherwise might not have happened on September 11, for both good and bad. Indeed, the attack on the World Trade Center was organized and implemented at least partly through mobile communication. The terrorists also communicated between planes by mobile phone as they sat on the tarmac that fateful morning.

As noted above, there were many false reports of mobile phone messages being received from people trapped under the wreckage of the World Trade Center. Although some of these reports to authorities were believed to be correct at the time by the callers, they were often caused by people's misunderstanding of signaling and confirmation records, and a few were malicious. It was important to investigate the validity of these signals before dispatching rescue workers to risk their lives in an attempt to save people who were already dead. Someone claimed that her husband had called her on his mobile phone, and this led rescue workers to risk their lives to follow up what turned out to be a false claim. Sadly, despite great hopes and huge efforts, no one was saved from the rubble because of mobile signals or other wireless signaling technology. One woman, Sugeil Mejia, was sentenced to three years in jail for leading rescue workers on a wild goose chase through the rubble of the World Trade Center. She had fabricated a story that her husband, who she said was a police officer, and ten colleagues, had contacted her by mobile phone from the depths of the rubble several days after the September 11 attack. But within minutes of beginning a rescue attempt, the emergency workers had to flee for fears the surrounding buildings were about to collapse.[28]

Many people began using their mobile phones to commemorate the September 11 incident, but not always in the way we would expect. In what was interpreted as an anti-American gesture, a graphic began circulating among mobile phone users in the Middle East. The message was described by the *Economist* as appealing to "terrorist sympathizers" throughout the Middle East. The graphic, which can be easily sent on the advanced phones commonly used in Europe and the Middle East, shows a crude airplane crashing into a skyscraper. The caption, in Arabic, was "It hit and did not miss."[29]

A Syntopian Perspective

This chapter explores how ordinary people (and a few extraordinary ones) used telecommunications to address their situation and needs during the terror attack on New York City and Washington. It does this within a general theoretical perspective called "syntopia." Syntopia emphasizes the human uses and social consequences of telecommunication technologies in modern society. It avoids a mandatory ideological perspective (whether historical determinism, postmodernism, or technological determinism), instead embracing an empirical-pragmatic tradition.[30]

We chose the word "syntopia" for several reasons. First, an important aspect of the syntopia concept is that new media such as the Internet or mobile phones are part of a much larger synthesis of communication and social interaction. People's physical and social situation and history influence their actions online or over the air or wires, and what they learn and do there spills over to their real-world experiences. The term syntopia underscores this synergy across media and between mediated and unmediated activities. Second, the term syntopia draws together the words "syn" and "utopia." Derived from ancient Greek, the word means literally "together place," which is how we see the Internet and associated mobile communication and its interaction with unmediated interpersonal and community relations. Third, the term syntopia invokes both utopian and dystopian visions of what new media such as the Internet and mobile telephony does and could mean.

Conclusion

Why is it worthwhile examining telecommunication technology, especially telephone-based media, in the context of the September 11 terror attack? Analyzing human behavior at the extreme can illuminate a great deal about what people value, what they feel they need to commit themselves to, and what their lives might mean to themselves and to others, regardless of the specific communication medium they use.

The particularly dramatic, tragic, and devastating event of September 11 provides many examples of how new communication technologies both represent and shape syntopia—a dynamic social context where media are used for diverse human purposes, often in combination with other media, both intentionally and unintentionally, both in expected and unexpected ways, to communicate intense emotions and immediacy as well as objectively command and control information, for ill and for good.

Our examples have suggested a variety of propositions about new media—especially telephonic media—that emphasize aspects of communication that more traditional media theories have overlooked. While we know that media can convey different kinds of social and nonverbal cues, in this extreme situation the telephone and related media were used for the most intense and immediate expressions (proposition 1). People get to speak their last words, telling others before they die that they love them. It allowed one to summarize one's life and preserve one's message, even if the intended recipient was not there to answer the phone (propositions 2 and 3). It also allowed those experiencing the devastation to communicate their situation to others outside, or for outside family and friends to provide information that was not directly available to those experiencing the attacks, along with subtle nuances (proposition 4). Computer-based media collect and provide residues, both message content and meta-data about the message process and participants, which can be used to reconstruct complex social interactions in the midst of devastation (proposition 5). And the use of such media, including situations where such media cannot be used to accomplish the initial communicative goal, provide opportunities for new social relations to develop, both because of shared information and interdependence, but also as an occasion for shared experiences (proposition 6). Central to a syntopian perspective, people with specific communication needs find ways to combine and integrate different media to overcome obstacles and achieve their social, informational, and emotional goals (proposition 7). What appear to be specific media are part of an increasingly interconnected web of communicative possibilities, and apparent boundaries between media are often artifactual. At the same time, the modern tools of technology, including mobile phones and jet aircraft, could be used for deception as well as tremendous destruction (proposition 8).

The insidiousness of a bin Laden in his boastful recounting of how he had tuned to an American news broadcast to hear how the attack was unfolding and the transcendent courage of a Rick Rescorla in his communication with his wife show many supremely social and complex aspects of the relationship between people and their technology. The uses of telephone technology as a medium of faith, hope, terror, and redemption in the September 11 event is not determined by material forces, but by the interrelations among the uses and capabilities of society's media, and by the heart, spirit, and emotional and social needs of humankind.

Notes

This chapter expands upon a paper originally published as James E. Katz and Ronald E. Rice, "The Telephone as a Medium of Faith, Hope, Terror, and Redemption: America, September 11, " in *Prometheus* 20, no. 3 (2002): 247–53.

1. J. E. Katz and R. E. Rice, *Social Consequences of Internet Use: Access, Involvement, and Interaction* (Cambridge: MIT Press, 2002).

2. J. E. Katz, *Connections: Social and Cultural Studies of the Telephone in American Life* (New Brunswick, N.J.: Transaction, 1999).

3. Reza Jafari, "Lessons Learned from September 11: A Brave New Mobile World," 2001. www.eds.com/about_eds/homepage/home_page_911_jafari_assess.shtml.

4. "Attack on America," 2001. www.theworldtradecenternewyork.com.

5. Michael Grunwald, "Washington Post Staff Writer: A Tower of Courage," *Washington Post*, October 28, 2001, F1.

6. J. Stewart, "The Real Heroes Are Dead," 2002. www.newyorker.com/fact/content/?020211fa_FACT1.

7. "RLMF." www.nycstories.com/places/911/40/48.html.

8. Peter Genovese, "Bob Lynch, 44, Went Back in to Help Out," 2001. www.nj.com/crisis/lr/index.ssf?/base/obits-0/10137873461661205.xml.

9. A. Clymer, "The Cord That Bound Them," December 11, 2001. www.nytimes.com/2001/12/11/national/portraits/POG-11YEE.html.

10. Dennis Roddy, "Echoing Voices of Erased Lives," *Pittsburgh-Post Gazette,* September 22, 2001. www.post-gazette.com/columnists/20010922roddy102col2p2.asp.

11. Joel Garreau, "Dead Man Talking," March 16, 2002. www.washingtonpost.com/ac2/wp-dyn/ A40816-2001Jun8.

12. Erik Kirschbaum, "German Firm Probes Final World Trade Center Deals," December 16, 2001. www.reuters.com. Story filed December 16, 2001.

13. Associated Press, "Victim's Father Seeks Help for Others," 2001. www.gazettenet.com/americantragedy/09262001/6823.htm.

14. Primo Levi, *The Drowned and the Saved* (New York: Abacus, 1989). It is worth noting a two-decade-old incident aboard a Japanese Airline Boeing jumbo jet. On a routine JAL night flight the rudder control assembly snapped. With enormous skill, the captain was able to keep the wildly bucking jumbo aloft for nearly an hour before plummeting from the sky, There were no survivors. But during the emergency a father seated in the plane's back was somehow able to scrawl a short note to his family. It was found by rescue workers among the strewn wreckage. It said: "Have courage."

15. Adam Mayblum, personal communication to author, March 2002.

16. Wendy Revers, "The Phone Rang," September 11, 2001. mystory.inter.net/browse.php? action=next&pt=36.

17. Karen Breslau, Eleanor Clift, and Evan Thomas, "The Real Story of Flight 93," *Newsweek*, December 3, 2001. www.msnbc.com/news/NW-WEBEXTRA_Front. asp?cp1=1.

18. Cheri Simmons, "Morning to remember," 2001. www.usatoday.com/news/ nation/2001/09/27/where-were-you.htm.

19. Carilyn Kolker, "BlackBerries Aided Dechert Lawyers," *New York Lawyer*, September 25, 2001. www.nylawyer.com/news/01/09/092501f.html.

20. Bob Braun, "From the Newsroom of *The Star-Ledger* (Newark, N.J.)," October 2, 2001. www.wels.net/pipermail/voice/2001October/000047.html.

21. Associated Press, "Terror Hits Home: Thousands Feared Dead as Nation Begins Recovery from Strikes," 2001. www.nd.edu/~observer/09122001/News/11.html.

22. Niall O'Dowd, "An Irish Journalist Speaks of Ground Zero," September 22, 2001. endtimespeculate.crosswinds.net/V.

23. J. E. Katz, *Connections: Social and Cultural Studies of the Telephone in American Life* (New Brunswick, N.J.: Transaction, 1999).

24. Aldo, "Notes from a Brooklyn Rooftop," 2001. stoozrecords.com/ World%20Trade%20Center.htm.

Two-thirds of the voice lines in Lower Manhattan that were cut after terrorist attacks on the World Trade Center were reconnected by Verizon, but 100,000 lines were still without service as of September 25, 2001, the telecommunications company said. Most were business lines. www.nando.net/special_reports/terrorism/rescue/story/ 105408p-1202534c.html.

25. Bill Singer, "The World Trade Center Tragedy," 2001. www.singerfru.com/ wtc.html.

26. Mikki Barry, 2001. mystory.inter.net/browse.php?action=next&pt=0.

27. Jere Longman, "Cockpit Tape Offers Few Answers but Points to Heroic Efforts," March 27, 2002. www.nytimes.com/2002/03/27/national/27TAPE.html.

28. Associated Press, "World Trade Center Hoaxster Sentenced to Three Years. Falsely Claimed She Received Call from under World Trade Center Rubble," January 23, 2002. cbsnewyork.com/terror/StoryFolder/story_1629942698_html.

29. "Hot Leads, Stolen Identities," *Economist*, September 20, 2001. www. economist.com/agenda/displayStory.cfm?Story_ID=789176.

30. J. Anigbogu and R. E. Rice, "Expectations and Experiences of Infertility Information Seeking via the Internet and Telephone Directory," in R. E. Rice and J. E. Katz, eds., *The Internet and Health Communication: Expectations and Experiences* (Thousand Oaks, Calif.: Sage, 2001), 121–41; James E. Katz and Ronald E. Rice, *Social Consequences of Internet Use: Access, Involvement, and Interaction* (Cambridge: MIT Press, 2002); James E. Katz and Mark Aakhus, eds., *Perpetual Contact* (New York: Cambridge University Press, 2002); R. E. Rice, "What's New about New Media? Artifacts and Paradoxes," *New Media and Society* 1, no. 1 (1999): 24–32.

8

A Content Analysis of American Network Newscasts before 9/11

Jeremy Harris Lipschultz

The year prior to the September 11 attack is examined by Jeremy Harris Lip-schultz for evidence that American network television news offered a wider defi-nition of terrorism than after the traumatic events. Qualitative content analysis, a method for studying the framing via language of news, offered some support for the idea that attack coverage focused the meaning of terrorism on Osama bin Laden and events in the Middle East. Further study of earlier news content might reveal that the cultural meaning of terrorism is linked to national interests, gov-ernmental relations and international politics.

Framing: The Media and September 11

MUCH OF THE DISCUSSION about how the nation and its news media pre-sumably changed dramatically following the attacks was based on anec-dotal accounts of big event coverage rather than empirical and systematic ev-idence of media content prior to September 11. In the months following the attacks on New York City and Washington, D.C., national media in the United States played key roles in framing events, defining a social construction of re-ality, and influencing public opinion (Lule 2002). By framing is meant that news media select a narrow slice of reality as newsworthy—specific people, facts, issues, and events—rejecting a majority of possibilities. The purpose of this chapter is to report a qualitative content analysis of American network TV news through a framing perspective. It is argued that media content is impor-tant in defining changes in national perception about the terrorist threat. As such, this chapter also considers the year before the attack.

In the case of the 9/11 attack on the United States, Lule (2002) argued that the *New York Times* editorial page (writing immediately following the attack) can be seen as rooted in myth and storytelling of four types:

- The end of innocence (everything has changed)
- The victims (we might have been)
- The heroes (amid the horror)
- The foreboding future (as horrible as it is to imagine) (p. 280)

Lule (2002) found that in the month following the attack, the editorial page avoided the myth of the Enemy, despite the president's statement that he would get Osama bin Laden "dead or alive." In rarely mentioning bin Laden, the editorials "focused inward and built a case for the sacrifice and suffering that had been and would be endured by the American people" (p. 386).

The results raise tantalizing questions about whether other print and electronic editorial and news coverage followed these themes, as well as the extent to which themes may be identified in broadcast coverage. The present study focused on the three major network television evening news broadcasts—ABC, CBS, and NBC. The interest was in determining how network framing of terror through terrorism and terrorists was linked to the usage of other language. The year before the 9/11 attack was examined to answer these questions: To what extent was terrorism a topic for discussion in the evening news broadcasts in the year prior to the attack? How was terrorism framed? Did the constructions of social reality focus on Osama bin Laden or others? If there were reports on bin Laden, how were these threats framed for the audience? What language was used to describe threats? Will specific frames of terrorism, security, victims, heroes, and enemies be useful in understanding network television news content before and after the attack?

The study examined the year prior to the 9/11 attack—September 11, 2000, through September 10, 2001—with a qualitative content analysis. The goal of such a study is to conduct a deep reading of the text for commonalities, patterns, and distinctions. American network news content is important for understanding the formation of public opinion and policy on issues, as well as for observing manipulation of the public sphere by powerful elites. The exploration of dominant themes began with a Lexis-Nexis search of ABC, CBS, and NBC transcripts using "terrorism or terrorist" and limiting the search to the "(6:30 PM ET)" broadcasts of each network. The search produced manageable numbers of stories for close reading—ABC (N = 131), CBS (N = 231), and NBC (N = 165). Duplicate stories were discarded. Each reference to terrorism or terrorist was examined to determine its cultural context and the framing of the news item.

The examination of network television news framing identified the importance of the weeks prior to the October 2000 attack on the USS *Cole,* the focusing after that attack on Osama bin Laden, the extensive coverage of ongoing Middle East violence, and their relation to a broad usage of the term "terrorism."

The Broader View of Terrorism before 9/11

Terrorism, one year before the attack, was framed in fairly broad terms. For example, the state funeral of a former Canadian prime minister was an opportunity for ABC News to look back: "Trudeau . . . put soldiers in the streets to crack down on Quebec terrorists" (October 3, 2000).

Also, terrorism was framed in the context of concerns for future Olympic athletes in Greece (October 4, 2000). Threats on "U.S. embassies throughout the Arab world," in a story discussing how U.S. and Egyptian leaders were meeting with Yasir Arafat to try "containing the violence in the Palestinian territories," also mentioned terror (October 5, 2000). And there were concerns about North Korea: "The U.S. accuses the North of supporting terrorism, of building nuclear weapons and long-range missiles" (ABC, October 10, 2000).

CBS began coverage the year before the attack with a clear link between terrorism and bin Laden: "CIA analysts have a new CD given to them by colleagues in Jordan, but it is not your basic top-40 collection. This is a digital copy of what's called a terrorist encyclopedia, a thousand-page training manual for followers of Saudi renegade millionaire Osama bin Laden, with instructions on everything from murdering individuals to building huge truck bombs" (September 18, 2000). NBC, like the other two major networks, used terrorism as a term to explain many types of violence. Four years after the Olympic bombing in Atlanta and days before the Sydney games, for example, an NBC interview with the vindicated Richard Jewell and the ongoing search for Eric Rudolph was an opportunity to talk about the "threat of terrorism" (September 13, 2000). NBC's exclusive Olympic broadcast contract meant that the network gave more time to "security" issues during the period (September 15, 2000). With Tom Brokaw anchoring from Sydney, the threat of terrorism was linked to none other than Osama bin Laden: "Good weather, genial host, and no protests—or worse, terrorist incidents. But that possibility is always on the minds of security officials who have a very tight system in place here. And tonight, there is a dramatic reminder of the constant danger of terrorism. A manual American officials say is a direct link to Osama bin Laden, the world's most wanted terrorist" (September 18, 2000).

The occasion was the sentencing of six terrorists in Jordan in a failed millennium plot, and evidence that included a computerized "terrorist training manual" recovered at a refugee camp along the Pakistan-Afghanistan border (September 18, 2000).

The *Cole* Attack: Terrorism against U.S. Interests Abroad

A pivotal moment came in mid-October, when the USS *Cole* was attacked in the port of Yemen. ABC reported that "the U.S. received information that suspected terrorist leader Osama bin Laden had signaled one of his hit squads to move out" (October 12, 2000).

CBS offered reaction to the *Cole* bombing from President Clinton, as well as the presidential candidates. An Al Gore sound bite emphasized a response: "Any terrorists should know that whoever is responsible for something like this will be met with a full and forceful and effective retaliatory response from the United States of America." A George W. Bush sound bite also was used: "I—I just don't think it's the role of the United States to walk into a country and say, 'We do it this way. So should you'" (October 12, 2000). CBS Reporter Jim Stewart offered an investigative frame : "U.S. officials said they . . . continue to believe that terrorist leader Osama bin Laden was behind the attack" (October 14, 2000).

For NBC, the "devastating terrorist attack" on the *Cole,* "the worst terrorist attack against a U.S. Navy ship in modern history," captured the news agenda as "senseless" and an "outrageous act of terrorism" (October 12, 2000). By the next day, the focus shifted to the search for terrorists: "Investigators have no firm evidence to identify those responsible, but tops on their list, the Egyptian Islamic Jihad with direct ties to terrorist Osama bin Laden" (October 13, 2000).

Events in the wake of the *Cole* attack reflected concern over Yemen as a nation that harbors terrorists, the continuing investigation into the terrorist attack, and the fallout. NBC's Jim Miklaszewski: "Terrorist Osama bin Laden is still considered a prime suspect in the *Cole* bombing. Today he warns the U.S. not to launch retaliatory strikes against him. Two years ago, the U.S. carried out air strikes against bin Laden targets in Sudan and Afghanistan, after he was linked to the bombings of two U.S. embassies in Africa" (October 17, 2000).

NBC also showed a videotape of "Egyptian militant Rifai Ahmed Taha, seen here with terrorist Osama bin Laden" three weeks before the *Cole* attack (October 19, 2000). A day later, the guilty plea in New York by Egyptian-born Ali Mohamed in the 1998 embassy bombings described him as "believed to be the highest ranking member of bin Laden's terrorist organization to turn state's evidence" (October 20, 2000). The use of the word "organization" is similar to the media framing of criminal groups, such as in organized crime.

The investigation into the *Cole* attack was a focal point for CBS, as reporting on the probe continued from Yemen. Anchor Dan Rather focused on Yemen: "it was considered to be a state sponsor of terrorism. And many of the young here fought with radical Islamic forces in Afghanistan and brought their anti-American, anti-Zionist sentiments back with them. Still, despite the fact that Osama bin Laden, the known terrorist with links to Yemen, has made recent specific threats against U.S. interests here, U.S. intelligence concluded there was no credible threat to the USS *Cole*" (October 19, 2000).

In the same broadcast, CBS reminded its audience that bin Laden was under indictment in the United States for his connection with the east African embassy bombings. CBS reported that authorities believed "the attack was ordered by terrorist mastermind Osama bin Laden" (January 8, 2001). Two days later, the network showed "rare pictures" of bin Laden at his son's wedding— he was "rumored to be seriously ill, but he seemed in good health" (January 10, 2001). The focus on bin Laden served media needs to put a face on terrorism in a way that framed the enemy rather than explained a violent political struggle for power in the Middle East.

A bin Laden videotape in June led ABC to reframe him as an "accused terrorist" in the *Cole* attack: "In this videotape, Osama bin Laden and his followers boast that they bombed the USS *Cole*, in which 17 American servicemen were killed. Bin Laden is also heard urging Muslims to prepare for a holy war, and young men are shown shooting at an image of Bill Clinton" (June 20, 2001). As American forces in the Persian Gulf were placed on "a very high state of alert" there were new fears. ABC Reporter Martha Raddatz observed: "U.S. intelligence intercepted transmissions from two known associates of Osama bin Laden" (June 22, 2001). Again the murky world of terrorism was implicitly defined in ways that suggested similar frames of the criminal underworld.

The Middle East as Ongoing Palestinian Terror

In the wake of the attack on the *Cole,* Middle East strife remained a frame in the ABC terrorism story: "At another rally in Gaza today, Islamic leaders called openly for terror attacks in Israel. Extremist groups have a lot of support these days and a lot of power. This afternoon, a crowd of angry Muslims set fire to a hotel and to homes of people whom they say sold alcohol" (October 14, 2000).

The words "terrorism" and "terrorist" were linked to Middle East violence, concerns for events such as the Olympics, and Osama bin Laden's threatening organization. CBS coverage of "a day of rage" in Israel focused on "Palestinian security" forces, "angry Palestinian teen-agers," and "Israeli riot police." The story left for a sound bite from an Israeli Knesset member to label the Palestinians as "terrorists" (October 6, 2000). The use of official sources produced a frame that pits terrorist enemies against security forces.

Event-driven Palestinian terrorism also made ongoing news on ABC: "The extremist group Islamic Jihad is claiming responsibility for an act of terror in Jerusalem that killed two Israelis and injured 11 others" (November 2, 2000). ABC coverage made linkages between the foiled millennium attacks and trouble in the Middle East.

Like the other networks, NBC described the ongoing Israeli–Palestinian conflict in connection with "Palestinians planning terrorist attacks" (October 10, 2000). Meantime, the Middle East conflict was portrayed in more heated terms as Israeli tanks fired on "Palestinian gunmen": "with more than 400 Islamic militants now out of jail, freed yesterday by Yasir Arafat, the threat of terrorism inside Israel is suddenly very real." The Islamic side was framed via militant gunmen, while Israeli forces were placed in a military context. In a profile on Arafat, reporter Andrea Mitchell called him "a walking contradiction," "a man of peace and war," and a "freedom fighter in the '60s to much of the world who U.S. officials say becomes a leading terrorist in the '70s, until he consolidates power and says he makes a commitment to peace" (October 13, 2000). At the same time, no frame for Ariel Sharon was offered. Ron Allen reported: "The militants from groups like Hamas are trying to seize the moment . . . urging Yasir Arafat to stay home and let the suicide bombers lead the war" (October 14, 2000). A day later, Martin Fletcher added: "The war is far from Israeli cities, but security officials worry that could change and that Palestinians are planning a wave of terror" (October 15, 2000).

Throughout the spring of 2001, the ongoing Middle East violence remained the most frequently reported story in connection with terrorism—using such words as "suicide bombing by a Palestinian terrorist" and "militant Islamic group Hamas" (May 19, 2001). During this period, terrorism also was mentioned in stories about the Taliban crackdown in Afghanistan and strife between Pakistan and India.

Terrorism in Its Many Forms

Despite an emerging new focus on bin Laden, ABC also reported on broader terrorism in Sierra Leone (December 3, 2000). Following the U.S. Supreme Court decision that decided the 2000 presidential election, there was a story that suggested terrorism would be a test for George W. Bush: "An immediate challenge for the new president: how to respond to the terrorist attack on the USS *Cole*. Intelligence already implicates Osama bin Laden, and Mr. Bush has said he will punish those responsible" (December 14, 2000).

While bin Laden's threat was framed as an overseas problem for the military, the execution date for Oklahoma City bomber Timothy McVeigh was an opportunity to frame the domestic terrorism story (December 28, 2000).

The guilty verdict of a Libyan agent in the Pan Am 103 bombing over Lockerbie, Scotland, twelve years earlier produced still another ABC frame of terrorism linked to Muammar Qaddafi (January 31, 2001). Still, the message remained overwhelmingly focused on bin Laden (February 7, 2001). A month later, bombings in England and Israel were linked to IRA and Hamas terrorists in a story that left international terrorism in an "over there" context (March 4, 2001). The six-year anniversary of the Oklahoma bombing, an opportunity in April for coverage of plans for the upcoming McVeigh execution, was portrayed in symbolic terms: "It was, we all remember," noted anchor Peter Jennings, "that horrible moment when Americans realized that terrorism had truly reached the heartland" (April 19, 2001).

In May, it was reported in a brief item on the weekend news that the president was concerned about the terrorism threat: "In other news tonight, the president wants a White House office on terrorism, and he wants the vice president, Dick Cheney, to run it. The office would coordinate the government's response to biological, chemical, and nuclear attacks, tasks currently being handled by the Justice Department" (May 5, 2001). Clearly it was not so much that networks avoided coverage of terrorism in favor of other news, as much as the threat of terrorism remained more abstract and generally beyond our borders. ABC reported that there was a "boom" in high technology designed to protect against terrorist attacks. The story lead was: "The State Department is warning Americans abroad to be on the alert for attacks by groups linked to the Saudi millionaire Osama bin Laden. Protecting against terrorism is part vigilance, but more and more it is also part high-tech gadgetry" (May 12, 2001).

Less than two months before the 9/11 attack, ABC reported its most specific terrorist threat against the United States in a John McWethy story: "A coded message, we are told, and it names two specific places. ABC News has learned it is Saudi Arabia and Kuwait they are most worried about, and the date they are worried about: tomorrow" (July 18, 2001). The story named "Osama bin Laden's terrorist organization" as the source of the threat. As that threat passed, ABC coverage again broadened to other sources of terrorism—including the failed search for accused U.S. bomber Eric Rudolph and the ongoing reporting of Palestinian terrorists. Beyond this focus, terrorism also was linked to a broader range of concerns involving many countries—North Korea, Libya, Iraq, Iran, Russia, Northern Ireland, Canada, Afghanistan, the Philippines, Pakistan, and India. In the United States, terrorism was linked to Oklahoma City bomber Tim McVeigh and fugitive Eric Rudolph. Terrorism was portrayed as a broad threat related to school shootings, missile defense systems, embassies, the Olympics, biological weapons, and technology designed to provide safety.

Terrorism and the Criminal Justice Frame

The trial of four for the bombing of two U.S. embassies in Africa in 1998 was occasion for CBS to offer a description that went beyond bin Laden to his organization. Said reporter Jim Stewart, "The terrorist millionaire accused of masterminding the bombings. He's been indicted for the attack but remains in hiding in Afghanistan, protected by the ruling Islamic chieftains. The government intends to present a case that portrays bin Laden as something like a godfather figure in charge of the terrorist group known as al-Qaeda, or the Base" (February 3, 2001). Again, the use of the phrase "something like a godfather figure" defined the accused in a criminal frame.

Two days later, with the trial under way, anchor Dan Rather noted twelve Americans had been killed in the attacks in which 224 people died: "Experts say they believe bin Laden will stop at nothing to strike back at the United States" (February 5, 2001). Reporter Jim Axelrod described testimony of the government's star witness in the case: "Al-Fadl said he was a founding member of al-Qaeda, an Islamic terrorist group started by Osama bin Laden to fight the Russians in Afghanistan. During the Gulf War, Al-Fadl testified today, bin Laden warned, 'We cannot let the American Army stay in our holy land and take our oil, our money. We have to do something to take them out,' and that bin Laden's religious advisers said not to worry if that meant killing civilians" (February 6, 2001). The testimony reported was a rare and isolated instance of explaining a cause for terrorism. The testimony also identified countries: "Al-Fadl, who's talking as part of his own plea deal, said bin Laden coordinated with Islamic radicals inside Algeria, Libya, Yemen, Egypt, Syria, and Chechnya about overthrowing those governments" (February 6, 2001).

In March, another federal criminal case was mentioned by CBS for the first time as a "cell" operating in the United States: "A federal grand jury in Charlotte, North Carolina, indicted four people today for allegedly conspiring to finance and supply the Islamic terrorist group Hezbollah. Prosecutors say they are part of a Charlotte-based Hezbollah cell that was charged last summer with smuggling and money laundering" (March 29, 2001). The release of a bin Laden recruiting video in June prompted a story by reporter Tom Fenton. Osama bin Laden is described as a "Saudi-born militant, renegade millionaire" planning more attacks against, according to a source, his "enemies, you know, the Americans, the Israelis." He is described by Fenton as "the prime suspect" in the Cole attack (June 20, 2001). Just a day later, reporting of a government indictment in the Khobar Towers "terrorist bombing" in Saudi Arabia focused on Iran: "The indictment alleges that the charged defendants reported their surveillance activities to Iranian officials and were supported and directed in those activities by Iranian officials" (June 21, 2001).

Overall, in the year before the 9/11 attack, there was significant focus by CBS on Osama bin Laden and the Israeli–Palestinian conflict. But terrorism was also linked to a wide array of incidents and nations—Afghanistan, Algeria,

Kosovo, Libya, Macedonia, Yemen, Syria, Iraq, Iran, Egypt, Peru, Ecuador, Columbia, Chechnya, Cuba, and the Philippines.

The conviction of a Libyan in the 1988 bombing of Pan Am flight 103 led to some of the harshest criticism on government policy. Susan Cohen, the mother of a twenty-two-year-old victim, lashed out in an interview with NBC News: "Qaddafi is the winner in this . . . Qaddafi has oil. Bush is an oil man. Cheney is an oil man" (January 31, 2000).

Such was the wider face of terrorism, even as the African embassies trial opened, and Dan Abrams reported on the government case against four men linked to Osama bin Laden—one that outlined the al-Qaeda organization and its "terrorist cells maintained around the world" (February 4, 2001). The trial was occasion to label bin Laden the "FBI's most wanted man," the "alleged mastermind" of the embassy attacks, head of an "alleged global terrorist network," and someone who was "waging war on the west, in particular, the United States" (February 10, 2001).

NBC's Dawna Friesen reported on civil war, drought, and famine in Afghanistan, as well as relief efforts hampered by "tough, new UN sanctions imposed last month, an attempt to force the Taliban to hand over Osama bin Laden who the U.S. accuses of masterminding a worldwide terrorist network" (February 17, 2001).

Like other networks, NBC linked terrorism to the Oklahoma City federal building bombing in 1995: "the site of the bloodiest terror bombing in the U.S. history," which became a new museum (February 18, 2001). In March, NBC showed new pictures of bin Laden, for the first time called an enemy: "And we have rare new pictures tonight of one of America's most feared enemies, the Islamic militant Osama bin Laden reciting a poem to praise the deadly terrorist bombing of the U.S. Navy ship the *Cole*" (March 1, 2001).

In June, a "Palestinian suicide bomber" killed eighteen at a discotheque and was labeled the "worst terror attack" in eight months (June 2, 2001). President Bush was quoted by NBC as calling it a "heinous terrorist attack." British Prime Minister Tony Blair's sound bite reflected frustration with the ongoing violence: "They will continue these ghastly and totally unforgivable terrorist attacks, and then Israel will feel it needs to respond."

The indictment of "14 Middle Eastern terrorists" charged in a truck bombing that killed nineteen servicemen in Saudi Arabia led to this sound bite by Attorney General John Ashcroft: "The indictment explains that elements of the Iranian government inspired, supported, and supervised members of the Saudi Hezbollah" (June 21, 2001). The threat of terrorism from "terrorist Osama bin Laden" was reported at the end of the month, as a "terrorist training video" became available and was considered a clue that bin Laden "may be preparing to unleash a new wave of terror" (June 25, 2001).

Elite Discourse and Terrorism as a Cultural Frame

Mass media constitute much of what is accepted as the culture at any given time or place. Because culture may be a very profitable social agreement on popularity, it is in the interests of social elites to control it. Media messages, in short, are embedded with social-cultural meanings that help define global-international context about nations, races, and religions. In the case of terrorism coverage, content is driven by elite sources and their power agenda.

Modern culture is often seen as having been transmitted through various mass media channels, including television. TV news plays an important role in reality construction by framing events. The manipulative political landscape of media, even when it comes to coverage of terrorism, produces limited frames: "Elites face a ceaseless threat of oversimplification and stereotype from opponents taking advantage of the volatile combination of aggressive reporting and uninformed public opinion" (Entman 1989, 125).

In the wake of 9/11, terror for most Americans became less of an abstraction and more of a concrete threat. Media coverage in the period following the *Cole* attack in October 2000 may have begun to reflect this change. The year before 9/11 represented a period in which, through the frames of the three major network television news operations, the public could have seen that Osama bin Laden's brand of terrorism and the ongoing Middle East violence combined to create a climate of danger.

The diffusion of new ideas about the threat of terrorism was dominated by a focus on Osama bin Laden and ongoing Middle East violence. The October 2000 attack on the USS *Cole* in Yemen led the networks to see bin Laden's threat as serious within a criminal frame. However, the network framing of terrorism and terrorists also included coverage of many other countries and characters. It tended to emphasize overseas rather than domestic targets.

Framing of international news, such as terrorism, involves definition, shared norms, themes, and meanings (Shah, Watts, Domke, and Fan 2002): "In essence, by organizing complex news topics around distinctive arguments and themes while concurrently downplaying others, journalists help shape an issue's deeper meanings and implications for the public" (p. 343). In the case of terrorism before 9/11, American networks treated Osama bin Laden as "mastermind" behind a somewhat vague terrorist criminal organization, Palestinians as terrorists, and people such as Timothy McVeigh and Eric Rudolph as domestic terrorists. The emphasis was on law enforcement efforts to investigate and prosecute terrorism. The criminal frame was emphasized by, for example, calling bin Laden "something like a godfather figure" and referring to his "organization" and "associates." Stories tended to focus on the terrorism threat and consequences of attacks rather than reasons for them—an oversimplified message for the public.

There were similarities and differences across the three networks. CBS offered more extensive coverage of Palestinian terrorism, and NBC seemed to take more seriously the threat of domestic terror—partly because of its Olympic contract. Overall, the framing in the year before 9/11 avoided the later focus on domestic security, enemies, victims, and heroes. Another study comparing the present data to the year after 9/11 may find a radically different framing of terrorism. When ABC's *Nightline* reported on a Washington, D.C., area sniper, for example, BBC correspondent Dennis Murray distinguished "random killings" from "politically-motivated terrorism" (Murray 2002). Media may report on people being terrorized by a wide range of events inflicted on them by a broad list of "terrorists." However, it is the limited framing of events in news that regularly defines public fears. "Operating within a particular ideological system (be it free market, socialist, or Islamic), mass media workers consciously or unconsciously produce integration propaganda that serves the overall interests of elites" (Karim 2002, 105). In other words, the terror label is a political tool utilized to claim power.

Framing, News, and Culture

It has been argued elsewhere that before the 9/11 attacks, news media did not have "a language" for terrorism (Schudson 2002, 39), failings of elites left Americans "baffled" (Carey 2002, 76), lack of context in coverage about the Middle East led to public ignorance (McChesney 2002), and previous events such as the 1991 Gulf War demonstrated the power of television news to shape politics (Robinson 2002). At the same time, however, an alternative view is that the meaning of terrorism is found among "experts" who are the powerful "owners of the dominant discourses on terrorism" (Karim 2002, 104).

Framing of news about terrorism may be understood from a cultural perspective. Carey (1992) linked culture to "unity" (p. 8) and common information. Culture focuses on media representations or "significant symbolic forms" (p. 30) and "expressive artifacts—words, images and objects that bore meanings" (p. 37). "Terrorism," then, is a matter of human language in which "myth, ritual . . . story, narrative, chronicle" help strengthen social bonds (p. 15). The labeling of terrorism by governmental, military, and academic sources may emphasize state security lapses: "Persons who are not agents of the state and who use violence for political reasons are portrayed as criminals, to be dealt with within the judicial structures (including military tribunals). Public attention is thus kept focused on the violence rather than the politics of political violence" (Karim 2002, 104).

In this way, the framing of terrorism is subject to domestic propaganda and ideology about Islam: "it dramatically reconfirms the well-established stereotypes about Muslims, namely those of violence, lust, and barbarism" (p. 110). Nowhere is framing so overt as in the case of the mythmaking in television news coverage.

The framing of myth surrounding the 1988 Yellowstone wildfires (Smith 1989) and the cultural ritual of the 1989 United Flight 232 disaster (Haarsager 1990) offered two examples of this in network TV news coverage. Framing involves a social construction of reality found in bits of social action pieced together to create meanings (Ryan and Sim 1990). When framing involves a political enemy, it inevitably leafs to stories that ignore certain facts and emphasize others (Lenart and Targ 1992).

The enduring power of network television news has been noted in defining media events (Jamieson and Waldman 2002). Framing of news involves sense making of complex facts (Andsager and Powers 2001), discussion of difficult social issues through the lenses of current events and people (Hasian and Flores 2000), policy preferences (Kellstedt 2000), political debate (Kruse 2001), and public deliberation (Simon and Xenos 2000). Thus framing often involves "elite discourse" (p. 364) by "elite political actors" (p. 365), and meaning making through manufacture of "context" (p 366).

Conclusion

The notion of a political enemy is intriguing. Osama bin Laden, during the war with the former Soviet Union in Afghanistan, was considered a friend of the United States. It is likely that a content analysis of terrorism in the early 1980s would produce a quite different media frame from what is found here. Likewise, political enemies such as Saddam Hussein have varying degrees of relationship with the U.S. government over time. To the extent that news media rely on government sources at the Pentagon and Department of State, it is likely that the frame changes with whatever is the politically expedient position.

This study of words is limited because we need to better understand the visual importance and the imaging of television news stories (DeLuca and Demo 2000). Powerful images, such as those of bin Laden or Saddam displaying and shooting weapons, are frequently repeated on network news as file footage and may overpower the more careful words chosen for a news report. The gatekeeping process of news, including news of terrorism, turns out to be a strange mix of news values, available sources, political concerns, nationalistic tendencies, economic realities, and cultural norms of interpretation. Framing terrorism, then, has at stake control of the political agenda (Jasperson et al 1998). The framing of political enemies in media content (Lenart and Targ 1992; Parenti 1996) in part appears to influence racial and cultural identities (Lind 2001). This complex cultural process belies journalism's adherence to the norm of objectivity. Far from the objective myth sold to the public by media people, news is frequently subjective manipulation of opinion utilized by elites to achieve political objectives. Those political actors with the skills to manipulate events to their benefit may use the malleable public mind by controlling media coverage.

Note

An earlier version of this work was presented at the Third World Conference, University of Nebraska-Omaha, October 11, 2002.

References

Andsager, Julie L., and Powers, Angela. 2001. "Framing Women's Health with a Sense-Making Approach: Magazine Coverage of Breast Cancer Implants." *Health Communication* 13, no. 2: 163–85.

Carey, James W. 2002. "American Journalism on, before, and after September 11." In *Journalism after September 11*, edited by Barbie Zelizer and Stuart Allan, 71–90. London: Routledge.

———. 1992. *Communication as Culture: Essays on Media and Society.* New York: Routledge.

DeLuca, Kevin M., and Demo, Anne T. 2000. "Imaging Nature: Watkins, Yosemite, and the Birth of Environmentalism." *Critical Studies in Media Communication* 17, no. 3: 241–60.

Entman, Robert M. 1989. *Democracy without Citizens: Media and the Decay of American Politics.* New York: Oxford University Press, 1989.

Haarsager, Sandra L. 1990. "Seeing Is Believing: News as Cultural Ritual in Times of Disaster." Paper presented to the Association for Education in Journalism and Mass Communication, Minneapolis, August.

Hasian, Marouf, Jr., and Flores, Lisa A. 2000. "Mass Mediated Representations of the Susan Smith Trial." *Howard Journal of Communications* 11: 163–78.

Jamieson, Kathleen Hall, and Waldman, Paul. 2002. "The Morning After: The Effect of the Network Call for Bush." *Political Communication* 19: 113–18.

Jasperson, Amy E., Shah, Dhavan V., Watts, Mark, Faber, Ronald J., and Fan, David P. 1998. "Framing and the Public Agenda: Media Effects on the Importance of the Federal Budget Deficit." *Political Communication* 15: 205–24.

Karim, Karim H. 2002. "Making Sense of the 'Islamic Peril': Journalism as Cultural Practice." In *Journalism after September 11*, edited by Barbie Zelizer and Stuart Allan, 101–16. London: Routledge.

Kellstedt, Paul M. 2000. "Media Framing and the Dynamics of Racial Policy Preferences." *American Journal of Political Science* 44, no. 2: 239–55.

Kruse, Corwin R. 2001. "The Movement and the Media: Framing the Debate Over Animal Experimentation." *Political Communication* 18: 67–87.

Lenart, Silvo, and Targ, Harry R. 1992. "Framing the Enemy: New York Times Coverage of Cuba in the 1980s." *Peace and Change* 17, no. 3: 341–62.

Lind, Rebecca A. 2001. "The Relevance of Cultural Identity: Relying upon Foundations of Race and Gender as Laypeople Plan a Newscast." *Journalism and Communication Monographs* 3, no. 2: 113–45.

Lule, Jack. 2002. "Myth and Terror on the Editorial Page: The New York Times Responds to September 11, 2001." *Journalism and Mass Communication Quarterly* 79, no. 2: 275–93.

McChesney, Robert W. 2002. "September 11 and the Structural Limitations of U.S. Journalism." In *Journalism after September 11*, edited by Barbie Zelizer and Stuart Allan, 91–100. London: Routledge.

Murray, Dennis. 2002. "In Cold Blood." *Nightline*, October 15. Lexis-Nexis transcript.

Parenti, Michael. 1996. *Dirty Truths*. San Francisco: City Lights.

Robinson, Piers. 2002. *The CNN Effect: The Myth of News, Foreign Policy, and Intervention*. London: Routledge.

Ryan, John, and Sim, Deborah A. 1990. "When Art Becomes News: Portrayals of Art and Artists on Network Television News." *Social Forces* 68, no. 3: 869–89.

Schudson, Michael. 2002. "What's Unusual about Covering Politics as Usual?" In *Journalism after September 11*, edited by Barbie Zelizer and Stuart Allan, 36–47. London: Routledge.

Shah, Dhavan V., Watts, Mark D., Domke, David, and Fan, David P. 2002. "News Framing and Cueing of Issue Regimes: Explaining Clinton's Approval in Spite of Scandal." *Public Opinion Quarterly* 66, no. 3: 339–70.

Simon, Adam, and Xenos, Michael. 2000. "Media Framing and Effective Deliberation." *Political Communication* 17: 363–76.

Smith, Conrad. 1989. "Brave Firefighters, Endangered National Icons, and Bumbling Land Managers: Network TV Myths about the 1988 Yellowstone Wildfires." A Paper presented to the Association for Education in Journalism and Mass Communication, Washington, D.C., August.

9

Something's Happened:
Fictional Media as a Recovery Mechanism

Fiona McNee

By the afternoon of September 11, entertainment executives were rushing to re-move media products containing "inappropriate" references from American tele-vision and movie screens. While references to terrorism were the starting point, their caution extended to themes of war and threats against America, all in the name of "public sensitivity" and "respect for the victims." Simultaneously, unin-terrupted news coverage was brimming with scenes of devastation and heart-break.

Fiona McNee analyzes an episode of the NBC series West Wing entitled "Some-thing's Happened" to show how fiction can help the viewer process fact and re-cover from a disaster. West Wing series author Aaron Sorkin created both an analogy for what was happening across America and a way to address the ques-tions and issues of tolerance, patriotism, and response. She concludes that "in-stead of requiring protection, audiences may indeed benefit from fictional media products in a time of crisis."

ON TUESDAY, SEPTEMBER 11, 2001, over fifty television channels across the United States were broadcasting news of a single event. In the four fol-lowing days, the major American broadcast television networks devoted their prime-time programming to commercial-free coverage of the attacks on New York and Washington, D.C. Over the weekend of September 15–16, each re-turned to some semblance of normal programming, but with comprehensive scheduling changes. Film studios were also reconsidering marketing and dis-tribution strategies, some because of an inability to secure television advertis-ing and others in acceptance that the nation was transfixed by the small screen.

Many of these decisions to postpone, cancel, or remove media products from American screens were couched in sensitivity and respect for the victims. As frantic as those first days were, the scope of projects affected on this basis was remarkable. With unbelievable scenes of destruction and heartbreak on almost every channel, why was it considered inappropriate to offer the audience fictional stories about war, terrorism, and political intrigue? Why were audiences considered ill-equipped to watch fictional good guys win battles against aliens,[1] but able to watch hour after hour of an increasingly hopeless search for real heroes? Why did the Twin Towers need to be immediately erased from our screens[2] when their rubble was still strewn over New York's streets?

Interpretative Frames

The traditional mass media response to tragedies such as the Oklahoma City bombing or war has been to focus on news gathering, with fictional treatments following months, if not years, later. These fictional treatments have focused principally on viewer empathy and identification with the people involved, on the heroes and their lives. Stories focused on issues and motivations, on moral judgments of policy issues, seem to need the distance that only time can give, emerging years later if at all. But is this in fact the case, or is there another role that fictional media can play?

Research shows that viewers of media products, both fictional and factual, use interpretive schemata or strategies to understand those products. Interpretive strategies are largely unconscious and are formed by individuals based on their experiences of media generally. For example, as familiarity with the rules and conventions of a genre increases, viewers are able to use these rules to construct meaning.

Other media representations and treatments also influence interpretive strategies. Research shows that audiences, in processing the meaning of a media product on an issue, draw on other media discourses, both factual and fictional, about that issue. This contextualizes the issue for the audience, not only producing meaning but potentially adding another layer to future interpretive frames. If a topic is extensively embedded in media culture, audiences have a broad inferential framework with which to build meaning, subordinating the impact of any one product.

This idea of cross-pollinating interpretive frames is at the heart of fictional media's potential role as a recovery mechanism. One school of thought sees mass media as a way individuals meet social and psychological needs such as gathering information, reducing personal insecurity, and finding support for their values. In times of social instability when established institutions and beliefs are challenged, people no longer have the social realities that usually provide frameworks for understanding, acting, or escaping. This makes them more likely to turn to the media to provide these frameworks.

Certainly the public's need for information was at the center of the networks' decisions to devote so much airtime to continuous, commercial-free news coverage despite the financial and human cost.[3] As MSNBC's president and general manager, Erik Sorensen, said, "This is what we do, and we can't let people down."[4] But news and factual programming are not the only way audiences obtain information. Storytelling has long been recognized as an effective technique of information dissemination, contextualizing information into the experience of the audience. In contrast to formal discourse, narrative approaches to communication engage audiences on conscious and subconscious levels, drawing on their imagination and sensation as well as reason.

If fictional and factual media products are both capable of having an educational or informational function, and viewers draw broadly on media discourses to interpret these products, there would seem to be little reason to protect audiences from fiction but not fact. But does its ability to engage on a subconscious level make fictional narrative discourse capable of a more profound function or role? Audiences are seldom merely seeking information in a time of crisis such as September 11, even from news services. Certainly uses and gratification theory has demonstrated that individuals use media generally to resolve more profound psychological needs than information gathering. But can the rules and conventions of fictional media give it the scope to inform, reassure, and influence at a deeper, emotional level than factual media is able?

Fiction in Times of Crisis: "Isaac and Ishmael"

With the entertainment industry continuing to remove "inappropriate" media products, ten days after the tragedies in New York, Washington, and Philadelphia, NBC announced that it had approved a script for its drama series *West Wing* that would deal directly with "some of the questions and issues facing the world in the wake of the recent terrorist attacks in the United States."[5] Series author Aaron Sorkin and his coexecutive producers John Wells and Thomas Schlamme felt not only that it was important to acknowledge the tragedy but to contribute something to the national discourse on how to move forward. As John Wells said, "Hopefully [this episode] will make people talk and think. You can't pretend it didn't happen."[6]

The challenge for Sorkin as author was to find a premise that allowed him to address these questions and issues without crossing into opportunism. Sorkin's simple premise gave him the distance he needed by taking the focus off the terrorists and the tragedy: As part of the Presidential Classroom program, a select group of high school students are being addressed by Deputy Chief of Staff Josh Lyman when the White House has to be sealed. Unbeknown to the students and Josh, a routine FBI database search has triggered an investigation in which the FBI, Secret Service, and White House Chief of Staff Leo McGarry are faced with a terrifying possibility: a terrorist agent successfully infiltrating the headquarters and home of the president of the United States.

This premise sets up two story lines, each with a distinct purpose. The one carried by Josh and the students has principally an information dissemination purpose. By educating and encouraging Josh's fictional audience to think rather than merely react, Sorkin challenges his literal audience to do the same. In contrast, the investigation story line is more subtle in reaching the literal audience, reflecting the more complex experiential approach it takes to conveying its message. Combined, they produce a media product that provides as much information as any factual media product and then goes further to offer the audience a constructive means to process, respond, and move on from the crisis event.

It is a *West Wing* convention that the scenes before the main titles serve as a prologue to the self-contained episode that follows. The prologue for this episode, "Isaac and Ishmael," closes with a seemingly simple but thematic statement by Josh to the increasingly frightened group: "Something's happened." On September 11, something did happen—something that wasn't supposed to be able to happen. As heartbreaking as the casualty lists in New York, Washington, and Pennsylvania were, in many ways they were not the most terrifying part of the attacks for most Americans. The real terror was that there was something in the world that could conceive of such evil, and it had their country in its sights.

Answering Questions and Issues

By placing Josh and the group from the Presidential Classroom in the middle of a crash situation, Sorkin created both an analogy for what was happening across America and a way to address the questions and issues to which NBC referred. Faced with an audience with only one thing on their mind, Josh leads a Socratic discussion that ultimately reassures both fictional and literal audiences by empowering them with knowledge. Americans are not renowned for their knowledge of global events, and Sorkin drew on almost his entire cast to help the audience build interpretive frames based on analogies: Islamic extremists and the Ku Klux Klan; the Taliban's actions in Afghanistan, and the Nazis' actions in Poland; the circumstances that create a terrorist and those that create a gang member.

With the parameters more clear, Sorkin has Josh pose the fundamental issue for the students and indeed for many Americans: Why are Islamic extremists trying to kill us? The students' responses mirror the rhetoric of world leaders and the news media in the days following the attacks, exhorting the values for which America stands. Unsatisfied, Josh observes: "I'll tell you: right or wrong—and I think they're wrong—it's probably a good idea to acknowledge that they do have specific complaints. I hear them every day. The people we support; troops in Saudi Arabia; sanctions against Iraq; support for Egypt. It's not just that they don't like Irving Berlin."

At the time, this was a speech not without risk. Suggestions in the days following the attacks that they had been the direct result of American foreign policy sparked considerable outrage and a brief but bitter public debate that went largely unresolved. Traditional fictional responses might have patriotically avoided this issue, but *West Wing* executive producers wanted to advance the national discourse and that meant exploring both views to some extent. Josh's assistant Donna voices the thoughts of a significant part of the viewing audience when she responds with:

D: Yes it is.
J: No, it's not.
D: I don't know about Irving Berlin, but your ridiculous search for rational reasons why somebody straps a bomb to their chest is ridiculous.

Again, rather than give a simplistic, populist reply, Josh explores her point and the difficult issue of how it is possible that simply being an American can make one the object of such hatred. To be condemned for being a citizen of a particular country is a concept Americans may intellectually understand but very few would have experienced, making the terrorist attacks even more incomprehensible. Through Josh, Sorkin tries to explain the unexplainable: His brief discussion of the beliefs of Islamic extremists contrasts them with basic tenets of the American way of life, from restrictions on women to acceptable cheers at soccer matches, and then asks:

So what bothers them about us? Well the variety of cheers alone coming from the cheap seats in Giants Stadium when they're playing the Cowboys is enough for a jihad, to say nothing of street corners lined church next to synagogue next to mosque; newspapers that can print anything they want and women who can do anything they want including taking a rocket ship to outer space, vote and play soccer. This is a plural society: that means we accept more than one idea. It offends them. So yes, she does have a point.

On one level, this passage presents a fairly evenhanded discussion of the issues. Both viewpoints are presented without any overt statement as to which is correct, leaving the interpretation in the hands of both fictional and literal audiences. However, when the dynamics of the entire scene are considered rather than simply the extracted dialogue, signposts toward the creator's preferred interpretation are revealed.

Beyond the fact that one viewpoint is shown making allowances to the other, suggesting dominance, particularly telling is which character presents which viewpoint. In the factual media, networks relied heavily on their established anchors—Peter Jennings (ABC), Dan Rather (CBS), and Tom Brokaw (NBC)—during their marathon coverage of the attacks' aftermath for one main reason: credibility. The American public trust these men: they "know" them and see them as a form of authority figure. This trust and respect makes the audience more likely to accept and respond to their messages at both a conscious and subconscious level.

This idea of credibility or fidelity is at the heart of Sorkin's allocation of dialogue to character. Donna is female, and previous scenes have established she is Josh's assistant. From the students' perspective, she has taken a subordinate, even subservient position in relation to Josh, staying a step back and to the side to allow him to be the center of the figurative stage. She has remained largely silent, not participating with the students in their discussion. Josh's only "public" comment to her at this point has been a terse command to which she immediately responded.

To both figurative and literal audiences, this signifies that while Donna's perspective is valid, it is not to be preferred. By contrasting both views, Sorkin encourages both audiences to engage in the process—to respond rather than react. In contrast, the narrative conventions of news reporting constrain emotional responses to factual media products, focusing on personal empathy rather than identification with values. Similarly, fidelity in news reporting is judged on a very different scale to that applied to dramatic discourse. Althogh both fictional and factual media were providing answers, Sorkin's fictional treatment may have been more able to address questions that remained unspoken.

A similar examination reveals Sorkin's support for one side of the civil liberties versus intelligence powers debate between communication director Toby Ziegler and press secretary CJ Craig. This issue, very topical in the mainstream media as people grappled with how the attacks could have happened, is also discussed in some detail by the students and Josh. The prointelligence debate may be more comprehensively explored, in part acknowledging its understandable appeal to a frightened public, but CJ's flippant responses and inability to answer some of her boss's impassioned challenges provide strong signs of Sorkin's views on the issue.

Themes of Tolerance

If Sorkin's first story line proved that fictional media can fulfill an information dissemination role at least as successfully as factual media, his second demonstrates the true potential of fictional media in a time of crisis. The strength of narrative discourse lies in its ability to bring the creator's message into the experience of the audience by appealing to all of their faculties. This makes narrative discourse ideal for communicating abstract concepts. Abstract concepts by their nature are difficult to convey in discourse that relies on rationality and reasoning. They are experienced rather than identified and, as such, do not easily fit within the rules and conventions of factual media. This is particularly so with a concept like tolerance, which is itself composed of other abstract concepts such as respect and compassion.

In the days following the attacks, there was great speculation in the factual media as to who had committed and authorized them. Many distasteful practices were proposed by a community unable to understand why the government, military, and intelligence community hadn't been able to prevent the tragedies. Many of these practices were aimed at Arab Americans, as was much of the public's fear and anger. While appeals from civic leaders for tolerance were widely reported in the news media, so were biographies of the suspected hijackers and montages of previous terrorist actions against America that had been attributed to terrorists from the Middle East.

The theme of tolerance is alluded to in the Presidential Classroom story line, particularly in the spirited debate on civil liberties. CJ and Toby's debate exists primarily on a rational plane. While one perspective is shown as preferable, in essence it is a debate of two intellectual philosophies. However, as chief of staff Leo McGarry interrogates White House staff member Rakeem Ali, Sorkin makes real the issue of tolerance and the inherently narrow-minded prejudices of racial profiling in a way no presidential address ever could. The coherence of Sorkin's narrative seduces the audience into identifying more deeply with Leo. Instead of merely understanding his actions intellectually, the audience shares the same emotions, makes the same judgments, and ideally faces the same unpleasant truths as this character.

To do this, Sorkin makes extensive use of the conventions of the espionage genre—the lighting, the set, the interrogation style and process—to progressively build both the interrogators' and audience's suspicions. Rakeem Ali has organized protests against the American presence in Saudi Arabia. He was questioned over bomb threats while in high school. He has an applied mathematics degree from MIT but chooses to work for a White House staff secretary. In the minds of Leo and the audience, Ali's answers are pat, almost too plausible. Finally, someone breaks:

RA: It's not uncommon for Arab Americans to be the first suspected when that sort of thing happens.
L: I can't imagine why.
RA: "Look . . .
L: (interrupting) No. I'm trying to figure out why anytime there's terrorist activity people always assume it's Arabs. I'm racking my brain.

RA: I don't know the answer to that, Mr. McGarry but I can tell you that it's horrible.

L: Well that's the price you pay.

RA: (after a long pause) Excuse me?

RA: (cut to L sitting in silence with a blank expression, then the camera returns to RA): The price I pay for what?

The White House of *West Wing* is liberal and democratic. Its chief of staff has always exemplified those beliefs and values. When Rakeem Ali is subsequently cleared, both the audience and Leo are left stranded, their outrage and frustration suddenly replaced by confusion and disbelief at finding themselves unexpectedly revealed as prejudiced and judgmental. Sorkin manipulates the audience's interpretative frames, built both from espionage and thriller genres but also from factual media reports and "investigations," to expose the prejudices inherent in them. We expect Rakeem Ali to be guilty—he fits the profile.

It is the potency of this particular cross-pollination between media and life that is Sorkin's true caution. Leo believes himself to be a civilized American, a man committed to the notion that all men are created equal and are innocent until proven guilty. Until he is tested. Until he is afraid and under pressure, and finds that he is less than the man he thought he was. Leo's disbelief is in sharp contrast to Rakeem Ali's grim acceptance of his perfunctory discharge when his innocence is established. There are no apologies, no explanations, and for Ali no surprises.

In accepting the normalcy of his treatment and returning to work, Rakeem Ali demonstrates real tolerance. He understands tolerance because, as a second-generation American of Middle Eastern descent, he has had to practice it his entire life. He has had to live with the sudden suspicions, the wariness, and presumptions he encounters because some of those who share his faith and heritage choose to act from hate. Intellectually the audience knows this occurs; they have seen news reports and current affairs programs exposing the impact of racial profiling on a variety of minority groups. But tolerance is not something that is known intellectually but rather understood emotionally and experientially. Factual media is ill-equipped to convey this understanding—fictional media is not. Similarly, it is difficult for a factual media product to suggest to a public, particularly a public in crisis, that it is prejudiced and judgmental. By allowing it to be suggested in a story about fictional characters, however, the narrative discourse is able to raise this issue with the audience in a nonthreatening way.

During the interrogation, Leo dismisses Ali's frustrated protests by remarking, "I don't think you understand the seriousness of what's happening right now." Instead of being suitably chastened, Ali vehemently responds, "I don't think you do." This reversal of power, the first hint of the reversal to come, is Sorkin's fundamental warning to America: do not allow your grief, fear, and anger cloud your appreciation of what is at risk. Steel, glass, and even lives may have been destroyed, but the terrorists could only destroy America's foundation if Americans allowed it. Since the newspapers that first reported the attacks also reported the first death threats against Arab Americans, this warning cannot be too often sounded.

Lessons for the Future

Instead of requiring protection, audiences may indeed benefit from fictional media products in a time of crisis. Of course, these media products need not have an explicit public policy purpose. For example, video stores reported significant increases in rentals for films featuring American heroes vanquishing terrorists in the days following September 11. Patriotic themes and battles already won may offer audiences much more than entertainment. Reassurance is not simply a function of knowledge and logic: belief and emotion are relevant factors, aspects in which fictional media excel.

However, fictional media's role in recovery has a second dimension distinct from meeting the audience's psychological needs. Other writers have considered the subversive potential of the factual media's disaster marathon in far greater detail and with far more authority than could be done by this author. Terrorists have long recognized the power of the media to amplify and disseminate the horror of their attacks. They understand the rules and conventions of factual media and exploit them to hold hostages far beyond the geographical confines of the terrorist act. Making available fictional media products, particularly products that interrupt the lingering emotional destruction with a constructive response, denies them at least in part the salience and exclusivity they crave. It offers a viable alternative to the disaster marathon, empowering the audience to reclaim the stage.

Conclusion

The attacks on New York and Washington, D.C., were, certainly in the eyes of the world leaders, attacks on the entire civilized world. In Australia, we were beset by the same fears, the same disbelief, and the same attacks on mosques and Muslims as in America, albeit on a smaller scale. To my knowledge, no media products were modified in the wake of the attacks, other than to accommodate news specials. But when "Isaac and Ishmael" aired in Australia on October 10, it was inexplicably without the modified title sequence that featured the cast speaking to the camera.

Three central issues feature in both story lines: racial tolerance, civil liberties, and American foreign policy. Unlike the other two issues, Sorkin's position on this third issue is not revealed as a simple for or against. Perhaps acknowledging that this was neither the time nor the place to make a value judgment on such an issue, Sorkin instead chose to advocate accepting responsibility: that the choices a country makes, even with the most noble of intentions, may not accord with or be appreciated by other countries.

Nonetheless, as part of the global rather than local audience, certain aspects of Sorkin's treatment irked but only because the underlying policies also irk. For example, for all his bravery and diplomacy in tackling the foreign policy issues inherent in the text, the only reference Sorkin made to another country suffering at the hands of terrorists was to Israel. But "Isaac and Ishmael" never claimed to have all the answers, and to spark foreign policy debate from numb disbelief and horror could well be seen as achieving its intent.

In America, critics were split on the merits of "Isaac and Ishmael," some accusing it of being "preachy" and others praising the contribution made by its approach and content to the national recovery. While the experts were divided as to whether the experiment was a success, audiences demonstrated their willingness to look for answers in fictional media. "Isaac and Ishmael" received the highest ratings ever for the series, with 25.24 million viewers.[7] To give this context, audience numbers fell by 10 percent the following week but still constituted one of the largest audiences for West Wing.

NBC, Warner Bros., and the executive producers of West Wing took a significant risk in "Isaac and Ishmael." Commercially, there were questions as to whether there would be an audience. Logistically, it required a virtually unheard-of turnaround time to make it to air just twenty-two days after the attacks. Financially, the interruption to the planned season premiere incurred significant costs in wasted promotion and lost advertising revenue. When it did air, Sorkin waived his writer's fees and all profits from the episode went to September 11 charities. But they proved that fictional media could play as important a role as factual media in meeting society's needs, should something ever happen again.

Notes

This chapter expands upon a paper originally published as Fiona McNee, "Something's Happened: Fictional Media as a Coping Mechanism," in *Prometheus* 20, no. 3 (2002): 281–87.

1. The Fox Network had planned to screen a repeat of the feature film *Independence Day*, which features the graphic destruction of New York City at the hands of aliens, and *The X-Files Movie*, which opens with an Oklahoma City-style bombing of an empty federal building by humans in league with aliens, on the weekend of September 15–16. Both films were pulled from the viewing schedule.

2. Within hours of the attacks, Columbia Tristar pulled from public release a poster advertisement for the upcoming release *SpiderMan* that showed a reflection of the Twin Towers in the eyes of Spider Man's mask. Twentieth Century Television also pulled from syndication a 1997 episode of the animated series *The Simpsons* titled *The City of New York vs. Homer Simpson*, in which the cartoon family visits the Twin Towers to reclaim their abandoned car.

3. Fianacially, various estimats put the total loss of advertising revenue to the networks at a minimum $600 million over the six-day period from September 11. In terms of the human cost, journalists were working minimum twelve-hour shifts; broadcast anchors Peter Jennings (ABC), Dan Rather (CBS, and Tom Brokaw (NBC) were reportedly on air an average fifteen hours a day throughtout that period.

4. Paula Bernstein and Rick Kissel, "Fatigue Frays Auds and Nets," Variety.com, September 13, 2001. www.variety.com/index.asp?layout=print_story&articleid=VR1117852673&categoryid=14.

5. Marcus Errico, "A Very Special 'West Wing,'" Eonline, September 22, 2001. www.eonline.com/News/Items/Pf/0,1527,8865,60.html.

6. Josef Adalian and Michael Schneider, "Plots Are Hot Spots for Nets," Variety.com, September 24, 2001.

7. Rick Kissel, "Wing Sings for Peacock," Variety.com, October 4, 2001. www.variety.com/index.asp?layout=print_story&articleid=VR1117853726&categoryid=14.

10

September 11 in Germany and the United States: Reporting, Reception, and Interpretation

Joachim W. H. Haes

Joachim W. H. Haes compares the reporting and the formation of interpretations of the terror attacks of September 11, 2001, in Germany and in the United States. He begins by comparing reporting style and diffusion figures in the two countries and shows far-reaching similarities. The interpretations, however, vary considerably. While Americans turned to increased patriotism and religion, German commentators stressed the importance of thorough investigation and international cooperation.

THE HUMAN AND POLITICAL crisis of September 11, 2001, had a counterpart in the realm of mass media because the crisis shed a light on the role of individual journalists in news reporting. How do journalists form opinions and interpretations? How much personal opinion is allowed and how much is necessary? How important are cultural borders for news reporting in moments of crisis? On this level, September 11 was unprecedented insofar as factual information on the events was immediately available all over the world: eight minutes after the first crash, the Associated Press (AP) reported, "Plane crashes into World Trade Center." Police, firefighters, and reporters arrived simultaneously at the towers and witnessed the second plane's impact at 9:03 A.M., enough time for CNN to broadcast live pictures of what later became the "War against America."

News reporting and reception in the United States is contrasted with news reporting and reception in Germany. If September 11 was really an event of global significance, we should be able to derive insights on the state of what might be called "cultural globalization"—the increasing interconnectedness of technical and purely interpersonal communication and interpretation networks on a global scale. Identical information does not automatically lead to identical interpretations, and this is even truer in an international and intercultural context. Immediate reactions to the attacks in Germany are described, data on the news diffusion in Germany and the United States is contrasted, and finally the interpretations that developed from this news are compared.

The empirical basis for this research was drawn from experience, published articles, and two surveys. The Institute for Media and Communication Science of the Technical University of Ilmenau interviewed 1,460 Germans in January–February 2002.[1] Everett Rogers and Nancy Seidel surveyed 127 individuals, mainly from New Mexico, in September 2001.[2] Additional data is drawn from studies of undisclosed size by the UCLA Internet Project and communication scholars Mary Step, Peggy Finucane, and Cary Horvath.

Reporting

On Tuesday, September 11, news reporting in all Western countries was probably the same: the same "special newsflashes" showing the same pictures, and long-time professional journalists telling the same little information while being visibly shocked. Americans agreed that it would "never be the same again" and expected worse to happen. They—and many in Europe—feared that the peaceful prosperity western nations enjoyed might be lost from tomorrow.

Being six hours ahead of eastern standard time (EST), radio stations in Germany broadcast the news about a (small) plane damaging the World Trade Center during the 3:00 P.M. news—four minutes after the AP announcement. The TV news channels N-TV and N 24 were even faster, as cooperation agreements enabled them to draw on CNN pictures. The first major TV channel/network to start live reporting was RTL, which canceled its regular program at 3:10 P.M. and sent its anchorman, Peter Kloeppel, on air. The public channels followed suit within the next two hours.[3]

On September 11, the news coverage was primarily by electronic media. Since all TV stations in the United States and abroad shared the few available pictures, most networks and channels aired virtually the same program. Meanwhile, radio had a hard time. The medium was bound to report verbally from the scene and on reactions by politicians and survivors, but most of the dramatic impact of the information was contained in the pictures. It could have been the hour of online media, but it was not. Though some websites updated their content continuously, many servers collapsed when millions of people wanted to know the full story simultaneously. Within the first few hours, however, many websites were again up and running. Sites like www.spiegel.de and www.welt.de reduced their content to one or very few pages with minimal multimedia content. A study by the UCLA Internet Project showed later that the Internet did not inform many but proved to be a viable tool for communication and news gathering in the weeks following September 11.[4]

Extraordinary, however, was the style of news reporting by professional journalists: Bewildered by the dreadful scenes, radio and TV reporters formed a union with their audience. Nobody knew what was going on. Too soon to explain, too soon to draw consequences, this was the time to describe the situation as it appeared, to inform people all over the world. Americans and Germans alike were shocked to view helpless victims trapped in the upper floors of the World Trade Center, some jumping to their certain death. The audience was moved to tears when the towers finally collapsed. These pictures, broadcast to a billion people, could have initiated a change in the way we watch the world and foreign politics. As the whole world saw the same pictures, a notion of community was generated. All civilized nations could equally condemn the attacks and call for global justice.

Knowledge Diffusion

In these hours, the similarity of German and American diffusion figures is striking: At 9:00 A.M. (EST), 10 percent of the German population had heard about the events and 7 percent of the American population had heard. In both countries, most people were informed before 10:00 A.M., 68 percent in Germany and 34 percent in the New Mexico (where it was 8:00 A.M.). Other sources speak of about 70 percent news diffusion before 10:00 A.M. (EST) and 90 percent before 10:30 A.M. in the United States.[5] In the next three hours, the diffusion curve had crossed the 90 percent line in both countries, with very few getting the initial information from newspapers or talk the next day.[6]

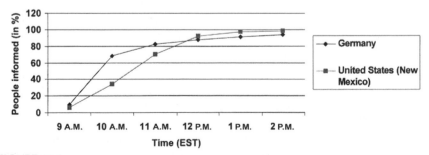

FIGURE 10.1
Knowledge Diffusion about the Attacks in Germany and the United States

In addition to the remarkably similar speed of diffusion, people obtained the information from the same media. About 50 percent saw the news on TV, about 25 percent were told by others, and 1–2 percent found it on the Internet. Only 18 percent of the Americans were informed about the attacks by radio, while 28 percent of the Germans heard about the events through this medium. This might be due to the time difference. As it was afternoon in Germany many were at work and did not have access to TV. The number of people informed by TV in the United States was about 8 percent higher. Newspapers can effectively be ruled out as a channel for primary information, as there was no significant minority left to be informed the next morning.

It is remarkable that 69 percent of Americans told others about the events, including complete strangers, and about 60 percent of Germans did the same. This hints toward people giving the attacks a similar (very high) level of importance. However, as only a fourth of the population got their primary information from others (including by e-mail, telephone, instant messaging, etc.), and interpersonal communication was rather slow: every sender must have heard about the news himself beforehand. Broadcast media, by comparison, could disseminate the information so fast that most people who were told about the events already knew about them. Because interpersonal communication was the only way to reach those who do not watch TV or listen to the radio, it became more important as a means of primary information over time. For Germany, the numbers suggest that after 9:30 A.M. (EST) interpersonal communication informed more than 30 percent of those who had not heard about the events before.[7]

In addition, people were interested in learning more about the attacks. In both countries, roughly 90 percent of those informed looked for further information. And this was definitely television's finest hour. Sixty-eight percent of those informed by radio or interpersonal communication in Germany turned on the TV, and those already watching preferred to stay in front of it. If they wanted a change, they switched to another channel. Only those informed by the Internet stayed with it in significant numbers, possibly because these people were usually at work with no TV available. The importance of TV information in this situation is obvious: no other mass medium can exercise such credibility and immediacy. Additionally most information available in these early hours was visual.

Interpretation

On Wednesday, September 12, 2001, politicians and journalists resumed their professional positions. Americans had found an interpretation and contextualization following President Bush, who had spoken to the nation announcing revenge against the terrorists and their supporters. Most newspapers had already printed that Osama bin Laden and his al-Qaeda organization were behind the attacks, even though the evidence was mainly speculative. This was the day when NATO and the Security Council of the United Nations voted to support American action against the terrorists whenever necessary. NATO declared the incident as an attack against all its nineteen members as specified in article 5 of the Washington Treaty, making it an official war of all member states against an unknown enemy.[8]

In general, the U.S. administration under President George W. Bush tried to transform sorrow into anger. The move was successful because it channeled the rage and helplessness of millions of Americans sitting at home. Many public media supported the move. An article on mismanagement in the New York fire department? Unthinkable! As Lance Morrow wrote in *Time:* "The worst times, as we see, separate the civilized of the world from the uncivilized. This is the moment of clarity. Let the civilized toughen up, and let the uncivilized take their chances in the game they started."[9]

In Germany, on the other hand, contextualization and interpretation were for a large part done by the press itself. Politicians quickly issued statements of sympathy for the victims and the United States. Regarding next steps, however, they stressed the importance of thorough investigation and analysis by intelligence and diplomats—and by the press, namely, *Der Spiegel,* the most influential newsmagazine in Germany, selling more than a million copies per week.[10] But what could a weekly magazine tell about September 11? Because it is published on Mondays, the editors had to expect the Sunday newspapers to give background reports first. And because there was little real information about the attacks other than that they happened, the magazine took a bold step: it published the next edition "Der Terror-Angriff: Krieg im 21. Jahrhundert" (The terror attack: War in the twenty-first century) on Saturday, September 15.[11]

Members of all departments reported from their perspectives—from the American correspondents to the art editors. The first twenty pages were completely devoted to the events. The three stories featured the attacks themselves, the "German connection" to Hamburg and national reactions like the chancellor signaling "total solidarity" with the United States. Contextualization meant connecting the events with the readers: even if they had never been to New York, they might have been to Hamburg, and many would have attended a German university as the terrorists had.

Further on in the issue, another nine pages analyzed economic consequences of the attacks, including an extensive interview with the leader of Deutsche Bank, Rolf Breuer, on the world economy's prospects. The media pages quoted TV ratings of September 11, the foreign affairs editors reported another ten pages on Osama bin Laden and religious fundamentalism. Two

Spiegel reporters who had witnessed the events in New York City reported their personal impressions on three pages each.

Personal, descriptive, painfully open, and sad in tone, reporters Thomas Huetlin and Alexander Osang described how they experienced the disaster. Independently from each other, they got to the site after the first plane crashed into the north tower, and they saw the second impact and the south tower collapsing. Initially, both underestimated the situation and came dangerously close. However, the attacks themselves were only minor in their reports. Osang managed to catch the individual level as he was stuck in the basement of Temple Court Building, hiding from dust and debris. He told the story of Sammy Fontanec, the policeman who washed his eyes, Steven Weiss, the student who wanted to break out and help. He wrote of Stefan Garrin, who was ashamed of his asthma, and Eileen McGuire, whose husband worked on the ninety-ninth floor of the north tower. On this individual level, the story of heroes and cowards, of good and bad, of right and wrong worked best.

In Germany too some tabloids demanded openly to "Hunt him down" (Osama bin Laden) or "May he suffer in hell forever!" (Mohammed Atta). But most publications, television channels, and commentators tried to calm things down: let's try to sort things out, identify who did what, and why and how we could have prevented the disaster.[12]

This is where *Der Spiegel* achieved its true success: While electronic media reacted adequately in informing people quickly of what happened, they lacked the amount of information necessary to thoroughly evaluate the situation for two or three days. While everybody knew what had happened, nobody knew why it happened or who did it. Rumors about Osama bin Laden being involved in the attacks were formulated quickly after the attacks, but it took investigators several weeks to present evidence to (national and international) political leaders, which was never made available to the public. In this situation, *Der Spiegel* could report on bin Laden, his CIA past and Muslim fundamentalism.

Der Spiegel suffered from not being able to transport the news itself anymore, but its Saturday edition aimed precisely at giving its audience the background information they had missed since Tuesday's events in an objective manner. The magazine asked openly if it makes any sense to declare war against an unknown enemy, and it cited politicians like Javier Solana, who vowed for dialogue and understanding instead of war and retaliation (September 15, 2001, pp. 19–22). *Der Spiegel* showed the German chancellor swearing "total solidarity" with the United States but also reported on anti-American sentiments in Latin America and around the world. This "why question" had hardly been raised before and turned out to be unwanted in the United States.[13] The magazine had already anticipated the call to stay calm and critical and not to engage in friend-and-foe rhetoric that was published by the German Press Council on September 19.[14]

Conclusion

News reporting and reception in Germany and the United States were very similar. All television stations shared the few available pictures; reporters could hardly interpret the dreadful scenes themselves and joined their audience in the search for terms and interpretations. The news was immediately passed all over the world and provoked emotional reactions. Members of all cultures were shocked and appalled, and this created a feeling of solidarity with all mankind. Even countries critical of the United States like Syria and Iran expressed their sympathy. Germans and Americans felt a closeness rarely experienced before.

The very next day, journalists fell back into their old positions. Americans vowed for war, Middle Eastern and Latin American countries saw their latent anti-Americanism confirmed, and U.S. politicians gave powerful speeches against all evil, which was generally seen abroad. Politics and media agreed to foster (American) patriotism instead of "true globalism."[15] The Europeans, namely the Germans, and their media stood aside asking for caution—often called "relativism" overseas. The results were easy to see: Other countries welcomed the newly available option of fighting "terrorism" abroad. Russia could now feel safe about Chechnya. China was happy to fight "terrorism" in Tibet. India and Israel escalated tensions with their "terrorism supporting" neighbors. In fact, all those countries had already contextualized the terror attacks in America with their national conflicts, interpreted the same information to their national advantage.[16]

The terror attacks against the United States turned out to be a humiliation of the world's most powerful nation that could only exercise its worldwide effect because of the globalization of media coverage, of culture. But the same pictures were interpreted differently, always according to the audience's sense of closeness. In Germany, reporters stressed the importance of international cooperation in order to fight terror against the "free world," while American reporters stressed the fact that the location where the "free world" had been attacked was in the United States, making it a matter of patriotism to fight back.

With the distance of a year, one can say that interpretations of the attacks in Germany and the United States grew closer again. But for the victims and their families it will "never be the same again." America and the West have recovered. The heat and anger recognizable in U.S. publications wore off just as the president returned to a strategy of international cooperation. Successful joint operations like the war in Afghanistan and the "war against terrorism" have convinced many observers in Europe and the United States alike that unilateral actions make little sense in a world of increasing complexity.

Notes

An earlier version of this chapter was originally published as Joachim W. H. Haes, "Catching the Wave: German Media on September 11," in *Prometheus* 20 no. 3 (2002): 277–80.

1. Martin Emmer, Christoph Kuhlmann, Gerhard Vowe, and Jens Wolling, "Der 11. September: Informationsverbreitung, Medienwahl, Anschlusskommunikation," *Media Perspektiven,* April 2002, 166–77.
2. Everett M. Rogers and Nancy Seidel, "Diffusion of News of the Terrorist Attacks of September 11, 2001," *Prometheus,* September 2002, 209–19.
3. Ulrike Kaiser, "Zeugen des Entsetzens," *Journalist,* October 2001, 10–14.
4. "Study by UCLA Internet Project Shows E-mail Transformed Personal Communication After Sept. 11 Attacks," *UCLA News,* February 2002.
5. Susan Griffith, "Communication Scientists Survey 9/11 Reactions," *Research in Arts and Sciences,* Case Western Reserve University, 2001. www.cwru.edu/menu/research/artsci911.htm. Originally published as Mary M. Step, Margaret O. Finucane, and Cary W. Horvath, "Emotional Involvement in the Attacks," in *Communication and Terrorism: Public and Media Responses to 9/11,* ed. Dradley S. Greenberg (Cresskill, N.J.: Hampton, 2002), 261–73.
6. Emmer et al., "Der 11. September"; Rogers and Seidel, "Diffusion of News."
7. Emmer et al., "Der 11. September," 171.
8. NATO, press release, September 12, 2001. www.nato.int/docu/pr/2001/p01-124e.htm.
9. Lance Morrow, "The Case for Rage and Retribution," *Time,* September 14, 2001, 48–50; quote on page 48.
10. Its influence on politics was demonstrated in the fall of 1962, when the minister of defense, Franz Josef Strauss, had to resign in what is now called the "Spiegel Affäre."
11. *Der Spiegel,* "Der Terror-Angriff: Krieg im 21. Jahrhundert," September 15, 2001.
12. Kaiser, "Zeugen des Entsetzens," 10.
13. Michael Kleff, "Wut und Patriotismus," *Journalist,* October 2001, 15–16.
14. Deutscher Presserat, "Medien sollen besonnen und kritisch bleiben," press release, September 19, 2001.
15. Ingrid Scheithauer, "Wenn das Frühwarnsystem Medien versagt," *Frankfurter Rundschau,* September 4, 2002, 20. See also Caroline Fetscher, "Der Journalist als Feind und Helfer," *Der Tagesspiegel,* August 31, 2002, 27.
16. Andreas Hepp, "Beziehungsgeflechte: Zur Globalisierung der Medienkommunikation," *EPD Medien,* September 11, 2002, 7–14.

11

The Internet as a News Medium for the Crisis News of Terrorist Attacks in the United States

Pille Vengerfeldt

In Estonia, conventional mass media is delayed because of the need to translate from English. Thus the role of the Internet will be increasingly important in such countries.

Pille Vengerfeldt looks at how people in Estonian cyberspace dealt with the tragic news of the September 11 terrorist attacks on the United States. The role of the Internet in receiving, discussing, and reacting to the news of the attacks is examined through survey, interviews, and text. She also compares different channels, such as online newspaper and chat rooms, to determine the similarities and differences of dealing with the news. She concludes that although Estonia is far away from United States, the terrorist attack still caused a lot of disruption in Estonian cyberspace. This shows that the Internet indeed can bring world events closer to everyone.

Relevance of Researching New Media

"NEW MEDIA" IS A LOADED TERM THAT refers to a variety of new technologies but also has a larger political connotation. We speak of the digital divide as something dividing people and nations: those who have better opportunities to cope with their lives due to access to the new media and others who don't. But in a small country like Estonia, the new media also carry the heavy burden of hopes, for instance, helping the country bridge the differences with more advanced societies. As Lauristin and Vihalemm put it, "The rapid introduction of the e-society in Estonia has provided an opportunity for a small post-communist country to take a 'shortcut' to being an advanced postindustrial society and to make use of the new opportunities for economic and social development" (Lauristin and Vihalemm 2001).

With such heavy expectations of the new media, the research done in this field aims constantly to show the relevance and importance of the subject. Although new media carry the name (and thus also the connotational framework) of media, in essence they are much more. The audiences of the new media are called users, giving them a more active role in participation and consumption than the audiences of the traditional media have.

This chapter aims to broaden the field of new media studies and connect them with traditional media studies. It aims to compare the new media environment with traditional news environment. There has not been much material published in which the new media have been viewed as a news reception context—a social context for adding values to traditional audience processes.

The aim here is to use the media coverage of the terrorist attacks in the United States on September 11 as a basis for researching audience reception processes. This study looks at the new media as an environment in which all kinds of media consumption can take place and where the reception process can be analyzed through written traces that users leave behind.

The issues raised in this chapter include how can one research Internet communities in their process of interpreting the news? And from the content side, is there a difference in news content in different new media channels?

New Media Audiences as Interpretative Communities

The object of this study is the September 11 news in the Estonian new media space. It is analyzed through a survey and interviews with students of Tartu University, and through text analysis of a sample of the new media environment in Estonia: the online forum of the largest daily newspaper, *Postimees*, and its online commentary forum and two Internet relay chat (IRC) channels #estonia and #linux.ee.

Communication researcher Denis McQuail notes in *Audience Analysis* (1997) that

> in practice, the interactive potential of new technology is as likely to strengthen the position of the media "sender" as to serve the "empowerment" of receivers. The greater potential for interactivity of new electronic media is actually a force for consolidation of the traditional audience since it opens up new possibilities for active relations between senders and receivers. (McQuail 1997, 147)

This chapter attempts to show that, in the case of September 11 news, the new technology enables interpretative communities to meet in virtual reality. (See figure 11.1.) People have more opportunities to access the news and relate to it more quickly through the Internet. As research indicates, in a crisis situation people open all kinds of channels to obtain more information: TV, radio, Internet, newspapers. (See, for instance, Cohen et al. 2002; Rogers and Seidel

2002.) The Internet chat rooms and comment pages at newspapers and portals may prove to be more than just information sources, possibly gathering points for different news sources and opinions. Previous experience shows that participants in chat rooms and comment pages turn out to be news gatekeepers for the community. They gather and spread the news among their own groups. A hypothesis was raised to see if this phenomenon can also be seen in the chat rooms. The Internet makes it possible to cite news items with web addresses; then these news items can be commented on and discussed. If the hypothesis can be proven, then Internet communities can be viewed as interpretative communities. "Media use is typically situation specific and oriented to social tasks that evolve out of participation in 'interpretative communities'" (McQuail 1997, 19). Community interpretations can go further than just interpreting concrete news pieces; the terrorist attack is referred to and interpreted in the local context and new information is added to traditional media sources. A shared interpretation process can be viewed as a process through which a common understanding of the news develops, empowering users of the new media in dealing with the news. (See also Poulsen 2002.)

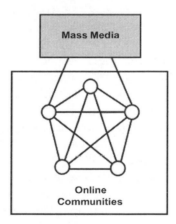

FIGURE 11.1
Online Communities as Media Audiences

Methodology: Combination of Different Methods

The aim of this research is to show how the Internet gives added value to the reception of crisis news. For that, three methods are selected: survey to show what kind of role the Internet played in crisis news reception; interviews to help understand people's opinions about the issues; and text analysis to see what actually happened in the new media environment.

First, a survey was used to determine the context of media use among students of Tartu University in order to see if the new media played any role in the crisis news situation. The survey also attempted to create the context of the new media environment to see how its qualities as a news source are rated in relation to other sources. One hundred and fifty six students from the departments of philology, informatics, medicine, social sciences, and media and communication studies participated in the surveys. The questionnaires were distributed in the classes and some were left in libraries to be filled out.

The second method used was dyadic semistructured interviews. This was basically a follow-up to the survey, even containing some of the same questions. Seven pairs of students who had used new media sources actively during the crisis were selected for interviews on the basis of their answers to the survey. In the interviews, people had a chance to expand and comment on the questions and results of the survey.

The third part of the data was gathered through text analysis. During the period from September 11 to September 19, 2001, electronic sources were monitored to gather data from the largest daily newspaper in Estonia, *Postimees*, and its online commentary forum and two chat rooms.

Postimees has had an online version since 1995. Currently the news is updated throughout the day. Analyzing articles in *Postimees* helps reveal the traditional pattern of news and, as most of the articles are also in the paper version of the newspaper, *Postimees* can be viewed as a representation of the traditional media. Analysis shows the topics used in the paper and it provides good reflective material to be compared with other sources.

The *Postimees* online commentary forum, in which people can comment in real time on the news that is published in *Postimees,* can be viewed as a virtual community that meets in electronic space based on the actuality, context, and content of the news. *Postimees* online commentators can be regarded as people who read the newspaper (a newspaper audience) and leave imprints in textual form in the new media environment of their news reception process.

Chat room logs were also a valuable source for this kind of research as they helped us conduct a virtual observation of what happened during those days in a relatively closed community. As the news in question was regarded as very important throughout the world (most people knew about it and talked about it), the logs helped to make clear how the news was actually discussed among people—they are like recordings of actual and authentic conversations in virtual space.

Text Analysis as Exploration of Method

The challenge of the method is that traditionally content analysis is made with equal-sized objects, but this time, the items of the content analysis are from different sources and therefore of different natures.

In our text analysis three things were analyzed: who spoke, what was said, and when. The idea was to compare those items across different genres in order to compare them as news environments. Text analysis consisted of three steps: qualitative, quantitative, and then once again qualitative.

First, a rough qualitative analysis was made in order to select content analysis categories. Altogether thirty topics and fifteen subtopics were identified in analyzing the September 11 attack. This part of the analysis was a preparation phase for the actual work.

Next, a content analysis was conducted on comments, dividing them into previously selected categories. This part was used to set up the timelines and quantitative content comparison.

Problems with the Content Analysis Categories

As the units for the comparison were rather difficult to set up, there are two levels of analyzed objects. First there were utterances—single items in content analysis that have their own category markings: who the speaker/writer was, what the content was, and when it was said. The utterances in IRC chat room logs were separate comments produced by a speaker. This might have been one sentence, one word, or one paragraph. They were separated by the speakers themselves as they pressed <enter> somewhere in the flow of communication, thus separating one statement from another. This probably can be compared to taking a breath in oral communication. In the *Postimees* online comments forum, one utterance is one single comment, varying in length from one-word exclamations to one page of reasoning. But they are clearly distinguishable by the intent of the commentator and in general their length is also comparable to the chat room utterances. The difficult part of using this method was deciding the length of the utterance in the newspaper. Finally, through discussion with a colleague with expertise in text analysis, we agreed that using the lead paragraph as the utterance unit for *Postimees* would be a good idea. This solved a number of problems. First, it is comparable in size. It also contains the leading thought of the article and is the most read (according to different theories about online newspapers; see, for instance, Hall 2001; Rich 1998). The total number of analyzed utterances can be seen in table 11.1.

TABLE 11.1
Sample for the Text Analysis

Channel	Number of Total Utterances	Number of Utterances on Terrorist Attacks in the U.S.
Postimees articles	1,412	406
Postimees editorials	2,957	1,022
IRC #linux.ee	28,498	3,187
IRC #estonia	34,802	1,850
Total	67,669	6,465

Problems with Comparing the Sequences of the Content Analysis

The second level of the analysis also presented a problem. In traditional content analysis the sequence of the objects is comparable, but in the new media environment, where there is a constant flow of information, it is more difficult to separate it into comparable pieces. The notion of a traditional twenty-four-hour day cannot be used because in IRC chat rooms communication is an ongoing process and is also quite active at night. Cutting it at midnight might result in cutting off someone's discussion in the middle of a sentence. So the idea of a news day was suggested by my colleague Veronika Kalmus. As everyone needs to sleep and as the chat rooms analyzed mostly involved Estonians, who are all in the same time zone, the idea was that there was bound to be a "night"—a natural pause in the continuous communication flow. That "night" is also present in newspapers, comment forums, and chat rooms—although occurring at a slightly different time. In newspapers it was from midnight until eight o'clock, but in chat rooms it was from 3:00 or 4:00 A.M. until 8:00 or 9:00 A.M. Dividing the utterances into news days made it possible to compare the results of the content analysis across channels. As each utterance is marked with a time stamp, it is easy to divide the flow of communication into different news days.

Problems with Identifying the Author of the Utterance

Log files, articles, and comments all have time identifiers of the talker. The talker is best identified in the newspaper, where the identity of the author of the article is clear. In the chat rooms under observation, in spite of the doubts of different Internet research classics (see for instance Turkle 1997; Rheingold 1993), the real identity of the people could easily be tracked and therefore the speaker could be a content analysis category. The most difficult problem was to identify the speaker in the online communities. Further investigation into anonymous online comments might involve the question of how often people change their nicknames to ones that already exist. The hypothesis here is that people either use one concrete nickname throughout their comments or change them randomly, according to the situation. Therefore we hoped that people would not take nicknames that were already in use. This still leaves the problem of how to identify/count those who randomly switch their identities, but in content analysis, we can also limit the sample to nicknames that are used several times.

After the content analysis was completed, the third step was to qualitatively review all utterances assigned to different categories and summarize some of what was talked about in broader categories. The qualitative revision process also provided the opportunity to compare the different discourses in different channels.

Timelines as Part of the Text Analysis

As each content analysis category also had a time stamp, a timeline analysis of the texts became possible. Timelines are well known in historical analysis, where they are used to map the historic processes of longer-term events. Media often use timelines to create a conclusive overview of a complicated event. In the case of this analysis, it is important to highlight the differences between the two kinds of timelines. One type might be called event lines as they record the date of different events. Others might be called news timelines, as they cover the sending and receiving process of the news. After the text analysis, it was possible to draw together four different timelines, one for each channel, so that the news timeline for the terrorist attack in the United States in *Postimees, Postimees* editorials, and the IRC channels #Estonia and #linux.ee could be compared in terms of speed, density, and variety.

The Internet as a News Medium: Where Students Found Out about the News

The terrorist attack news follows the classical news diffusion pattern (Ganz 1983; Bantz, Petronio, and Rarick 1983), the most important source being other people in face-to-face conversations (see table 11.2). The next most common source is radio and the third is local television. A total of 10 percent of respondents claimed to have learned about the news in new media space such as online newspapers, portals, and chat rooms. The reception of the news is very much context related. Terrorist attacks on the United States had occurred around 3:00 P.M. in Estonia, when most people were at work and students were on campus. This probably accounts for the high level of face-to-face news reception. As can be seen in table 11.2, local television and Internet channels together had the same proportion of people using them as the first source. This indicates that, at least among students, television and the Internet played equal roles.

What Channels Were Used for the Follow-Up on the News

Assuming that learning about the news is a rather random activity and depends on the situation and context, where and when the news is received, then following the news is a matter of choice. We can also see how people regard electronic channels—do they use them in a crisis situation and how important do they consider them to be?

In the case of the terrorist attacks (see figure 11.2), all sources are mentioned as being used to follow the news. Almost everyone (133 people out of 156) used local television to follow the event. Radio and newspapers were the

TABLE 11.2
How Estonians First Learned of the
Terrorist Attack on the United States

Source	Number of People Mentioning Source
Friends and family	47
Radio	34
Friends over phone	19
Estonian TV	18
International TV	11
Newspapers	9
Internet portals	6
Newspapers in the Internet	6
Chat rooms	3
Other	9

next most commonly used sources. In looking at the different sources people mentioned in the open questions, it is clear that in this case the range of different sources was wider. For instance, the Internet portals were not limited to local Estonian portals but included foreign news portals. The chat room logs show that people who were using one IRC channel usually used not only Estonian but also another, preferably American, portal to get first-hand information.

In general, although traditional channels were used more heavily in following the news than new media channels, around one-third of my respondents used the Internet in following the news. This shows that, for this group, the Internet is an important and reliable news source. In order to present the results of the content analysis, four figures help compare agendas, topics, time density and variety in four different channels.

Results of the Content Analysis

In order to present the results of the content analysis, figures 11.3, 11.4, 11.5, 11.6 help compare agendas, topics, time density, and variety in four different channels.

Each figure represents one channel: with the top five most-used categories on one axis and the days of the event on the other axis. The cylinders on the figure show how many utterances were made on each topic each day. Where there is no cone, this means that the topic was not mentioned in discussion

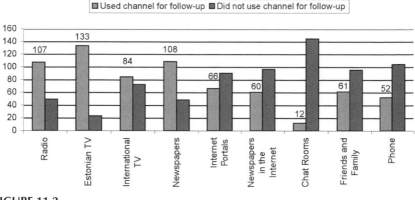

FIGURE 11.2
Channels Used for Follow-up

that day. As can be seen in the figures, the four channels have some similarities and differences in their agendas. From the thirty categories, thirteen were represented in the top five agendas of the four channels.

Similarities of the Content of Different Channels

What happened is that the most-used category is present in all channels and in *Postimees* Online and IRC channels. It is also first in their agendas. Under this category everything that reports about different activities is filed. This reporting is done in a neutral manner. The high position of this category shows that IRC chat rooms have acquired an almost news agency–like quality in reporting events to members of the community. *Postimees* Online comments do not have a great need to report the events as they rely on the newspaper to perform that function. But in this channel the role of media category is in the highest position and within this category it is possible to find links to other media sources and critiques of existing ones. As *Postimees* itself does not refer often to other sources, this topic is very low in their agenda, but it is there as self-reflection to analyze the media's role in this crisis. This category also shows the variety of different channels that chat rooms used to provide the community with information. In the combination of those two categories—what happened and role of media—it is possible to see the gatekeeping nature of chat room community members and how the chat room itself becomes a news agency for its members.

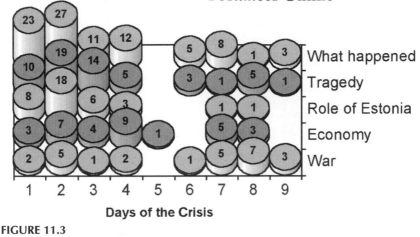

Days of the Crisis

FIGURE 11.3
Content Analysis Results of *Postimees* Online
Note: The numbers in the circles are how many utterances were made for each topic.

The next most actively used category is tragedy. This contains all compassionate utterances related to the sadness of the event. This tone is more represented in traditional media and online commentaries. Other channels also express their compassion but do not deal with those issues as extensively.

The topic somewhat related to the issues of tragedy is jokes. Making fun of the issues—funny pictures, stories, and speculations—helped people deal with the tragedy more easily and the online communities offered plenty of possibilities for this kind of shared experience. As there are more jokes in chat rooms and fewer in online comments, this might mean that in chat rooms people feel more connected to each other, and the closer relationship enables them to use jokes as a tool to get over the tragic events.

Complementary Nature of *Postimees* Comments

In the *Postimees* commentary forum, the topics relevant to helping people get over the tragedy are the content categories "revenge," "arrogance of the United States," and "terrorism." All these categories cover different aspects of the same topic. Under "revenge," people speculated on what the United States would do with the culprits and how they would punish them. In the

Postimees **Online Comments**

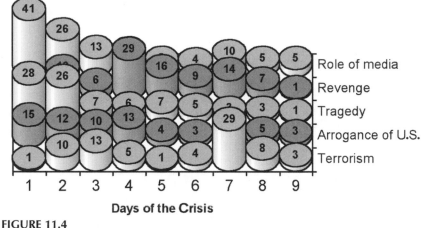

FIGURE 11.4
Content Analysis Results of *Postimees* Online Comments

"arrogance of the United States" category people discussed whether a major power has the right to use particular kinds of methods to punish culprits. There are people who said that maybe the United States deserved what happened, while others scolded them for such opinions and disrespect for the tragedy and dead. The issue of possible arrogance is also present in the chat rooms, where the revenge and activities of the United States are also often joked about. In online comment forums, the topic is discussed in a little more serious tone.

The "terrorism" content category covers discussions about the background of the event, issues about terrorists' worldviews, and how they are connected to issues of Islam. People discussed those issues in a serious and educated manner, to some extent filling the gaps left by the traditional media, which failed to cover background issues in depth.

It is interesting to see how these three categories filled gaps in the traditional media that come from the lack of genres. Although the traditional media also tried to cover the background of the conflict and discuss the issues of terrorism and war, the comments in the online forum and chat room hinted that they were not very successful. Therefore the audience in the forum combined their interpretative knowledge in discussion and covered the background of the tragedy in their own way.

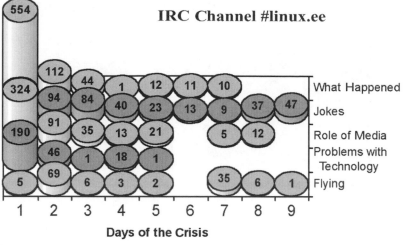

FIGURE 11.5
Content Analysis Results of IRC Channel #linux.ee

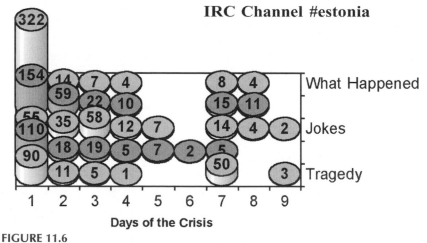

FIGURE 11.6
Content Analysis Results of IRC Channel #estonia

News Characteristic for the Traditional Media

The "war" category is related to the three content categories and is connected with the way that traditional media discussed the issues of the terrorist attacks in editorials. Traditional media reported on actual war activities much less than might be anticipated. Rather they attempted to discuss the possibility of a third world war and what might be the contending powers in the case of such a crisis.

A very interesting category for the traditional media is the "role of Estonia." Sources for this category were local people in authority who used the media to report on how they sent notes of condolence to someone in the United States. Another main theme here is how Estonia is ready to assist the United States in rescue operations, and so on. Other channels responded rather critically to this kind of self-promotion. This category is strongly related to Estonia's wish to join NATO.

Economy is also a category often present in the traditional media, as the "economy" topic includes discussion of how the crisis influenced economic changes.

Interactive Role of Chat Rooms

The "personal experience" category is mostly represented in one chat room. This topic revealed the interactiveness of the new media. In IRC #estonia this category revealed instances of support and comfort given to a regular member of the chat room, who was in New York at the time. The IRC channel was used to keep in contact with people. The member in New York asked friends to call her family, to help her to search the Net, and used people on the channel as her personal support network to help her through the crisis. This category was also present in other channels, but there it took the form of self-expression rather than support.

"Problems with technology" is a content category that looks at technology-related issues: what kind of pressure this attack posed on technology as the source of more information. Here the broken Internet connection, speed and availability of the news sites, and online video streams were discussed. This category helps reveal what kind of role the Internet played in this crisis for technology-oriented people. The last category in the #linux.ee channel is called "flying," and it is used to illustrate discussion about planes, learning to fly, and flight simulators.

Density of the Utterances in Different Channels

Timeline methodology makes it possible to compare the agendas of the different channels in relation to time. From the four figures we can see how the different channels have different densities in the discussion of the issues of the September 11 attacks. While chat rooms had very active discussions on the first days, the discussion seemed to die down later. The most enduring interest community seemed to be the one that formed around *Postimees* Online. They posted different utterances on almost all topics and their interest did not seem to fade as events developed. Even in *Postimees*, within nine days of the terrorist attack there was significantly less news. Seemingly *Postimees* commentators found a topic with community-forming strength and, at least for the nine days under consideration, some kind of community formed.

Conclusion and Notes for Further Research

In conclusion, *Postimees* and *Postimees* Online comments are complementary channels—comments filling in the gaps of traditional media with analysis and discussion (figures 11.2 and 11.3). The IRC channels are similar, giving information and support to community members from a perspective that seems most relevant to their communities (figures 11.5 and 11.6).

Topics in the newspaper are dominated by the source of the news—the agendas of the what happened, tragedy, and economy topics were set by international news agencies, while the agenda of the role of Estonia category was set by the state. Topics in the chat rooms seemed to form out of the needs and interests of the chat room communities.

There are also theoretical and methodological perspectives that this research opened. First, the Internet provides us a unique opportunity to explore the creation of the news from different perspectives. The chat room logs, although quite demanding in terms of workload, provide us valuable online recordings of real discussions previously unavailable to researchers. Carefully selected chat rooms that the researcher knows well enough to be able to distinguish cynical comments and jokes from real opinions could be used in further investigations as a valuable source of people's everyday conversations. At least in the case in question, the chat rooms and discussions were in no way edited, arranged, or directed. The researcher can, after announcing his or her presence, remain as a more or less active participant in the community, as long as he or she remains impartial. This would provide a unique opportunity to peek into people's workplaces and homes to see what they talk about, without researcher influence. We could argue about the validity of the data from a practical perspective, as one might claim that the existence of computer mediation influences the way people think and talk. But my seven years of experience in participatory investigation of both online and offline situations convinces me that the data available from chat room logs is appropriate and valuable material worth considering, not only as a method of researching cyber communities but also as an opportunity to research everyday life and practices. It is worth analyzing whether opinions vary in relation to the channel through which they are presented. A possible hypothesis here would be that the opinions of people do not vary so much in relation to the channel, but more in relation to the participants. Therefore it is possible that opinions given in online space are closer to personal communication than those given in the presence of a researcher.

Second, online comments help us see how important news events have the power to unite people through discussion and by providing a valuable forum that fills the gaps left by traditional sources. It is important to investigate what kinds of topics online communities gather around. What kinds of events influence people's opinions enough to encourage them to share those opinions extensively in online forums? As this research has shown, online comments provide an opportunity to share support and information. Often those online communities attract educated people whose opinions are worth considering and add something extra to the traditional news reception process.

Third, the timelines method is an interesting methodology that provides an opportunity to look at the development of the news over time. It is possible to see when new strands are brought in and, with extensive ethnographic study, we can also see how the news is built. With the timeline pictures presented here, we can determine the most important influences and where they fall in the daily scale. However, the method itself should provide a much more detailed overview and is certainly worth testing through further research.

The interesting points mentioned above about how online communities received the news and how they discussed it call for a model to describe audience processes in the new media environment. A model is needed to describe news reception online, as well as community formation. This model should show the added value of how the Internet enabled communities to gather in the face of crisis news. It would be interesting to consider what kinds of news facilitate the gathering of online communities in the newspaper's online space. Another point of interest would be what kind of news attracts people's attention enough to start discussions in chat rooms. That could give newspapers valuable feedback and would enable researchers to explain some of the aural processes that are otherwise out of reach.

A model that would describe the new media audience processes would be a valuable addition to audience analysis, as this would make it possible to see the audiences as active participants in the news reception process, a reception process where traces of the interpretation are left in the same environment and those traces are used by other people, giving added value to other audience members.

The data presented indicate that this attack was important and interesting to the people of Estonia as well as the rest of the world. Our small nation neglected its own tragedies and turned its face toward the suffering major power. While the traditional media relied heavily on the data provided by the United States, the new media used all sources possible to provide balanced discussion and compassionate support for the people who suffered most.

Note

An earlier version of this chapter was originally published as Pille Vengerfeldt, "The September 11 Attacks on the U.S. in the New Interactive Media Space in Estonia," in *Prometheus* 20, no. 3 (2002): 229–36.

Bibliography

Bantz, C. R., S. G. Petronio, and D. L. Rarick. "News Diffusion after the Reagan Shooting." *Quarterly Journal of Speech* 69 (1983): 317–27.

Cohen, Elisia L., et al. "Civic Actions after September 11: Exploring the Role of Multilevel Storytelling." *Prometheus* 20, no. 3 (2002): 221–28.

Ganz, W. "The Diffusion of News about the Attempted Reagan Assassination." *Journal of Communication* 33, no. 1 (1983): 56–66.

Hall, Jim. *Online Journalism: A Critical Primer*. London: Pluto, 2001.

Lauristin, Marju, and Peeter Vihalemm. "Development of a New Media Society in Estonia." Paper presented at the Fifth Conference of European Sociological Association, Helsinki, August 2001.

McQuail, Denis. *Audience Analysis*. Thousand Oaks, Calif.: Sage, 1997.

Poulsen, Jens. "Use of News on the Internet: As Part of the Social Construction of Meaning, Identity, Social Practice, and Democracy." Paper presented at 23rd Conference of IAMCR: Intercultural Communication, Barcelona, July 2002.

Rheingold, Howard. *Virtual Community: Homesteading on the Electronic Frontier*. Reading, Mass.: Addison-Wesley, 1993.

Rich, Carole. *Creating Online Media: A Guide to Research, Writing, and Design on the Internet*. Boston: McGraw Hill College, 1998.

Rogers, Everett M., and Nancy Seidel. "Diffusion of News of the Terrorist Attacks of September 11, 2001." *Prometheus* 20, no. 3 (2002): 209–19.

Turkle, Sherry. *Life on the Screen: Identity in the Age of Internet*. New York: Simon & Schuster, 1997.

12

The Internet and the Demand for News: Macro- and Microevidence

Paul N. Rappoport and James Alleman

Paul Rappoport and James Alleman explore data about the use of the Internet during the tragedy. The data shows a dramatic increase in the usage of Internet news sites on September 11. Their analysis shows that this increased usage of Internet news sites seems significant even after the tragedy.

THE TRAGIC EVENTS OF SEPTEMBER 11, 2001, unleashed a voracious demand for news and information. All media channels were busy reporting on the tragedy. These included traditional broadcast, cable news channels, radio, and, for the first time as a serious news channel, the Internet.

On September 11, cable news channels, with their attention on covering breaking news, were clearly beneficiaries of the tragedy. Nielson Media Research reported that over 100 million people, or close to 50 percent of all TV households, watched at least part of CNN's coverage the day of the attacks.[1] A typical share for CNN is 10 percent. Broadcast television and radio ratings were also high.[2] These numbers underscore the fact that traditional communications media were clearly the channels of choice for most households.

Not everyone was satisfied with these established media channels. The demand for more coverage and instantaneous updates of news and events on September 11 led increasing numbers of households that had Internet access to use the Internet to augment their access to news. For some commentators, this increased demand legitimized the Internet as an alternative channel for obtaining in-depth news and information. There were also detractors of the view that the Internet was a serious channel for news. They simply point to anecdotal evidence that the Internet quickly became overwhelmed and left millions of users without access or reasonable connections. Still other commentators noted that while "the Web was slow to catch up to the news of the devastation of the World Trade Center and the Pentagon, when they did, many sites served as a nice supplement to TV."[3]

On one point there is little debate concerning the value of the Internet during and after September 11: It proved to be adaptive in supporting the demand for news and information. Immediately after the attack, community websites, discussion groups, alternative news sites, mailing lists, and reference sites "lit up" the web. According to one analyst, the web did not fall apart. "Under the radar, the Net responded magnificently; it was just a matter of knowing where to look."[4]

This chapter examines the demand for Internet news sites. Two sources of data are used to analyze demand. The first dataset represents estimates of daily aggregate traffic to news sites and nonnews sites. Traffic is measured in terms of unique visits to specific sites. The aggregate data support the view that September 11 marked a turning point in the acceptance and use of Internet news sites. The second dataset covers the use of the Internet from a sample of 5,000 households. The assessment of this data supports the view that September 11 was an important factor in the demand for Internet news. However, the magnitude of this demand was neither as large nor as permanent as what was found from the aggregate data. What is the evidence on the demand for Internet news?

The Datasets

The first dataset provides an aggregate view of Internet activity. This dataset presents a macroview of overall Internet traffic before and after September 11 and provides an opportunity to evaluate the importance of the Internet as a channel for news. The traffic analysis uses data that was obtained from tracking Internet activity of over 500,000 households. The information was obtained from Plurimus, a company that specialized in monitoring and measuring Internet traffic.[5] The large volume of transactions in the database provided the basis for estimating total demand with a great deal of precision. The second perspective is based on the detailed examination of household Internet usage for a set of 5,000 households. This second dataset, also from Plurimus, provides an opportunity to look at the microbehavior of a household's usage patterns, before and after September 11.[6]

The aggregate database tracks unique visits estimated from the populations of Internet users. This evidence shows that after the initial surge of activity was digested, minor bottlenecks notwithstanding, the Internet played an increasingly important role in providing access to information and news. The micro- or household database provides an opportunity to evaluate household behavior. An examination of household behavior yields a number of different insights regarding the demand for Internet news. First, while the microdata show there were significant increases in households visiting Internet news sites, the numbers were still modest compared to household activity at other Internet sites. Second, this increased usage and interest in Internet news sites did not appear to last long. This finding is also in contrast to the longevity result found in the analysis of the aggregate data.

An Overwhelmed Internet: An Aggregate View

At midmorning on September 11, it was almost impossible to log onto any major news site. For some, this was evidence that the Internet failed. These users were unable to access well-known news sites. This was perhaps the first time the Internet failed to deliver on this scale. For example, between the hours of 9:00 and 10:00 A.M. on September 11, MSNBC.com experienced almost a 500 percent increase in traffic. CNN.com experienced almost a 450 percent increase in traffic. Needless to say, the network sites and their servers were not prepared for surges of that magnitude. On Tuesday alone, according to a study commissioned by the Pew Foundation, 29 percent of Internet users—or more than 30 million people—sought news online.[7] That is one-third greater than the normal news-seeking population during a typical day online. Yahoo, Google, and other portals and search engines reported huge surges in activity.[8-9] For many users, initial attempts to access the Internet were thwarted. Those who could log on were met with very slow response times. Indeed, the initial congestion caused by the surge in traffic brought most portals down to a crawl. The Internet search engine Google directed news seekers to radio and television. "Many online news services are not available, because of extremely high demand," a statement said on the site's home page.[10]

Initial problems regarding access notwithstanding, a more complete review of the aggregate data suggests that overall interest in Internet news sites continued to remain high despite early problems due to bottlenecks. This suggests that (1) Internet news sites were able to adjust their format to relieve a significant portion of their bottleneck by limiting streaming video and large graphics and (2) the value individuals placed on accessing these sites was greater than the problems associated with gaining access. In a follow-up survey commissioned in December, the Pew researchers found that "the change in news interest in the post-Sept. 11 period was striking. On average, just 23 percent of the public paid very close attention to the typical news story before the attacks, which is comparable to yearly averages since 1990. But after the attacks, that number more than doubled, to 48 percent."[11] A more recent Pew study, *The Broadband Difference,* indicates that 46 percent of all broadband users get news online on a typical day.[12]

Prior to September 11, on any given day, approximately 12 percent of Internet households visited online news sites. On September 11, estimates suggest that close to 40 percent of all Internet households accessed news sites.

Viewed from a macroperspective, the Internet emerged from September 11 as a mainstream channel for obtaining news. The events of September 11 empowered users to become active participants in the organization, collection, and dissemination of news. It appears these efforts were long lasting. After September 11, a larger percentage of Internet households continued to rely on Internet news sites when compared to pre–September 11 levels. That reliance has grown. For example, as of January 2003, there were multiple news hubs and search engines.[13] Note that this finding is predicated on an implicit correlation between the number of visits and the number of households or users. This correlation cannot be tested using the aggregate data.[14]

Aggregate Evidence

Pre-September Baseline

Figure 12.1 shows the average number of unique visits that were associated with a visit to a news site between August 2001 and mid-December 2001.[15] Figure 12.1 provides a macroview of average activity at Internet news sites. Levels of activity rose dramatically in September and, while falling thereafter, nonetheless remain significantly higher than the pre-September levels.

The average number of visits for August was 6 million. This can be considered a base number for visits prior to September 11. The average for the period from September 11 through September 30 was 11.5 million visits, or an

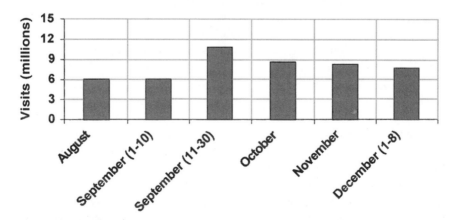

FIGURE 12.1
Average Number of Online Visitors to News Sites

increase of 92 percent over the pre–September 11 base. Relative to this baseline, the average number of visits to news sites continued to remain high long after September 11. By mid-December, the average number of visits to news sites was still 48 percent higher than the period before September 11. As suggested by the December Pew survey, this increase in activity was not due to chance but rather to an acceptance of online news sites and the value these sites provided. This change in usage is significant and points to an increased demand for Internet news sites after September 11. This shift occurred despite the problems accessing sites that many households encountered on September 11. One conclusion drawn from these results is that September 11 represented a watershed event in terms of both the acceptance and role of Internet news.

Figure 12.2 looks at online visits to news sites over a shorter interval. Figure 12.2 displays average daily visits to news sites. On September 11, almost 19 million visitors successfully accessed a news site. The numbers decline after September 11 but remain close to 100 percent greater by September 20. Put another way, on September 11, close to 40 percent of all sites visited were news sites.[16]

These numbers further underscore the significant increase in the use of the Internet. The data point to a more intense and immediate focus on news. To be sure, there were significant news events prior to September 11. However, it appears that no single event prior to September 11 came close to matching the numbers turning to Internet news sites that was observed on September 11. Clearly, September 11 was a defining event for news sites on the Internet.

Daily Activity

Figure 12.3 displays the demand for CNN.com by hour of the day for September 10 and September 11. The comparison between the two days illustrates the enormous surges in demand experienced on September 11. On September 10, peak demand reached 300,000 at 11:00 P.M.

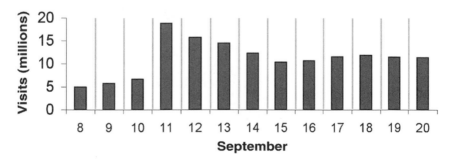

FIGURE 12.2
Number of Online Visitors to News Sites

Figure 12.3 illustrates the dramatic surge in CNN.com traffic. On September 11, traffic surged after 9:00 A.M. Bottlenecks and delays occurred. The demand for access remained high throughout September 11. However, the numbers suggest that by midafternoon, CNN.com was able to manage its network and accommodate most of its traffic. Within hours, most of the major news sites were able to reconfigure their networks and accommodate the increased traffic.

Internet monitoring company Keynote[17] reported on overall Internet performance for September 11, 2001: "Starting at 9:00 am EDT, coinciding with the start of the attacks, overall Internet performance, as indicated by the results of the Keynote Business 40 Internet Performance Index (KB40 Index), started to slow." The KB40 Index measures the performance of forty top business websites, including major news sites and search engines, as experienced by users at work over high-speed connections. The KB40 Index has become an industry-standard barometer for the overall health and performance of the Internet. On Monday, September 10, the overall Index average at the same time, 10:15 A.M. EDT, was approximately 5.0 seconds, which was a slight but normal fluctuation from the usual daily average of 2.5–3.5 seconds. On Tuesday at 10:15 A.M., following the attacks, the index average reached 12.9 seconds—a performance degradation over twice what it was at the same time when it peaked on Monday and three to four times the normal daily average. Over the next few hours, the index average improved until it returned to normal by midafternoon. Keynote has rarely seen this kind of performance effect on the overall KB40 Index.

Table 12.1 displays the traffic for eight Internet news sites. All these sites experienced significant increases in demand. The increased demand peaked on September 11 but maintained higher levels after September 11.

During September 11, the surge in visits to Internet news sites suggests that activity to other sites declined. Not surprisingly, traffic to Amazon and eBay declined on September 11. However, this decline was short-lived as traffic to

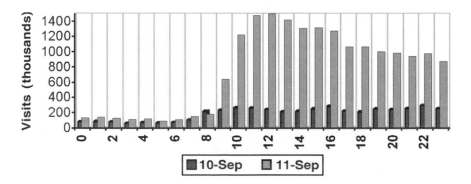

FIGURE 12.3
CNN.com Hourly Traffic

TABLE 12.1
Visitors to Selected Internet News Sites

Date	ABC	CBS	CNN	FOXNEW	MSNBC	NYTIMES	WASH POST	YAHOO
9/7	288,512	98,540	1,147,034	271,984	1,992,256	470,273	328,584	1,145,931
9/8	184,997	72,034	1,039,491	152,712	1,496,945	408,051	232,817	834,665
9/9	207,127	97,738	1,237,364	142,517	1,662,019	475,849	315,734	1,011,322
9/10	258,247	87,346	1,329,792	223,285	2,031,645	533,693	376,072	1,201,107
9/11	1,461,078	679,792	4,822,568	794,059	5,027,384	1,141,144	1,138,586	2,553,101
9/12	1,053,505	536,154	3,898,313	675,597	4,284,271	1,082,916	1,076,979	2,002,495
9/13	853,544	472,732	3,462,922	552,262	4,026,349	1,087,908	874,202	2,108,412
9/14	681,154	332,133	2,795,355	488,314	3,503,299	825,593	901,130	1,896,147
9/15	514,984	274,579	2,364,923	360,612	2,854,317	712,644	680,403	1,833,748
9/16	470,766	269,430	2,506,396	433,384	2,919,849	774,605	590,287	2,043,227
9/17	497,386	255,246	2,529,715	468,671	3,346,584	739,123	724,693	2,049,015

Source: Plurimus (an Internet research company that assimilated data from a pool of 3.5 million Internet users).

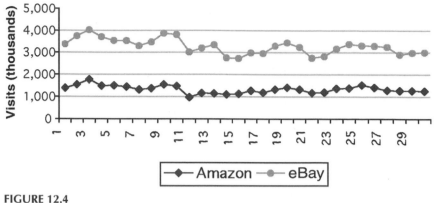
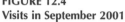

FIGURE 12.4
Visits in September 2001

these sites recovered to "near normal" levels quickly. These results suggest that increased interest and activity in Internet news sites was not occurring at the expense of other Internet activity.

Long-Term Changes in Activity

One way to test the increased role of the Internet as a channel for obtaining news and information is to track changes in Internet activity to news sites for "significant" national events that occurred after September 11. Figure 12.5 displays the increase in traffic to CNN.com and MSNBC.com for November 2001 relative to the average daily traffic to those sites prior to September 11. A value of 25 implies that traffic for that day in November was 25 percent greater than traffic prior to September 11. For both sites, the increase in traffic was noticeable, with November 12 standing out as significant.

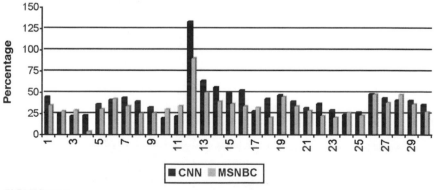

FIGURE 12.5
Lift to CNN.com and MSNBC.com in November 2001

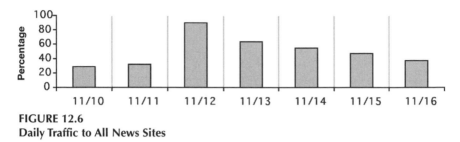

FIGURE 12.6
Daily Traffic to All News Sites

The November 12 spike in activity coincided with the crash of American Airlines Flight 587. That event generated Internet activity to the major news sites on the order of the activity observed on September 11. This surge in activity suggests that households were quick to use the Internet to learn more about the news. Figure 12.6 displays the percentage increase in daily traffic to all news sites for the period November 10 to November 16, 2001, relative to the average traffic prior to September 11. Note that Internet activity to news sites was still over 30 percent greater than pre–September 11 levels just prior to November 12. On November 12, Internet activity to news sites jumped dramatically on news of the crash. Activity levels remained high after November 12, mimicking the pattern of use observed after September 11.

The anthrax scare provides another example of the increased use of Internet news sites after September 11. On October 5 the first victim of anthrax poisoning died. On October 8, the news of the anthrax-laced letter to Senator Daschle was reported. During this time frame, the bombing of Afghanistan was also well under way and very much in the news.[18] These events were noteworthy and closely followed by households that had Internet access.

The percentage increase in total activity to Internet news sites is displayed in figure 12.7.

A Microanalysis

The macroperspective provides support for upgrading the role that Internet news played on and after September 11. The aggregate nature of the

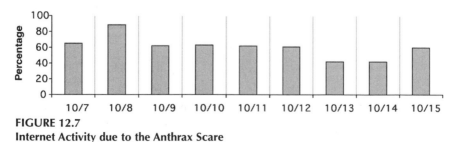

FIGURE 12.7
Internet Activity due to the Anthrax Scare

macroview, however, limits the assessment of a number of additional issues including:

- Was the increased activity at Internet news sites indicative of an increase in the number of households visiting Internet news sites or simply a few households using the Internet more intensively?
- Did household usage patterns change after the events of September 11? Specifically, is there evidence to support the notion that household demand for Internet news sites increased after September 11? Further, was this change in demand long-lived?
- Did broadband subscribers to the Internet visit news sites more frequently than their dial-up counterparts?

In this section we examine the Internet usage of a sample of 5,000 unique households. This database provides a comprehensive view of a household's complete Internet activity and thus provides an opportunity to estimate household responses to the events before, during, and after September 11 in terms of:

- The number of times a household accessed Internet news sites
- The average duration of a visit
- The time of day of visits
- The share of visits to nonnews sites

Both dial-up households and broadband households were included in this dataset. Consequently, a comparison of speed of access and demand for news sites can be made.

Household Behavior

Figure 12.8 displays the percentage of daily visits to Internet news sites for August, September, and October 2001. Figure 12.8 presents a surprising picture of traffic. Prior to September 11, the share of Internet traffic to Internet news sites was under 3 percent. That share increased to 8 percent on September 11 and then gradually declined to typical levels by the end of September. The October share was similar to the August share of approximately 2 percent. The rapid decline in visits stands in marked contrast to the results suggested by an examination of the macrodata.

Figure 12.9 displays the daily total number of visits to non-Internet news sites for September 2001. A review of figure 12.9 shows:

1. The number of nonnews visits is far greater than the number of news visits. For example, on September 11, the number of nonnews visits was

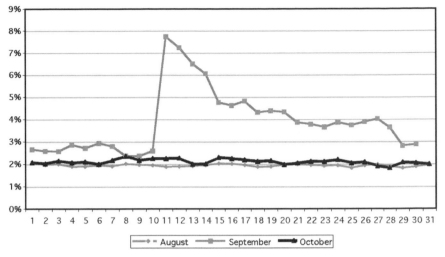

FIGURE 12.8
Percentage of Total Visits to Internet News Sites

50,449. The number of visits to news sites was 4,294, or 7.8 percent of all visits.

2. While the percentage of news visits to the total number of visits increased dramatically after September 11, the percentage of total visits was nonetheless under 8 percent.

3. There was not a major shift away from non-Internet news sites to other sites after September 11, suggesting minimal substitution of activity or changes in surfing habits.

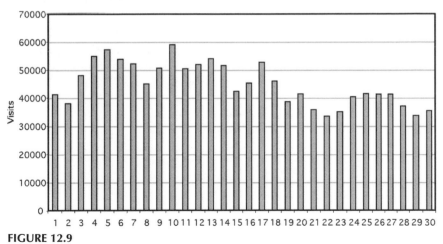

FIGURE 12.9
Daily Visits to Nonnews Sites, September 2001

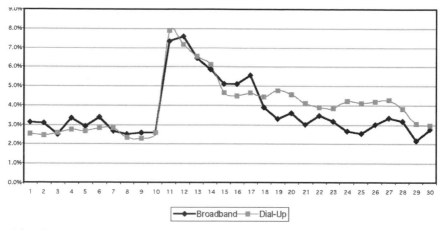

FIGURE 12.10
Percentage of Visits to News Sites by Type of Internet Access, September 2001

Figure 12.10 looks at activity by type of access. The graph displays the percentage of visits to Internet news sites by type of access for September. There is no major difference in the number of visits by type of access. A similar pattern holds for August and October.

Household Internet Activity

At the peak on September 11, visits to Internet news sites accounted for, at most, 8 percent of household visits. The Internet was lauded as a channel that facilitated communications. How much of the remaining activity was for chat, e-mail, and related activities such as searching for additional information, logging on to government sites, and participating in online forums?

The household database provides a complete picture of individual household Internet behavior. Measuring this component of activity requires the ability to summarize visits by site type. In the analysis that follows we adopt the site classification scheme developed by Plurimus.

TABLE 12.2
Plurimus Classification System

Site Classification	Number of Subcategories
Finance and insurance	5
Internet services	11
Online shopping	16
Travel	13
Business and companies	10
Entertainment	15
Information services	5

The Plurimus classification scheme places Internet sites (URLs) into seven primary groups. Each primary group is then divided into subgroups.

The group Information Services includes the subcategories of employment and classified ads, general news, local portals, maps, organizations, politics, special interest sites, and weather. Internet Services includes the subcategories of chat and community sites, e-mail, hosting, portals, search engines, security, and streaming media.

Figure 12.11 displays the distribution of the most popular sites visited on September 11. The total number of sites visited for the 5,000 households was 1,946,277.

Communications-related sites might include portals, news, and chat. On September 11, these sites represented approximately 24 percent of the total number of sites visited. While up from the peak of 8 percent, this implies that 75 percent of Internet traffic does not appear to be related to the events of September 11. This finding is surprising, given the estimates from macro-analysis of the percentage of households that were using the Internet to obtain information.

Figure 12.12 displays the relative amount of hourly activity on September 11 for Information Services, Internet Services, Entertainment, and Online Shopping. Activity on September 11 is measured against a baseline period prior to September 11. For example, a value of 1 for 7:00 A.M. in Entertainment implies that the number of visits to an entertainment site on September 11 was equal to the number of visits to entertainment sites during a baseline period prior to September 11. A ratio less than 1 on September 11 would indicate less than typical activity. A value greater than 1 would indicate increased activity.

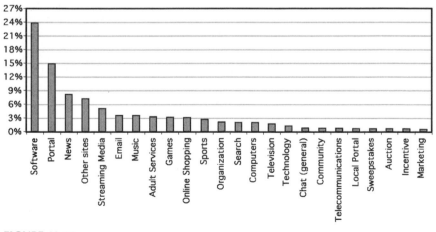

FIGURE 12.11
Distribution of Site Visits by Category on September 11, 2001

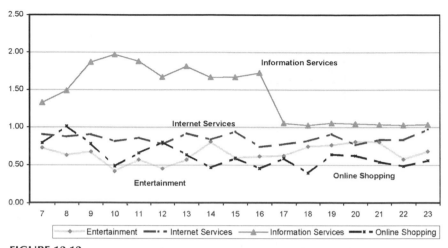

FIGURE 12.12
Internet Activity Relative to Baseline by Hour of Day (7:00 A.M. to midnight)
Note: 1.00 equals no change

By 9:00 A.M. there was almost a doubling of visits to Information Service sites. On September 11, the only category with a ratio greater than 1 was Information Services. Activity at the other categories was less than the baseline, indicating that during the early part of September 11, significant attention was focused on news, e-mail, and associated sites at the expense of other sites. This is indicative of substitution. However, by 5:00 P.M., the level of interest in Information Services sites dropped to the baseline, implying that household returned to their pre–September 11 behavior. Again, these results appear to be at odds with the increased demand for Internet news sites after September 11 found in the aggregate data.

Figure 12.13 displays activity at chat, e-mail, and news sites. The distribution of activity by type of site is displayed in figure 12.14. The vertical measure is 100 percent. It was suggested by a number of commentators that chat sites provided an additional level of communication during September 11. The graph underscores the increased activity at Internet news sites from 9:00 A.M. to 12:00 P.M. Thereafter, the share of e-mail increases. Again, the evidence suggests a relatively rapid return to pre–September 11 habits.

Figure 12.14 displays the average duration of a visit to a news site by time of day on September 11. There is a noticeable increase in duration after 8:00 A.M. This increase could be driven by the slowness of the Internet or by an increased interest in collecting information about the events of the day.

Not surprisingly, the average duration of a visit increases dramatically at 9:00 A.M. The duration of a visit to a news site stays high throughout the day.

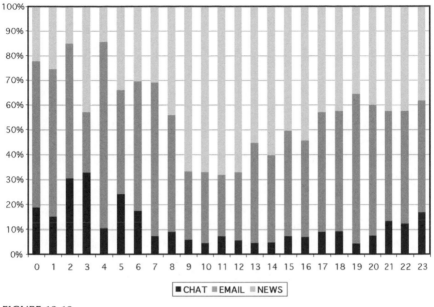

FIGURE 12.13
Relationship among News, E-mail, and Chat on September 11, 2001

Discussion

The analysis of aggregate Internet traffic before and after September 11 points to an increased level of interest regarding online news sites after the events of September 11. To many, the Internet had proven capable of providing value for those seeking news, commentary and analysis, and information. The

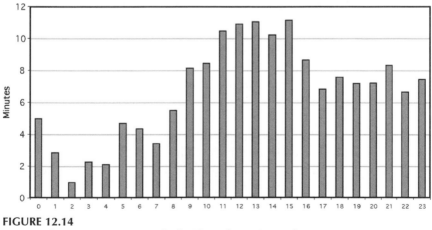

FIGURE 12.14
Average Time Spent at a News Site by Time of Day, September 2001

major Internet news sites such as CNN.com, MSNBC.com, ABCNEWS.com, and Yahoo.dailynews.com all benefited from this increased reliance on the Internet.

The Internet, however, provided more than access to established news sites. After September 11, the Internet witnessed a period of growth that could only be described as unique. Overnight, thousands of "September 11" websites emerged to fill the demand for information. The speed and success of this movement suggests that future news events are likely to build on the platforms created from the September 11 disaster.

For many, the value of the Internet can be measured by the following functions:

- First, information searches could be tailored to meet the specific objectives of the user. This provided users with freedom to explore leads they found interesting and useful. Search results could be bookmarked for later review.
- Second, the Internet provided the user with freedom to conduct research at any time. This provided a measure of convenience that was unique to the Internet. Unlike broadcast news, the Internet was not dependent on the scheduling of news reports. Interviews could be played at the convenience of the user.
- Third, news could be easily linked to other sources. The Internet facilitates exploration through hyperlinks.
- Fourth, with the growth of broadband access, video and streaming audio could be played often without bringing the system to a crawl.
- Fifth, Internet news sites provided a wealth of backup information, ranging from in-depth analysis of events to background information about the participants. This last point implies that one could dig as deep as desired without bumping into a time or information constraints. Internet news sites were of value because these functions were not available via traditional media.
- Sixth, the Internet encouraged the creation of multiple communities of interest. These communities helped account for the growth of network externalities and thus the value and power of the Internet.

A recent report by the Online News Association sums up the current status of online news sites. The report finds that (1) the public has accepted digital news as another option on its menu of credible news sources and that (2) in the digital age, people still rely on conventional media. News sites currently act as complementary sources of news for the public.[19] That study was commissioned prior to the events of September 11. Those events could only strengthen the reports' conclusions.

The evidence for an increased demand requires a more detailed analysis. At the aggregate level, the data point to an increase in demand, as measured by unique visits. At the household level, the data suggest that interest in Internet news, while increasing on September 11, was not as significant as suggested by an examination of the macrodata. The sample of households represented a random drawing from twelve cities. The sample selection and sample size make it unlikely that the household sample was not representative of Internet households. The results suggest that at the aggregate level there were a large number of users who were intensive in their use of the Internet to obtain access to and information from Internet news sites. Since identifying specific household activity is difficult using aggregate statistics such as the number of unique visits, care should be taken when estimating the share of households using the Internet for any purpose. However, the results of the microanalysis are profound. The results suggest that there was an increased demand for news from the Internet even if this demand was far less than previously thought.

Care must be taken in assessing the household results. First, there are many possible places where the microdata fails to account for specific visits. The analysis depends on the correct classification of sites. At this time, we have no way to check the Plurimus classification system. Second, the specific sample used might not have underreported households with high demand for Internet news. Finally, the aggregate data may well include nonhousehold activity. There is no reason to believe that those working who had access to the Internet were not online during the events of September 11.

With those data caveats, we note that whereas September 11 brought with it an increased demand for Internet news, the size of this demand depends on the unit of measurement. A focus on total visits provides a different picture than results obtained when the focus is on individual households. These results need to be evaluated with information on demand obtained from self-reported information. For example, the 46 percent rates reported recently by the Pew Foundation and others are at odds with the results of the microanalysis but not with the results of the aggregate analysis.

Notes

An earlier version of this chapter was originally published as Paul Rappaport, "The Internet and the Demand for News," in *Prometheus* 20, no. 3 (2002): 255–62.

1. www.medialifemagazine.com/news2001/sep01/sep17/3wed/news1wednesday.html.
2. "Arbitron: Radio Listening Surged during Week of September 11." www.gavin.com/news/article.php?art_id=753.
3. Bard Palser, *American Journalism Review,* November 2001.

4. Leander Kahney at www.wired.com/news/culture/0,1284,46766,00.html.

5. Plurimus is currently in Chapter 7 bankruptcy, having met the fate of many Internet startups. Through partnerships with more than fifty Internet service providers (ISPs) across the United States, Plurimus collected the clickstream data from over 500,000 households across the United States. The ISPs were strategically chosen to offer Plurimus adequate coverage geographically, demographically, and across different types of access. Plurimus made use of poststratification adjustment techniques to weight and project its estimates of behavior to the population.

6. The microdataset was composed of user logs for a random sample of 5,000 Internet users.

7. "Internet Relieves Communications Overload after September 11 Crisis," based on a survey of 1,200 households conducted for the Pew Research Center for the People and the Press. http://people-press.org/reports/display.php3?PageID=612.

8. www.acnielson.com/news/corp/2001/20011029.htm.

9. Richard W. Wiggins, "The Effects of a September 11 on a Leading Search Engine." www.firstmonday.dk/issues/issue6_10/wiggins/#author.

10. stacks.msnbc.com/local/knsd/nbclmx9nhrc.asp?cp1=1.

11. http://people-press.org/reports/display.php3?ReportID=146.

12. www.pewinternet.org.

13. Examples include www.alltheweb.com, news.yahoo.com, news.google.com, www.moreover.com/news, www.newstrawler.com, www.newsindex.com, www.headlinespot.com, newsdirectory.com, www.infogrid.com, www.newsisfree.com.

14. Plurimus utilized a number of filters to ensure privacy. Household information was deleted in the compilation of the aggregate data.

15. The dataset provides counts of unique household sessions, not unique households. Consequently, care should be used in projecting these data to estimate the overall number of online households.

16. National Telecommunications and Information Agency, February 5, 2002. www.ntia.doc.gov.

17. www.keynote.com/news_events/public_services_portal/09-11-02_media_report.html.

18. Percentage increase in activity is the level of activity in October relative to pre–September 11 visits.

19. Digital Journalism Credibility Study, commissioned by the Online News Association. www.journalists.org/programs/research.html.

13

History and September 11: A Comparison of Online and Network TV Discourses

Patrick Martin and Sean Phelan

The September 11 attacks were represented immediately by U.S. television news as events of immense historical importance and history and were largely spoken about in terms of comparisons with other epic, and traumatic, moments in the collective memory of the United States. In contrast, public discussants on CNN's online message board invoked a greater spectrum of historical references when seeking to understand, and explain, the consequences and genesis of the attacks.

IN OUR PREVIOUS RESEARCH into September 11–related television and message board discourse,[1] we showed how, despite some interesting comparative differences, Islamic culture was represented within a generally inflexible and mythical framework, in which it was explicitly indicted for its supposed tolerance of terrorism and promotion of religious fundamentalism.[2] Indeed, in some extreme cases, the discourse seemed to encourage the idea that Islam and militant violence exist together in some ahistorical and apolitical bind. Removed from history and geopolitics in this fashion, the attacks, putatively committed in the name of Islam, could therefore be viewed as an unparalleled "evil"—an inexplicable event, which suggests that there is no need to examine why it happened.

However, history was hardly absent from the media and political discourse in the aftermath of the attacks. The invocation of historical parallels informed television's framing of what had happened and speculation about what the future might bring. This much is to be expected: media narratives—underpinned by historical analogy—provide necessary cues for the public expression of grief and anger and are a means of understanding events within a framework of culturally salient and available information. In the context of the September 11 attacks, these historical analogies also serve an important political function, namely, the removal of Arab and Islamic discontent with the West from the historical context (dehistoricization) and a parallel placement of the attacks within the affirmative history of U.S. "war" time experiences (rehistoricization).

This chapter shows how American television networks participated in a patriotic reconstitution of American self-identity using a reservoir of images, ideas, and narratives against which the attacks could be contrasted and understood. By studying the same features of CNN's online message board discussion, we then consider to what extent this dominant view of history is received by message board participants, and we examine whether the language and ideas used by television media are challenged or uncritically accepted in this quasi-public discussion environment.[3]

Methodology

Using linguistic analysis software (Wordsmith,[4] Concordance[5]), we based cross-media comparisons on an analysis of the following sets of texts: (1) A 4.18 million word set of transcripts of news broadcasts, between September 11 and 17 inclusively, from five U.S.-based television networks: ABC, CBS, CNN, FOX, and NBC.[6] (2) A CNN message board that contained 2.39 million words. This message board was set up to facilitate discussion among CNN community members within one hour of the attacks and had a total of 30,836 individual messages before midnight, September 17.[7]

The quantitative (or corpus linguistic) approach allows us to measure and tabulate particular types of language use: the choice of words in particular contexts, the overall presence of certain themes, and words that are routinely inflected with a particular meaning by being repeatedly used in adjacent positions (e.g., "history teaches"). Having discerned patterns of language use that are relevant to the analysis of the discourse of historicization, we then apply a critical discourse analysis approach to ask certain politically resonant questions about the different discourse practices within both media contexts.

Historicizing September 11: An Overview of Elite Political Discourse

"History" is reconfigured in many ways by different discourse agents within the "order of discourse" surrounding September 11.[8] When we speak of an order of discourse(s), we are simply referring to the prioritization within media texts of certain kinds of ideologically resonant language and assumptions, in other words, the ideological implications of the talk typically used by social actors such as politicians, media pundits, journalists, and—in the case of the message board—the writing of public contributors. The invocation of history by elite political agents typically served to intensify appeals for particular responses—imputed not to political expediency or emotional need but to the remote and inscrutable agency of historical wisdom (e.g., history teaches us that military force is the best response; history teaches us that evil prospers when good men do nothing).

"Americans do not yet have the distance of history but our responsibility to history is already clear, to answer these attacks and rid the world of evil. War has been waged against us by stealth, and deceit and murder" (President George W. Bush).[9] Here we have two very different, even paradoxical, conceptualizations of history side by side in the same sentence. There is explicit acknowledgment that "Americans do not have the distance of history"—the implication being that "Americans" are temporally too close to the attacks to understand their possible historical consequences. This is immediately followed by the disclaimer "but our responsibility to history is already clear"—which, in its cancellation of the previous doubt, implies that tacit moral and historical imperatives will clearly dictate what September 11 "means": that the United States is at "war" and will not rest until "evil" has been vanquished.

History is thus regarded as a concept—an educator and a guardian whose values must be respected. But it can also be spoken about as a repository of images and narratives from which discourse agents may pick to strengthen, and give emotional resonance to, particular political interpretations. For example, Pearl Harbor is the most frequent and unambiguously historical analogy invoked by politicians, television media, and online message board participants in connection with September 11: the clear implication being that the attacks are an "act of war" and that the militaristic response which worked in 1941 is the best response for 2001.

Within political discourse, history is used as a symbolic resource that legitimates current political attitudes and future political actions. For instance, the common formulations "history teaches us" and "history will judge" are typical instances where historical truth is posited as a singular, authoritative, and active agent. As Ruth Wodak points out, the discursive construction of history in political discourse not only offers a legitimacy to the argumentative points being presented but also works as a moral force: a form of compulsion for whatever remedy is prescribed by historical logic.[10] We can therefore say that a hegemonic use of history in political discourse reveals itself through a "freezing" of the concept—seeing it as unchanging, stable, and singular. In such cases, linguistic analysis would see the word "history" disproportionately associated with particular word forms: imperative and active verbs, verbs connoting instruction and education. Contestation, in turn, would be marked by a greater association of history with pluralization, the use of "hedges" (such as "perhaps" and "maybe") or, more directly, by the explicit questioning of "official" history.[11]

Some strands of contemporary historicism concerned with ascertaining the knowability of the past observe how historical, and historicized, narratives can be used to legitimate past and present practices of exclusion and subordination.[12] This points to a wider dilemma about history's social function—particularly when the desire for contemporary appraisals of the past, to illuminate what should be done now, cannot but lend itself toward a simplification of the relationship between past, present, and future. Faith in the lessons of history certainly seems to have returned in the aftermath of the September 11 attacks. Hegemonic narratives that were most consoling—and also best suited to the political goal of unifying the American nation in a sustained and militaristic response—were much more likely to be aired on television than on the message board.

With respect to history and September 11, the television and message board discourses are examined here in terms of three of the most salient characteristics of elite political discourse:

- Dehistoricization of Arab resentment about U.S. foreign policy—particularly with regard to the Middle East
- Positive affirmation of U.S. self-identity and those moments in U.S. history that best encourage civic unity of purpose
- Emphasis on how history can inform a response to the attacks, as opposed to how it might help explain its origins

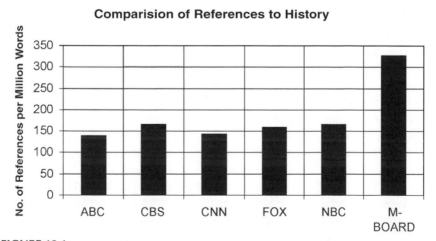

Comparision of References to History

FIGURE 13.1
Comparison of References to History per Million Words

"History" and Truth Claims

Figure 13.1 gives a quantitative overview of the invocation of history on each television network and on the CNN message board. Contributors to the message board made approximately twice as many references to history—perhaps indicating that, in times of social crisis and confusion, the need to refer to the past is a reflex of personal and social cognition and is heavily mediated by the cognitive and discursive resources which are most easily availed of. "Meaningful" or content terms (such as nouns, adjectives, and categorical markers)[13] are statistically more the province of the message board; value terms occur more frequently on the message board than on television. This can be accounted for by many of the situational factors that are typical of the use of personal telecommunications technology:[14] the brevity of the messages that people send ensures less repetition and circumlocution and hence more direct allusions to the theme of the contribution; the messages are frequently personalized and marked by emotive reasoning, which results in an intensification and iteration of key terms; and the fact that peer-to-peer textual communication, on this occasion, does not work with any of the strictures that shape TV media language, such as the need for the recapitulation of headlines or the pursuit of tangential news stories that bear little relation to the central political theme.

The differences between the television networks are marginal. However, when we consider the presence and use of historians in the respective media, we discover that the standard overpresence of meaningful terms on the message board completely reversed. Historians are alluded to or introduced as sources of authority eleven times more often on television. Their expert status ensures that they have greater "symbolic capital"[15] as "readers" of history than other sources and are more likely to be invoked, by other discourse agents, to add cachet to an interpretation. This is evident in the tendency of interviewers and anchors to repeatedly introduce guests as historians—sometimes a number of times in the same interview. There are also examples of military and political pundits having their historian credentials alluded to, as if the imprimatur itself is shorthand for professional expertise and authority. David Halberstam is categorized variously as a Pulitzer Prize–winning journalist, historian, military expert, and New Yorker—qualifying him for expertise and relevance on all possible grounds. He appeared on four of the networks during the course of the week and, tellingly, endorsed the highly charged analogy between September 11 and Pearl Harbor by associating American identity with military strength:

> David Halberstam (Historian): I'd like to think that the adversary, the enemy in this case, you know, perhaps made a crucial mistake in the way—the same way

the Japanese at Pearl Harbor did, in the sense they may have succeeded too well, and they've gotten on our radar screen, they've allowed, therefore, the political fabric to unite, the political leadership to go deep into the bloodstream of the country and, therefore, we can, you know, use our enormous power and strength and resilience to address it and to be aware that we now live in a changed world.[16]

Inflecting History

There are significant differences in the words with which "history" is collocated in the two media: the propensity of broadcasters, television pundits, and "experts" to use American history as the primary resource from which to frame a historically based interpretation of the attacks manifests itself in incessant allusions to American history, U.S. history, and national history (figure 13.2). Conversely, the possibility of expanding the fields of reference to include other international attacks in which civilians died is not availed of (see the comparative references to geopolitical conflicts in figure 13.3). In fact, one of the most frequently referenced "nonmilitary" events was the Oklahoma City bombing of 1994 (365 references), which once more points to the tendency to localize the historical context (i.e., domestic insurgency is seen as a better analogy for the attacks than overseas terrorism). These are the defining markers for the way in which historical discussion proceeds on television.

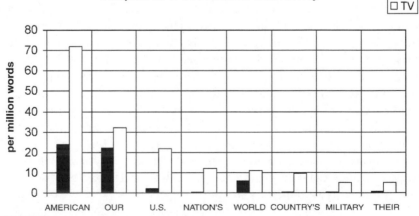

FIGURE 13.2
Comparison of Collocations with History
Note: A "collocation" is the use of two words beside each other in a text. For example, "American" and "history" in this figure. (References per Million Words)

TABLE 13.1
Words That Are Explicitly Associated or Collocated
with "History" on the Message Board and Not on TV

Word	Reference per Million Words
How	15
Etc.	14
Civilians	14
Afghanistan	13
Palestinians	13
U.S.	13
Millions	12
Innocent	11
Arab	10
Every	10
Nuclear	10
Yugoslavia	10
Bombed	10
Oil	9

The message board, on the other hand, finds history used in a broader category of contexts. There is a much greater distribution of associations across the contributions (see table 13.1) and no evident tendency to frame the historical aspects of the attacks in a purely domestic setting—history is "Americanized" three times more often on television, and Afghanistan, Yugoslavia, and Palestine do not warrant a single mention in the explicit discussion of history.[17] This reflects a prevailing trend in the two discourses: the (understandable) "localization" of the event on U.S. television networks and a greater internationalization of the historical context on the message board (perhaps indicative of CNN's more global reach).

Truth Claims

Resorting to declarations of the truth of a statement ("It is a fact that . . ." or "The reality is . . .") is a typical trait of adversarial discourse: The speaker implicitly acknowledges the existence of an opposing perspective with which his or her perspective is competing.[18] Reaffirmation—through the truth claim—can be interpreted in a number of ways: as a subjective ideological assertion purporting to be a proposition about a universal state-of-affairs or, more beneficially perhaps, as an indicator of the speaker's self-conscious awareness that he or she is proposing an interpretation which runs counter to that of others. To openly declare something as the truth is to bespeak an awareness that others will, or have, contested the fact.

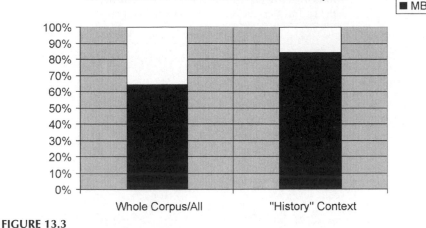

FIGURE 13.3
Distribution of Truth Claims between Corpora

Analysis of the two media, shown in figure 13.4, reveals that the message board contains nearly twice as many truth claims and, when discussing history, that contributors are even more inclined to intensify their claims by asserting a clause's truthfulness, basis in fact, or commonsense value.

Generally, analysis of truth claims within a discourse tends to provide a useful indicator of the degree of resoluteness and inflexibility of the attitudes therein expressed. For example, consider the anticipation and dismissal of dissenting views in General Norman Schwarzkopf's distinction between U.S. military activities in Iraq and the September 11 attacks:

> Schwarzkopf: A lot of people have criticized what we did in Iraq and Desert Storm, but the truth of the matter is we went to extraordinary limits to try and avoid any civilian casualties, to try and avoid, even at the risk of—a greater risk to our own pilots. And—but you look at these bastards and what they did yesterday; they deliberately went after civilians and innocent people. And that's what makes the difference between us and them.[19]

This is atypical for TV discourse where, compared to the message board, there is far less commingling of historical events and truth assertions, suggesting that fewer closed, dogmatic assertions are made in TV discussion. However, it also suggests that there is less of a *need* to make dogmatic assertions in the structures of consensual television discourse, particularly when one's truth assertions are unlikely to be challenged with anything like the same ferocity we find on the message board.[20]

Historical Analogies and Antecedents

"Presidents don't call on history enough. Now is the time that I think George Bush should remind us of what we're all about and what we've been through together as a nation."[21]

Historical analogies that seek to understand an event such as September 11 arguably become political on being articulated—especially when they become fixed and reused in a discourse. It is difficult to assess where language use becomes political: Analogical reasoning is a human heuristic function, a sense-making reaction to new experiences.[22] To look for analogies—and then formulate them in language—is such an all-pervasive and rudimentary human activity that it should not in itself be usefully considered political. However, in the choice of source and target (the choice of "what" is compared to "what") the cognitive clearly becomes politicized and as the specific features of the analogy become an established part of discourse and social practice, they become more than rules of thumb for allowing us to "understand" one event in terms of another already "understood."[23]

When looking at the historical context in which September 11 was framed by television and message board discourse, we can ask the following questions:

- What historical events is it most readily compared to?
- How is September 11 said to differ from these other events?
- What actions and behaviors do the analogies predict?
- Who is making the analogy?

Table 13.2 gives an overview of some of the geopolitical and historical allusions made in both media contexts (they appear in descending order of their usage on television). Although more of an immediate, geopolitical issue than a historical one, references to the Middle East conflict are included in the table. It shows that Israel and Palestine are the most frequently occurring references in both media contexts, but that they are roughly six times more likely to feature in message board discourse. The crucial distinction between both contexts is the dearth of critical attitudes to Israel on television—in contrast to what is a much broader spectrum of critical and (sometimes) partisan discourses on the message board.

One strong indication of this is evident in the contrasting noun phrases used to talk about Israel in each medium. Israel or, more precisely, the Israeli government is associated with terrorism, killing, and occupation approximately eleven times more often on the message board (figure 13.5).

TABLE 13.2
References to Historical Conflicts and Figures

Reference	TV	Messageboard
Israel*	1005	2877
Palestin*	638	1862
Iraq*	379	801
Pearl Harbor	416	278
Gulf War	371	182
Vietnam	141	239
Kosovo	46	103
Hiroshima	10	96
Roosevelt	85	14
Somalia	26	45
Iwo Jima	36	4
Churchill	11	25
Nicaragua	0	19
Neville Chamberlain	0	11
Guatemala	5	5
Grenada	0	8
Salvador	0	6
Lusitania	2	4
Sabra & Shatilla	0	5
Laos	1	4

Denotes a wildcard (lemma) search. Thus Israel would capture Israel, Israeli, Israel's, and so on.

The hypothesis that the U.S. mass media systematically repress aspects of
America's political past that reflect less positively on the nation's self-image as
a liberating, democratic force (conflicts such as Nicaragua, Somalia, Salvador,
Grenada) gains partial credence through a study of the television omissions.[24]

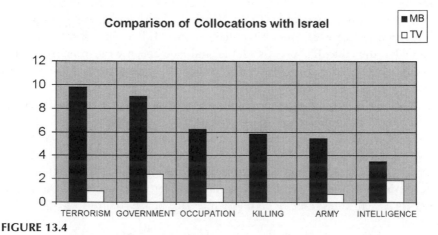

FIGURE 13.4
Comparison of Collocations with Israel per Million Words

These critical discourses may have no great presence on the message board either, but the simple fact of their being articulated does point to the existence of an alternative view of U.S. history—a view that is largely absent from television's partisan, historical narrative. Indeed, the fact that Vietnam—one of the more inglorious moments in U.S. history—is invoked three times more frequently on the message board is very much indicative of this pattern.

Comparisons with Pearl Harbor

"Rep. Gephart: 'We need to be united. This is like the time after Pearl Harbor in 1941, the whole country is being challenged, and we need to unite shoulder to shoulder and fight this thing and try to win this difficult challenge that we face.'"[25]

Unlike the other major comparisons, Pearl Harbor is not "overrepresented" in message board discussion and, proportionally, is mentioned less frequently online than it is on CBS and NBC.

Characteristically invoked as a direct comparison by television media, the ensuing discussions focus largely on the same question: Is September 11 like Pearl Harbor? Indeed, backed up by their own opinion polls, many of the networks focused exceptional attention on this question:

> Compared to the attack on Pearl Harbor, how do you rate this—this attack two days ago? Sixty-six percent said it's more serious, 25 percent said equally serious, five percent not as serious. Does—does this tell us about the enormity of this event, or that people tend to feel most strongly about what's most recent? When 90 percent of American people believe this is as serious or more serious than Pearl Harbor, we understand the magnitude. The fact is, 2400 people died at Pearl Harbor, military personnel, one government attacking another, one army

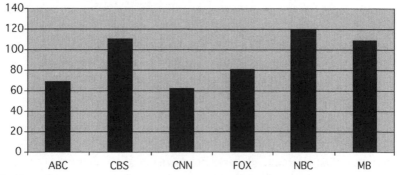

References to Pearl Harbor

FIGURE 13.5
Comparison of Frequency of References to Pearl Harbor per Million Words

attacking another. This was an attack on civilians, brothers and sisters, people who had not signed up for the military, and the death toll is going to be tens of thousands.[26]

There were three consistently used caveats or qualifications to the Pearl Harbor comparison, each of them premised on the idea that September 11 was worse than Pearl Harbor. The above excerpt is typical: the attack on Pearl Harbor was less invidious because it was a legitimate military target; the (Japanese) enemy was visible and a legitimate, state-constituted military force; and the fact that the September 11 death count was greater (this was before the estimated number of casualties was scaled down).

Although these qualifications were commonly made in both media contexts, there were differences too, mainly the attitudes toward the function and type of remembrance. On the message board, the memory of Pearl Harbor was based around a consoling and unifying narrative of recovery from attack and, in particular, the words of General Yamamoto: "I fear we have awoken a slumbering giant." In addition, message board contributors found comfort in imaginatively revisiting the idealized state of national unity of 1941.[27] This wartime nostalgia found other expressions too (in both media forums), for instance, in the reverential allusions to Churchill and Roosevelt as archetypal (and victorious) wartime politicians.

Historical discourse is heavily mediated by the cultural choices and practices that impact the representation of a nation's history. Pearl Harbor is presented as a focal point of the nation's coming of age in international conflict in the Jerry Bruckheimer/Touchstone Pictures film of the preceding year. With its strong narrative of an unprovoked assault on the United States and the nation's attendant "loss of innocence," the implied self-image was one of an isolationist, freedom-loving, and benevolent superpower reluctantly forced to confront belligerent nondemocratic forces. Consequently, the effect of choosing Pearl Harbor as a historical parallel is partly to anticipate a similarly heroic and militaristic response to the September 11 attacks.

The television references to Pearl Harbor were often framed as part of an alignment with other seminal historical moments. For instance, Tom Brokaw juxtaposes September 11 with Pearl Harbor, the assassinations of the Kennedy brothers and Martin Luther King, and the landing on the moon.[28] It is a particular type of historicity: accentuating the "historical magnitude" of the event while making little attempt to place it in a critical context. Indeed, it effectively balks at reflecting on U.S. involvement in geopolitical issues such as the Middle East, which are plausibly linked—however opportunistically—to the attacks.

Finally, there is the question of who produces the historical analogy and how it is maintained over time. The day and network on which the Pearl Harbor comparison was most frequently aired on television was September 12 on NBC. The categories of those making the comparison are outlined in figure 13.6.

As figure 13.7 illustrates, NBC's senior news anchor, Tom Brokaw, was far and away the most frequent user of the Pearl Harbor analogy. There are situational factors that might explain this, particularly his need, as anchor, to continually recap on the contributions made by others. But the figure certainly indicates the key role he played in framing the attacks in terms of a Pearl Harbor narrative. Thereafter, the analogy is most commonly invoked by a bipartisan range of present-day and former political figures (including William Cohen, former defense secretary; Warren Rudman, former U.S. senator; Warren Christopher, former secretary of state; Senator Wayne Allard). Interestingly, the analogy becomes headline news when invoked by Senator John McCain on the afternoon of September 12.[29]

Implications and Conclusion

In contextualizing the relationship between history and the September 11 attacks, our findings indicate that the mediated political discourse[30] of American television does not support the same spectrum of value judgments as the CNN message board. This difference can be explained prosaically, for of all the news networks in the sample CNN is the one with the most ambitious global reach—which presumably will be reflected in the international profile of its message board contributors. Which begs the fundamental question: To what degree does American television, primarily addressed to the American collective, tacitly collude with elite political imperatives in limiting the range of "acceptable" historical analogy?

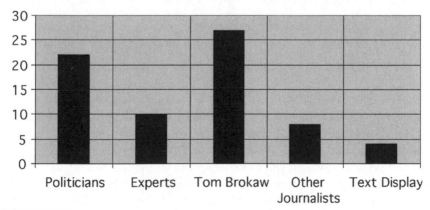

FIGURE 13.6
Authorship of Pearl Harbor Comparisons on NBC, September 12, 2001

Our findings highlight the degree to which TV discourse absolves the United States of critical introspection about its own geopolitical past and ignores possible international comparisons with September 11 (the obvious exception being the empathetic parallels between the United States and its close ally Israel). There is of course a compelling, and understandable, reason for this: the strong public need to ignore such questions in a time of shock. Anger and grief do not need discussions about U.S. cultural hegemony and imperialist foreign policy. However, given the extent to which critical discourses about U.S. foreign policy seem to have taken root in the mainstream media of other countries, but not the United States, since September 11, one can at least surmise that these discourses are structurally inhibited from flourishing on U.S. television—particularly now that the militarism roused by September 11 has extended to a U.S. military invasion of Iraq.[31]

References to history in the context of a crisis of global dimensions carry a particular force and suggest particular responses. Television practitioners operating in such an environment are liable to adapt particular themes and proliferate them, due to the pressures of time and the need for continuity that the medium can demand. Often the implications of these comparisons are left unspoken, as though the outcome, the corollary of the historical analogy is self-evident and does not need any further explanation.

In terms of the choice of historical analogy, one cannot realistically ask questions about whether particular analogies are chosen because, based on some abstract index or some "expert" barometer of appraisal, they are the most historically accurate. The issue of accuracy—or more precisely social conceptions of accuracy—will always be refracted through the cultural knowledge about particular moments in U.S. history. For example, some on the message board contract World War II to a causal relationship between Pearl Harbor and Hiroshima.[32] The same reductions, and emphatic assertions of truth, may not be present on American television. Nevertheless, discussions of history are generally limited to moments that reflect best on U.S. self-identity and affirm—even moralize—the use of military force.

The aptness of an analogy can clearly be contested at its coinage. But contestation is never as easy as it seems—particularly in a discourse environment as symbolically and emotionally averse to dissent as America in the immediate aftermath of the attacks. Consequently, once a particular analogy becomes an accepted part of a discourse, its spread is not arrested and it becomes firmly anchored by continued usage (often for reasons of expediency and the narrative demands that "rolling" news places on presenters). Of course, the same can be said, a fortiori, for the commonsense assumption that history speaks with some singular, uncomplicated voice. Indeed, one has only to consider how simple assumptions about the "lessons" of history still buttress the rhetoric of the Bush administration: "The business about more time, how much time do we need to see clearly that he's [Saddam] not disarming?" Mr. Bush told reporters, adding with a flash of impatience, "surely [note the modality of certitude] our friends [in Europe] have learned lessons from the past?"[33]

Peer-to-peer networks, which foster the development of communication between disparate and globally dispersed groups of people, have an unknown political function. Our findings suggest that they have a clear galvanizing effect on those who do not see their (hi)stories reflected in mainstream television discourse. At the same time, the Internet is increasingly being used as an auxiliary form of public relations for the dissemination of mainstream party political literature and—in an American context—further anchoring the firmly established tenets of bipartisan discussion.[34] Therefore, while it would seem to encourage diverse forms of democratic participation and provide a platform for the articulation of critical perspectives not aired on broadcast media, the Internet's long-term impact (if its values do not impact on the representational styles of the more influential medium) cannot be confidently affirmed.

Notes

1. This chapter and previous work (see reference in note 2) are both based around a sample of discourse from the same sources and covering the same time frame (September 11–17). See methodology section for more information.

2. P. Martin and S. Phelan, "Representing Islam in the Wake of September 11," *Prometheus* 20, no. 3 (2002): 263–69.

3. We use the word "public" here in a qualified sense. Contributors to the CNN message board are not taken to represent a democratic forum to which all members of the American—and global—public have equal access. Issues of nationality, religion, political affiliation, socioeconomic status, and cyberliteracy would ideally be considered in attempts to construct a profile of the message board contributors. However, in the absence of this information, we turn to regarding the message board community as a large, self-selected group of media consumers whose commonality is simply this: they have access to the Internet, speak English, watch television, and had a desire to become involved in a discussion about September 11.

4. A demonstration version of Wordsmith is available at www.hit.uib.no/wordsmith.

5. Technical information about Concordance is available at www.rjcw.freeserve.co.uk.

6. Based around a mixture of news and discussion programs, the transcripts were all downloaded from the Lexis-Nexis database at www.lexis-nexis.com. They were "cleaned" to ensure that there were no double entries of transcripts.

7. One of many message boards previously located at community.cnn.com. A local copy has been retained for the purposes of analysis. Quantitative analysis of the message board took into account the tendency of contributors to reproduce the text of the comment that they are rebutting or commending. These repetitions were removed

prior to the quantitative analysis and in fact were less plentiful than might have been anticipated, due perhaps to the exceedingly high number of contributions, which would undermine attempts at one-to-one engagement.

8. See Lille Chouliaraki and Norman Fairclough, *Discourse in Late Modernity: Rethinking Critical Discourse Analysis* (Great Britain: Edinburgh University Press, 1999); N. Fairclough, "Critical Discourse Analysis," in Allan Bell and Peter Garret, eds., *Approaches to Media Discourse* (Great Britain: Blackwell, 1998).

9. Cited during the following broadcasts: ABC News *Nightline* (11:35 P.M. ET), September 14, 2001, Friday; *NBC News Special Report: America on Alert* (7:00 P.M. ET), September 16, 2001, Sunday; *CBS Evening News* (6:30 P.M. ET), September 14, 2001, Friday; *CNN Live Event/Special* (12:58), September 14, 2001, Friday; *Fox Special Report with Brit Hume* (6:44 P.M.), September 14, 2001, Friday; *NBC News Special Report: America Mourns* (11:45 A.M. ET), September 14, 2001, Friday.

10. See Ruth Wodak, "The Discourse-Historical Approach," in *Methods of Critical Discourse Analysis*, ed. Ruth Wodak and Michael Meyer London (New Delhi: Sage, 2001), 63–94.

11. See Pierre Bourdieu, *Language and Symbolic Power* (Cambridge, U.K.: Polity, 1991).

12. See A. Dirlik, "Whither History? Encounters with Historicism, Postmodernism, Postcolonialism," *Futures* 34, no. 1 (2002): 75–90.

13. See Saeed, *Semantics* (London: Blackwell, 1997), for a general introduction to semantics and the distinction between content words (nouns, verb, adjectives, adverbs) and function words (conjunctives, prepositions, determiners, etc.).

14. For background literature on these aspects of computer-mediated communication, see R. Upitis, "Real and Contrived Uses of Electronic Mail in Elementary Schools," *Computers and Education* 15, no. 1–3 (1990): 233–43; H. McKee, "YOUR VIEWS SHOWED TRUE IGNORANCE!!!: (Mis)Communication in an Online Interracial Discussion Forum," *Computers and Composition* 19, no. 4 (2002): 411–34.

15. Bourdieu, "Language and Symbolic Power."

16. ABC News, *Nightline* (11:35 P.M. ET), September 14, 2001.

17. Because of the size of the text under examination here, this chapter limits itself to *explicit* mentions to history. We are not denying the obvious relevance of references to the past that avoid the word "history" (or its lemma).

18. This is not to deny that the dialogic function of a truth claim is partly to implicate the opposing viewpoint as "irrational" or "irrelevant."

19. General Norman Schwarzkopf, NBC's *Today* (7:00 A.M. ET), September 12.

20. Consider this message board example: "W******: It is truly a shame you are so consumed by hate for something the vast majority of Americans are not responsible for. Remember that ALL of the coalition governments that embargoed Iraq for its UNPROVOKED attack on a neighbor. I do not hear you saying sorry to those 5000+ kuwaitians killed by a sadistic leader bent on expanding his domain under the banner of 'our lost territory.' You need to grow up and get your facts straight and then talk about what REALLY happened."

21. Doris Kearns Goodwin (biographer and former aide to President Lyndon Johnson and member of Harvard University's Board of Overseers) speaking on *NBC News Special Report: Attack on America* (11:00 P.M. ET), September 11, 2001.

22. This is a wide area of research in the disciplines of cognitive science, political science and critical theory. For an overview of metaphor and analogy in human reasoning, see G. Lakoff and M. Johnson, *Metaphors We Live By* (Chicago: University of Chicago Press, 1980). For a case study on the heuristic aspect of analogical reasoning, read D. D. Sadler and E. J. Shoben, "Context Effects on Semantic Domains as Seen in Analogy Solution," *Journal of Experimental Psychology: Learning, Memory, and Cognition* 19, no. 1 (1993): 128–47.

23. T. Van Dijk, *Ideology: A Multidisciplinary Approach* (Thousand Oaks, Calif.: Sage, 1998).

24. This, of course, is the ongoing contention of Noam Chomsky. See, for example, Noam Chomsky and Edward S. Herman, *Manufacturing Consent: The Political Economy of the Mass Media* (New York: Pantheon, 2002).

25. Representative Dick Gephardt, *America under Attack,* ABC News, September 14, 2001.

26. Matt Lauer, NBC's *Today,* 7:00 A.M. EDT, September 13, 2001.

27. As one contributor to the message board phrased it: "We have to rise above the chaos and madness and keep our resolve. They have awoken a sleeping giant, and we will now act with the determination we did 60 years ago after Pearl Harbor."

28. Tom Brokaw, *NBC News Special: Attack on America,* 10:00 P.M., September 12. Full quotation (which, interestingly, doesn't draw on exclusively American moments): "This day you'll remember forever, whatever your age, wherever you live in this country. There are those days that for the people who are alive in America are etched forever in their minds: December 7, 1941, Pearl Harbor; 1945, the end of World War II, victory over Germany and Japan, the death of FDR; November 22, 1963, the assassination of John F. Kennedy, the age of innocence came to an end in America; 1968, the assassination of his brother and Martin Luther King; 1974, the resignation of Richard Nixon; 1989, the death of Communism, the fall of the Berlin wall, the liberation of Poland and Czechoslovakia; 1990, the release of Nelson Mandela; and of course 1989, as well, Tiananmen Square and all that that meant to this country; 1968 also saw the landing of the man on the moon. And then the millennium, a new century, a new beginning of a thousand years, new hope for this world and for America. One year in, on the 11th of September, the ninth month, 9-11-01, an act of terrorism that is tantamount to war, the most serious attack on this country since Pearl Harbor, the most devastating attack within the continental United States ever by a foreign force of some kind in more than a hundred years."

29. The headline announcing Senator McCain's Pearl Harbor comparison appeared four times on NBC on September 12.

30. John B. Thompson, *The Media and Modernity: A Social Theory of the Media* (Cambridge, U.K.: Polity, 1995).

31. Tony Karon, "US-Europe Clash Deepens Blair's Iraq Dilemma," *Time,* January 23, 2003, discusses the differences between (media-mediated) popular attitudes in Europe and America to the threat of U.S. military intervention in Iraq. Of course, this is to not deny the growing American skepticism about the war (see also *The Nation*).

32. Some contributors habitually referred to the bombing of Hiroshima as a direct response to the attacks on Pearl Harbor and suggested that the same response was required to avenge 9/11.

33. *Irish Times,* January 22, 2003.

34. Grounded in the libertarian-inspired narrative of empowerment that surrounds discourse about ICTs, Zysman and Weber discuss the anticipated "radical" impact of network technology on forms of political participation (see J. Zysman and S. Weber, "Governance and Politics of the Internet Economy: Historical Transformations or Ordinary Politics with a New Vocabulary?" BRIE Working Paper 16, 2000). What is absent from their critique, however, is acknowledgment of the Internet's low status as a form of social and political networking. The U.S. party political system has little to fear from online grassroots activism, if these "alternative" political discourses fail to have an impact on the TV-dominated world of mainstream party politics.

14

From Disaster Marathon to Media Event: Live Television's Performance on September 11, 2001, and September 11, 2002

Menahem Blondheim and Tamar Liebes

Menahem Blondheim and Tamar Liebes show how television's coverage of the events of September 11 was a prominent example of its power to engage in "the live broadcast of history" and the increasing difficulty in distinguishing between television's coverage of an event and its becoming part of it. They discuss the two overlapping genres of live broadcasting, first, the media event, featuring the deliberate staging and dramatic coverage of preplanned symbol-laden moments in the social process, and then its sequel, the disaster marathon, featuring the live broadcast of catastrophe—natural, accidental, or meditated—and its aftermath. In both genres television interrupts its routine, switches into live broadcasting, and whole societies are riveted to the screen for long hours, sometimes days.

They propose to understand television's performance on September 11 as a paradigmatic disaster marathon, which focused the attention of an audience not only of worried Americans but also of voyeurs from along the sidelines of the entire globe. They proceed by discussing the texture and implications of the September 11 disaster marathon, highlighting a number of problems it poses for society as well as the profession of journalism. They conclude by juxtaposing the disaster marathon of September 2001 and the commemorative media event of September 11, 2002. The chapter concludes with advice that the goal of the media should be "strategies that would diminish incentives for the ruthless to engage in violence in order to reap the fruits of media coverage."

Disaster Marathons

IN DESCRIBING THE MEDIA-EVENT GENRE, Dayan and Katz suggest that television's intervention in the staging of what are perceived as great moments in history produces an experience in which private and public become one. These historical moments may be of various types: "contests" such as the presidential debates or the Super Bowl; "conquests," or giant steps for mankind, such as the landing on the moon or Sadat's visit to Jerusalem; and "coronations," as in the case of Charles and Diana's royal wedding, or, for that matter, the latter's funeral. At such moments, television moves from its presence as noisy wallpaper to center stage in the home and in society. In these highly charged events, people gather in front of the screen seeking ways to stay in touch with the collectivity. For their part, media clear the space, devoting all their airtime to the event, and journalists cooperate with the powers that be to enhance the festive spirit or the performative significance of the event. Coming close to the collusion of journalists in nondemocratic states, media journalists in the West can only refuse the hegemonic interest by not staging the event or by adding skeptical notes to the framing. Once they acquiesce, they become part of an irrevocable tripartite covenant with the initiators of the event and the public. They are in the loop.

When major debacles occur, television interrupts its schedule for the live, open-ended "celebration" of the momentous event—the disaster marathon. To qualify, a fiasco needs victims in substantial numbers or victims of celebrity status, the dramatic failure of visible and supposedly foolproof technologies, or the collapse of a well-established and salient institutional practice. Disaster marathons may be launched by natural disasters (e.g., the Los Angeles earthquake), high-profile accidents (e.g., the failed launching of the *Challenger* or landing of the *Columbia*), or purposive public acts of major violence (e.g., a gory terrorist strike). The genre is at its most effective when television arrives in time to cover the ongoing event while it still lacks symbolic or even narrative closure, rather than landing in its bloody aftermath, when the structure of the event is already established and involves easily identifiable villains and heroes. In the repertoire of debacles, terrorist attacks of the "developing" type (Tuchman 1978)—such as the hijacking of airplanes and holding hostages—have all the ingredients that fit the bill.

Both media events and disaster marathons draw active, socially involved audiences (in the case of disaster anxious and vulnerable ones) and keep them riveted to the screen. Unlike previous audiences, the audience of 2001 may be zapping among globalized channels only to find the same recycled footage and sound bites, introduced by different anchors wearing identically severe expressions. Audiences may follow the event on different channels, amid endless speculations based on the same meager scraps of evidence. But there are also significant dissimilarities between the genres. Although media events are carefully preplanned, in disaster marathons television is not prewarned and in most cases cannot fathom that it could happen (Dobkin 1992; Weimann 1994). This element of surprise, inherent in disaster marathons, underscores its diametrically opposite relationship with the establishment. If in media events the political establishment takes over the media and the public, during disasters forces external to the political establishment capture the attention of media and public. They may originate within society or beyond it.

A major distinction must be made between different kinds of disaster marathons, as typologized above. In the case of natural disaster or technological collapse, the event is arbitrary and not purposive. In the case of manmade disruption of order or radical institutional change, however, there is human motivation and a mastermind launching the drama. Moreover, the instigators of the disaster may well have the modus operandi of journalists in mind, and they may factor it into their plan of action. What we get in such cases is not very different from a media event, although one turned on its head: Normative society's disaster marathon is the terrorist's media event. The perpetrator of the disaster, as in a media event, preplans the staging of the dramatic moment. The public's engrossment and participation are assured, and media's cooperation, although not amicably prearranged, can be counted on. Television is sure to play its role in this subverted triangular covenant with the stagers and the public.

Theoretically, the media can resist its inadvertent covenant with terror. But three types of constraints combine to give them no choice but to play the game set up for them by the likes of bin Laden. First, there are the technological capabilities, facilitating live transmission from various sites in parallel, bypassing in the process traditional editorial practices (with their stress on careful selection and cross-checking of sources). Second, there are the economic pressures of ever increasing competition, the rules of which dictate that every channel has to outdo, or at least keep up with, its competitors. This pushes for the relaxation of standards in favor of the juiciest sound bites, the goriest photographs, and the most unlikely rumors. Third, there is the professional ethos—the perception by electronic journalists of the norms of reporting and of their role in democracy. These include the requirement of comprehensive surveillance of the environment (Wright 1986; cf. McQuail 1987) and efforts to frame events so that the logic of past patterns molds present comprehension and serves as the script for projecting future possibilities (Carey 1986). The latter, on such occasions, may be quite threatening to individuals and to their society and may produce anxiety and vulnerability.

Thus television must carry and does carry terrorists' performances live, and it is bound to do so in a professionally prescribed way. It follows that perpetrators can control the staging of what is in effect a co-opted media event and can also send a message by manipulating the structure and normative constraints of media's inevitable disaster marathon. In the disaster marathon routine, once television's news editors are pushed to open-ended live coverage, they discover they have no "script." In the classic media-events situation, television provides closure to the dramatic proceedings—intended to preserve social stability in the first place—by locating it within a consensual, well worked-out frame. It positions itself as narrator and interpreter of the ceremony so that everyone can join in. By contrast, large-scale disasters, sometimes considered an indication of more to come, have no ascribed symbolic closures: They neither resonate with a salient integrative social credo nor provide immediate or long-term solutions. The chaotic, improvised nature of the disaster marathon telecast amplifies the message of uncertainty, instability, and anxiety.

An attack of the September 11 magnitude thus signifies that things are out of control. It happens and is made public against the government's interest, making leadership look vulnerable, and it supplies journalists with a crack (in this case a collapse) through which to peer past the facade and see how the system operates. Journalists at such situations seem at their most powerful (Molotch and Lester 1974). But, paradoxically, TV journalists are allocated this power under conditions that make responsible journalism all but impossible. These conditions, in effect, put television in the position of an inadvertent accomplice of the perpetrators.

In addressing the routines of source–journalist relations, Molotch and Lester (1974) have highlighted the potential of the two players to work at cross-purposes. The extent to which the source's actions give it good or bad publicity is the crucial variable in the dynamic relationship between newsmaker and journalist. The newsmaker is interested in collaboration with the journalist when his deeds can be considered positive (e.g., by convening a press conference), but prefers to dissociate himself from the coverage of an event that is either normatively or practically damaging. In other words, the power of the journalist to expose undermines the newsmaker's interest to conceal. Scandal epitomizes the journalist's independence from his sources, exercised in the interest of the public.

The rules of this game of agent and journalist break down when rather than shying away from publicity of antinormative acts, perpetrators are free of society's norms or even wish to challenge them explicitly. In such cases, the central variables in the journalist–newsmaker relationship become publicizing the newsmakers' acts and the disclosure of their identity. The repertoire of antisocial behaviors emerging from the intersection of these variables is schematically presented in figure 14.1.

As the figure demonstrates, in workaday crime, all perpetrators are averse to publicity, but they may differ in their attitude toward disclosure of their identity. For those engaged in "normal," private crime, it is crucial to the criminal that his identity not be disclosed; however, in cases of extortion—kidnapping, protection, and so on—success may depend on the victim's knowledge of who dropped the bloody pig head on his doorstep. But whether it is in their interest or not, small-time criminals and "normal" private criminality inspire only small headlines.

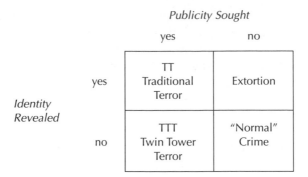

Publicity Sought

		yes	no
Identity Revealed	yes	TT Traditional Terror	Extortion
	no	TTT Twin Tower Terror	"Normal" Crime

FIGURE 14.1
Nature of Criminal Acts by Perpetrators' Preferences
with Regard to Publicity and Identity Disclosure

In recent years, we have increasingly witnessed antinormative acts that, far from shying away from publicity, are manufactured precisely for that purpose. However, here too there may be a difference as to the newsmaker's interest to disclose his identity. In "classic" terror, by now its traditional mode, the perpetrators use both the publicity of their actions and the disclosure of their identity for their cause. Bin Laden (and McVeigh before him) fills in the missing cell in the publicity/identity matrix: Publicity is a central element of their acts, but their identity is not disclosed. We argue that it is precisely this reticence in disclosing identity that adds tremendous power and unique dimensions to the inevitable disaster marathon. We posit that anonymity was a crucial aspect shaping television's coverage of the Twin Towers disaster. Before turning to that analysis, we want to make clear that although we specifically refer to bin Laden, his name is used merely as a peg on which to hang the structural relationship between perpetrator and media in this particular cell in our publicity/identity matrix. The nature of bin Laden's intentions, the extent of his involvement in, and responsibility for, the event, even his mere existence, are in no way taken for granted. In fact, they are irrelevant to our interest in defining how the perpetrator of such an event gets the highest return for his actions by mobilizing media. In what follows, we zero in on television's actual coverage of September 11, observing how the disaster marathon format could be manipulated by a perpetrator such as bin Laden to serve his cause.

The Disaster Marathon of September 11, 2001

The perpetrators of the September 11 attack managed to spread alarm and uncertainty, even cause national trauma, through the nexus of their acts and television's practices. The attack meant an automatic interruption of the schedules of all networks, and their rededication to an exclusive focus on the horror picture show indirectly directed by bin Laden. But bin Laden, as the missing participant, managed to extend his domination, maintain exclusivity, and keep up the suspense for days. We propose three devices made to fit the needs of the medium of television, the rules of the disaster marathon genre, and the hermeneutics of the story he spun.

Special Effects

Bin Laden's choice of targets meant maximizing the attack's visual impact, providing him with long-term *salience* on television the world over. Television could not but hypnotize viewers by recycling and repeating the apocalyptic image of the falling towers, as in the most vulgar genre of horror movie come true. The damage on the screen meant witnessing (1) material damage, underscored by the physical collapse, which caused direct fear ("it could happen to me"); (2) human suffering, expressed by interviews with relatives, witnesses, and firefighters (mostly on the days after); this exposure of emotional suffering exacerbated existential anxiety through empathy with the tragedy of other human beings; (3) the symbolic-semiotic aspects of witnessing the collapse of the Twin Towers, an emblem of America's spirit and achievement, instantly transformed into punishable hubris by bin Laden playing in effect the role of God in the Tower of Babel myth.

It should be noted, however, that a fourth potential spectacle did not come into play. The sight of physical damage to humans—injured individuals in pain, deformed and mutilated bodies so prominent in the image of other disasters—was not a major element in the broadcast of September 11. This lack was due to the overwhelming degree of material damage, which tragically left few injured and little of visible human remains; it also prevented the approach of TV crews. In turn, this deficiency worked to focus attention on the mythological dimensions of the physical destruction and to abstract the event and highlight its symbolic dimensions.

Temporal Effects

Whether the outcome of a carefully planned strategy or a contingency of operational constraints, bin Laden managed to maintain long-term exclusivity on the little screen by carrying out a series of repetitious acts, spaced in time. This magnified the attacks' psychological effect by (1) enhancing the visual impact of the second attack on the Twin Towers by having the cameras on the spot, ready for live broadcasting of the next attack, and (2) creating uncertainty about how many attacks were imminent, as well as anxiety in anticipation of further attacks. The "continuing" nature of the event (Tuchman 1978) also meant that the president and his men were kept busy not only with damage control but with their personal safety. Consequently bin Laden's handiwork ruled supreme on the global stage, with the voice of a protagonist (from the public's point of view) badly missing. This void in contesting bin Laden's dominance was underscored by the failure of Bush's first public response—agitated, unspontaneous, and conspicuously transmitted from a hiding place. In contrast, the public's rallying around Mayor Rudy Giuliani, when he appeared as the self-appointed true hero to balance the horror pictures, demonstrated how a solid performance of on-the-spot leadership could allay fears of vulnerability and chaos.

Narrative Effects

In contrast to the visibility of the collapse and its unequivocal symbolism, it was precisely the enigmatic invisibility of the actors, and the lack of any coherent and/or explicit rationale, that clinched bin Laden's media effectiveness. Since the September 11 attacks were not aimed at striking a specific bargain, bin Laden did not have to identify himself as the perpetrator or make demands; he was also silent for a long time as to his rationale. With no "who" and "why," only the what, when, and where, the narrative remained incomplete and therefore engrossing and tantalizing. This inexplicability and lack of closure enhanced the dependence on the media. Television was expected to come up with some answer. The engrossing effect of unsolved mystery also foregrounded the media celebrations around the belated appearance of bin Laden's video tapes. Here he achieved one of his greatest coups: he leveraged the enigma of "who" to capture his audience with his own ideological narrative of "why."

As the September 11 attack was not the kind aimed at achieving a tangible and/or manageable purpose, there was only one message that could be discerned from the enormity and ruthlessness of the planned destruction, and from the attackers' readiness to die for their cause. It was their wish to put us (Americans, capitalists, the Western world) in our place and show up our vulnerability.[1] It was a statement larger than life, open-ended, and motivated by deep frustration, one that could only be addressed in the time span of decades or generations. The magnitude of the claim, the impossibility of translating it into some form of immediate redress, and the notion of a globally spread network of perpetrators acting in the name of millions, were congruent to the invisibility and lack of identification of the attackers. The sinister anonymity of the perpetrators, moving the story from painful melodrama to a mystery thriller, injected suspense and foreboding into the experience of viewing it.

Compared to the story of classic terrorism, which plays out in the Proppian drama, with villains creating harm and heroes prevailing by addressing the damage, the bin Laden–type story plays out as a mystery play in which the villain still has to be detected. There is nothing like "unfinished business" to keep TV audiences glued to the set, and nothing like invisibility and inscrutability to give them the notion they are viewing, or participating in, a thriller with a ghostly, or godly, presence.

First Anniversary: September 11, 2002

With so much remaining unresolved, no appropriate occasion presented itself for a ceremonial retrospect. That is, until September 11 reappeared on the calendar. Lacking narrative, ideological, political, or even personal or spatial coherence, the event's date represented a refreshingly unambiguous marker. Thus, by default, "September 11" was universally seized on to definitely tag an equivocal affair. Its anniversary could thus serve as a focus for coming to terms with change, for reckoning with its implications and arriving at closure. This would be done by launching a carefully planned and intensively hyped media event. Such an event would both bring back and transform the memorable experience of the previous year.

Television's role on that fateful day would also be invoked and transformed. On the "original" September 11 it was the terrorists who set the agenda and shaped the event and, to a surprising extent, its coverage. Television, in bringing it to the public, followed the terrorists' script and stepped into the leadership vacuum of that day and framed the momentous experience for millions. One year later television once again addressed a global audience from downtown New York, the Pentagon, and Shanksville, Pennsylvania, but it played an entirely different role. This time it collaborated with lawful government, in the best media-event tradition, to leverage a meticulously planned ceremony to forge a remedial collective experience and ultimately, perhaps, collective memory.

The media event of September 11, 2002, was carefully orchestrated. It took shape on the various global and national channels as a combination of a series of live broadcasts of public commemorations, interlaced with flashbacks to the live broadcast of death a year earlier, and of original commemorative productions. This pattern was followed by each of the major national and international networks. Just as it did a year earlier, television radiated powerful images from New York, Washington, and Pennsylvania the world over, in real time; but in practically every other aspect of its role and its performance, the television of September 11, 2001, and September 11, 2002, was a mirror image of itself, generating opposite public experiences. We shall try, in the following, to compactly demonstrate this contrariety and to point out its significance.

From Macro to Micro

The ceremonies composing the 2002 media event were minimalist affairs. They were staged at the bare, humble, vault of Ground Zero, the ordinary and bureaucratic looking facade of the rebuilt Pentagon, and the rustic green fields of rural western Pennsylvania. Nothing could contrast more sharply with the larger-than-life images of the previous year: the hubris of New York's magnificent skyscraping landmark—not merely one tower but two of them—penetrated by giant airliners, then collapsing to the ground in a column of dust visible even from outer space, or the massive, smoking cavity ruining the geometry of the largest office building of the world—one that housed its most powerful establishment, and finally, the images of the White House and Capitol, the ultimate emblems of America's power, shown over and over again as the probable targets of the airliner downed near Shanksville.

Moments of silence and the quivering, fragile wailing of bagpipes playing "Amazing Grace" stood in stark relief to the echoes of the previous year's din of jets and the roar of their impact with glass and concrete, then the screams of uncounted sirens. The 272 perfectly balanced words composing the cliché-less Gettysburg Address were recited on September 11, 2002, without altering or adding a single word to its economic, time-glass shaped, edifice binding a glorious distant past, fateful recent event, and promising future. It contrasted starkly with the disjointed deluge of words and scattered thoughts of the year before.

Thus, if in 2001 it was the long shot, the open microphone, and overstatement that characterized coverage, in 2002 it was the close-up, silence, and tennis telecast–like soft, understated staccato that prevailed. Flashbacks from the media event to the disaster marathon served to highlight the contrast between the incomprehensibly gigantic, too-big-to-be-true images of the previous year, and the compact and manageable sights and sounds of their second coming on the screen a year later.

From Foreign to Familiar

One of the most striking features of the commemorative media event was the extent to which it ignored the perpetrators of the September 11 attacks. If the heroes of the disaster marathon were, by default, the diabolic attackers coming out of the blue skies aboard airliners, and the anonymous masterminds that sent them, in 2002 they all seemed to have vanished, as mysteriously as they had appeared. Television simply ignored them, focusing instead on how the familiar human and geographical landscape was transformed by their attack. The sinister and grasping anonymity of the perpetrators gave way to reassuring if tragic familiarity: A central feature of both the ceremonies broadcast live on that day and of the network-specific productions was putting faces on the victims and giving them social identities. Reading out the names of the victims was the chilling, if dignified, centerpiece of the New York City ceremony; the life and death stories of casualties and their families was a major theme of the repertoire each of the major channels prepared for the broadcast.[2]

In the same vein, the ghastly, outlandish bravery and sacrifice of the suicide warriors—so difficult to penetrate and comprehend—was radically de-emphasized. In its stead, stories of familiar and socially esteemed types of courage and sacrifice, such as those performed by officers of law, order, and public service—firefighters, policemen, medical and municipal crews—were celebrated. The unsettling enigma of bin Laden, his culpability and his design, was but a fleeting shadow in the media event of September 11, 2002. And if the outlandish, even mythical central figure of the previous year's event was nowhere, Bush was everywhere: in Washington, New York, and Shanksville, on the podium, behind the lectern, and in the crowd, accessible and holding intimate, informal conversations with the bereaved. Television, in turn, was not interfacing with the unknown this time around. It did not have to ask unanswerable questions or give a prominent voice to alarmist speculation. It had moved from the genre of apocalyptic science fiction and exotic mystery to the conservative and reassuring genre of the elevated documentary.

From Chaos to Control

Downsizing the dimensions of the attack to comprehensible proportions and delivering the event from the realm of the threateningly bizarre to the manageably familiar, together with containment of the tone of the coverage, produced an overall sense of control. The dimension of control was conveyed more directly, and at least as effectively, by other features of the media event. One was temporal: every programming detail of the cable and terrestrial network telecasts was preannounced, leaving no sense of open-endedness. The train of events and filler programs progressed on each of the networks in clockwork precision, leaving nothing unexpected or improvised. The orderly unfolding of the ceremonies seemed not only to take place but also to constitute an element of the rhetoric of the telecast. Time and again audiences were walked through the exact scheduled sequencing of exercises and filler.

Another dimension of control emerged from the temporal and spatial location of the cast performing the acts characteristic of a coronation-type media event. New York's chain of command—governor, mayor, ex-mayor, and bureau chiefs, even clergymen—each performed his part, highlighting the dominance and orderliness of institutional structure. Similarly, in Washington, the commander in chief was conspicuously and repeatedly shown surrounded by members of his army, his cabinet, and his administration, and in the company of representatives of government's other branches. These sights could serve as a soothing corrective to the conspicuous absence of leadership from the screen the year before, the president being shuttled away for safety, and New York's mayor stepping into the gap to single-handedly deliver control from the clutches of chaos in impromptu appearances.

These dimensions of the anniversary on television were in diametric opposition to the broadcast of the year before. They were also sure-fire ingredients of a media event that would be not only memorable but also a therapeutic collective experience. By looking inward and underscoring familiar American ways, the experience produced by television could reaffirm the prevailing social values and reintegrate a shaken society around them. It seemed to be calling audiences to take civic responsibility by merely being there, that is, in front of the screen. By focusing on individuals and on the performance of individuals, the event could serve the merging of the private, personal experience of viewers with the public, collective life of the community. Finally, through respectfully presenting leadership at center stage and strategically collaborating with it in staging the event, television's live broadcast of history on September 11, 2002, could win one for the status quo.

Discussion: An Assessment

Many observers have criticized the performance of American media in the year that followed the September 11 disaster. It was accused of collusion with the administration, uncritically propagating its agenda and neglecting media's responsibilities as a watchdog to critically review government's policies and give voice to alternatives. Media was charged with excessive patriotism, neglecting its duty to interpose on behalf of the public and the American way in cases of abuse of power on the domestic front, and irresponsibility in foreign affairs. The complacency of American media since September 11 has been most marked, it is alleged, in its failure to contest the abridgement of civil and human liberties in the wake of the war on terrorism, in particular in cases of infringements on freedom of speech and privacy.

The foregoing may conceivably help interpret such alleged complacency and collusion attributed to post–September 11 American television. The events of September 11, 2001, thrust television into the position of foremost player in the events. As we have seen, the combination of television's modus operandi, of the professional standards that guide it, and of the competitive market it plays in had effectively made it an agent of the terrorists' goals on that tragic day. Further, given the leadership void immediately after the attack, television emerged as the major public institution managing the crisis in the public sphere, in the absence of an effective contingency plan by government for managing a national emergency via the media. Television, as a player in the affair whose performance raises inevitable questions as to whether it indeed served the public interest in the emergency in the best possible way, eagerly passed responsibility on to government as soon as the latter was ready and then stood by its side.[3] It perhaps passed on this responsibility too complacently and too completely. In fact, it may even have tried—consciously or otherwise—to divert criticism of the disaster marathon it aired by displaying excessive patriotism thereafter.

In the anniversary media event, television cooperated with government in shaping and disseminating a prominent public memorial exercise that paradoxically distanced the audience from the experience of the previous year. It put the disaster marathon on its head (albeit replaying its elements excessively), signaling the return to familiar workaday order and control, symbolically acknowledging a return to the status quo ante. One hopes that for television too, the live broadcast of the commemorative event will signal the completion of a full cycle: that its collaborative effort with government in staging the media event will signal the resumption of its traditional critical distance from events and from government, returning to its traditional role in American democracy.

However, television should not return to its preattack routine as if nothing had happened. It owes itself and the public a careful review and reevaluation of its ethics and standards in serving the public when disaster strikes. Professional soul-searching and public debate on the proper standards for broadcasting disaster marathons are necessary. Their goal should be arriving at strategies that diminish the incentives for the ruthless to engage in violence in order to reap the fruits of media coverage—the very media that must remain free in order to sustain life, liberty, and happiness. One hopes, of course, that such a review will prove no more than an academic exercise.

Notes

The authors wish to thank Professor Elihu Katz, who coined the phrase "the live broadcast of history," for his helpful comments and advice.

An earlier version of this chapter was originally published as Menahem Blondheim, "Live Television's Diaster Marathon of September 11 and Its Subversive Potential," in *Prometheus* 20, no. 3 (2002): 271–76.

1. Recent interpretations of the attack suggest that bin Laden's message may have been intended for the Islamic world, more than America, in an attempt to mobilize and empower it.

2. A similar focus on the persona of the tragic heroes of disaster was evident in the

most recent ceremonial in commemoration of an event that was covered in the disaster marathon—the loss of space shuttle *Columbia* ("We Lost Them So Close to Home," *Washington Post*, February 5, 2003).

3. Media organizations became targets of chemical terrorism in attacks that focused on government institutions.

References

Barber, J. D. 1965. "Peer Group Discussion and Recovery from the Kennedy Assassination." In B. S. Greenberg and E. B. Parker, eds., *The Kennedy Assassination and the American Public: Social Communication in Crisis.* Stanford: Stanford University Press.

Carey, James W. 1986. "Why?" In Robert Karl Manoff and Michael Schudson, eds., *Reading the News.* New York: Pantheon.

Dayan, D., and E. Katz. 1985. "Media Events: On the Experience of Not Being There." *Religion* 15: 305–14.

Dayan, Daniel, and Elihu Katz. 1992. *Media Events: The Live Broadcasting of History.* Cambridge: Harvard University Press.

Dobkin, Bethami A. 1992. *Tales of Terror: Television News and the Construction of the Terrorist Threat.* New York: Praeger.

Liebes, T. 1998. "Television's Disaster Marathons: A Danger for Democratic Processes?" In T. Liebes and J. Curran, eds., *Media, Ritual, and Identity*, 71–84. London: Routledge.

Liebes, T., and Y. Peri. 1998. "Electronic Journalism in Segmented Societies: Lessons from the 1966 Israeli Elections." *Political Communication* 15: 27–43.

McQuail, D. 1987. "The Functions of Communication: A Non-Functionalist Overview." In *Handbook of Communication Science*, 327–49. Beverly Hills: Sage.

Molotch, H., and M. Lester. 1974. "News as Purposive Behavior." *American Sociological Review* 39: 101–12.

Parton, J. 1866. "The New York Herald." *North American Review*, April, 373–410.

Peri, Y. 1999. "The Media and Collective Memory of Yitzhak Rabin's Remembrance." *Journal of Communication* 49, no. 3: 106–24.

Tuchman, Gaye. 1978. *Making News: A Study in the Construction of Reality*, 49–58. New York: Free Press.

Weimann, Gabriel. 1994. *The Theater of Terror: Mass Media and International Terrorism.* New York: Longman, 1994.

Wright, Charles R. 1986. *Mass Communication: A Sociological Perspective*, 3–27. New York: Random House.

Will, Garry. 1992. *Lincoln at Gettysburg: The Words that Remade America.* New York: Simon & Schuster.

———. 2002. "How to Speak to a Nation's Suffering." *New York Times*, August 18.

15

Globalization Isn't New, and Antiglobalization Isn't Either: September 11 and the History of Nations

James William Carey

The September 11 attack on the Pentagon and the World Trade Center reveals, among other things, a colossal failure of intelligence and radical deficiencies in our understanding of communications in the modern world. The history of nations and the history of communications are continuous, though contradictory, since the eighteenth century and those continuities and contradictions are revealed by way of analysis of 9/11 and its aftermath. In this chapter, James William Carey discusses the role of communications in the formation of nations and as the stimulus for the creation of conditions conducive to terrorism.

A Holiday from History

FOR THE PAST DECADE or more, aficionados and enthusiasts of cyberspace have proclaimed the emergence of a new, borderless world thanks to the computer and satellite. Nations, as they correctly observed, were losing control of their frontiers whether understood as geographic or symbolic. Nations were more easily penetrated, not only by transnational flows of communications but also by flows of people. Even island nations like Britain and Japan, always the most resistant to these flows, had, relatively speaking, lost control of their borders. The words on everyone's lips and pens were globalization, privatization, deregulation, innovation, Internet, and World Wide Web. A new economy, new politics, and new culture were under construction and Americans were to be the first beneficiaries. We were on a holiday from history.

All that came to at least a temporary halt on September 11, but the consequences of that day for the real world of politics and communications, as well as for understanding the underlying processes of social change, will not be known for a very long time. However, the heady atmosphere of the 1990s, the vision of a world united in theory and practice—one market, one culture, one politics, one seamless global communications system—is over, just as assuredly as the guns of August 1914 ended an earlier phase of globalization driven by the telegraph, railroad, underwater cable, the steamship, and the gold standard. Whether the consequences will be as devastating—two world wars and a cold war—whether the interregnum will last as long—world trade recovered to 1914 levels only in 1970, capital flows in 1985—no one knows.

At the instant commercial airliners, brimming with jet fuel, slammed into the Twin Towers of the World Trade Center and the Pentagon on September 11, 2001, the people of the United States experienced in a moment of nonplussed apprehension an apparent massive failure of intelligence. The news media, the political class, intellectuals—all the distant and early warning systems of the culture—had failed and Americans were armed only with obsolete historical analogies. "It's Pearl Harbor all over again."

In the decade following the end of the Cold War, journalists had been preoccupied with one media event after another: OJ, Tanya, Monica-Linda-Bill, and Gary. The political class was turned inward, focused on economic growth, the stock market, interest rates, social security and health insurance, affirmative action, and the so-called cultural war. The first report from the U.S. Commission on National Security, containing a devastating indictment of the fragmented and inadequate structures and strategies in place to prevent and respond to attacks on U.S. cities, was issued in September 1999. It was studiously ignored by not only leading news outlets but Congress as well. The keyword and framework was globalization, which was understood on a model that was primarily economic and, to use an awkward but necessary neologism, U.S.-centric. As a result of the events of September 11, history, politics, and the study of human nature are back on the agenda.

Communications and the Building of Nations

One context for understanding the events of September 11 is the intersection of communications and nation building. The major project of the modern era is making nations out of fragments of historic cultures: tribes, principalities, kingdoms, and religions. We understand that in the aftermath of World War II new nations were made across the globe out of the remains of European empire. Less obviously, the nations of Europe and the Americas are not preternatural but themselves historical creations. There are few if any nations—France, perhaps England but not Great Britain, Japan—that predate the modern era. In the eighteenth and nineteenth centuries the nations of Europe and the Americas were built just as assuredly as Czechoslovakia was built early and Somalia late in the twentieth century.

The original instrument of nation building was the printing press, which by creating a "free trade" zone in culture built the imaginary community of the nation. Printing was merely the software, of course; the hardware was the network of roads and post offices, schools and government offices that carried the printed word in the regulatory form of a lingua franca. Simultaneously, the printing press erected barriers between geographic spaces driving a high, if often invisible, wall into a landscape of continuously blending languages.

If the printing press could unify the relatively small nations in Europe and, when wedded to new arts of navigation and transoceanic transport, permit these nations to leap boundaries into new worlds, it proved hopelessly inefficient at policing and maintaining such newly enlarged spaces. It was the railroad and the telegraph, in combination, that turned a loose collection of political sovereignties into integrated nations, ones in which a national identity and a national community predominated. The same technology that permitted the integration of large nations allowed much smaller European states to secure an effective empire. Unlike the empires of the eighteenth century, it could be governed and controlled from a center that continuously monitored its margins in something close to real time.

The creation of large nations and the integration of empire were aspects of the same process; one integrated contiguous land masses—Russia, Canada, the United States—and the other leaped oceanic barriers. The spread of nation-states and modern empires produced everywhere a characteristic reaction formation: ethnic nationalisms sprang up at their margins—distant margins, thousands of miles from the center, or internal colonies close to home.

Television completed and perfected the national system, finished what the printing press, telegraph, telephone, wire services, and national magazine began. The first cable systems, the last mile of the national system of communication, and, as it turned out, the first mile of the new global system, linked places inaccessible to over-the-air signals and fulfilled the social imaginary of the nineteenth century—the eclipse of time and space: one nation under a common system of communication. The great audience, as Gilbert Seldes called it, was implicitly addressed as members of nation, exposed to one national culture and a consensus narrative exploring the underlying agreements and schisms within the nation.

The Unraveling of Communication

The national system of communication that embodied, symbolized, and ritualized a common national narrative, indeed a civil religion, held until sometime in the 1970s, when a decisive unraveling began with the launching of satellites for direct pay television, the inauguration of Home Box Office, and the subsequent transformation of small cable systems into independent competitors of the networks.

With the end of the Cold War, the restraints imposed by world politics were shattered, and the new configuration of cable, satellite, and computer technologies, reinforced by changes in public policy, opened up novel conceptions of time and space, individual identity and social action; opened up, in fact, social, political, and economic possibilities that transcended the boundaries and restraints of national communication, national identity, and national religion.

In the wake of these technological changes, every modern nation has witnessed a dazzling array of new communication services and, disturbingly, dangerous political phenomena: proliferation of computers and cell phones as consumer goods, the breakdown of the structure of national broadcasting, disarray in political parties and processes, alterations in patterns of settlement, the emergence of new dominating firms, a new cosmopolitan plutocracy unknown two decades ago, and the bursting of borders and boundaries of all kinds, political as well as personal. At the international level there has been a breakdown in governmental authority, a breakup of states, an intensification of tribal ethnic and religious conflict, the migration, forced and voluntary, of large numbers of people, the proliferation of weapons of aggression, the spread of terrorism, and a new wave of massacres and ethnic cleansing.

We learn again that as communication erases some borders, it erects others, though the latter are much less visible and difficult to detect than the former. Fragmentation and homogenization are not opposites but mutually related trends of a single global reality. Nations, caught in the contradiction between homogenizing and fragmenting forces, unable to reconcile them, are torn as sovereignty simultaneously evolves upward to the transnational and devolves downward into regional, class, ethnic, and racial segments.

We exist, then, in a "verge" in the sense Daniel Boorstin gave that word: a moment between two different forms of social life in which technology, among other things, has dislodged all human relations and nothing stable has replaced them. The world seems to be imploding and exploding at the same moment, experienced imaginatively as simultaneously coming together and falling apart. In the mid-1970s we entered a new phase in the history of the compression of space and time. As telecommunications burst the constraining boundaries of the nation-state, social structures that had defined the modern world and established its direction were thrown into disarray and national cultures forced into cognitive and affective meltdown.

September 11: A New Symbolism

On September 11 that verge became strikingly, undeniably apparent. Global communication, including television, had taken the world, not just the nation, as its domain. In the commercial sector it was proclaimed that "The world is our audience" (Time-Warner) and "We see the world as one civilization" (Archer, Daniels, Midland). But if commerce, commercials, and currency were globalized, so was terrorism. It occurs across state boundaries rather than within, erasing the distinction at the root of our thinking between the domestic and the foreign.

We are not at the end of history, as Francis Fukayama predicted a few years back, but perhaps at the beginning of a new historical phase in which nations thrash about like beached whales, unable to adequately cope, despite a lot of brave talk, with political and cultural processes both within and without their borders. As the capacity of governments to control the traffic in persons, goods, and information that flows across borders decreases, other social formations, usually weaker and less cohesively imagined communities, are better able to transcend the confines of the state. With that, myths of regional, continental, and hemispheric unity grow in tandem with an unstable mix of racial, ethnic, religious, and gender-based myths of particularity. The Internet dream of nonspatial communities turns out to be an illusion, for it gives rise to communities lodged in a new dimension of space where they are beyond any form of control, democratic or otherwise.

Samuel Huntington has described this development as a return to a "pre-Westphalian condition" in which culture breaks loose from its national moorings and is realigned in transnational and subnational linkages. Huntington's primary example of this change is religion. As he puts it, "the separation of church and state, an idiosyncratic product of western rationalization, is coming to an end and religion is increasingly likely to intrude in international" and domestic politics as well. The age of ecumenism, cultural as well as religious, may have passed at both the local and international levels. A period in which moral values and cultural outlooks were taken to be private matters and tolerance a shared value may be giving way to antagonism and difference as cultures universalize their particularity in transnational movements and particularize their universality in more rigidly bound local communities and formations.

The nation is no longer the focus, explicit and implicit, of the social imaginary. Peoples and countries with similar cultures are coming together. Peoples and countries with different cultures are coming apart. Alignments defined by ideology and superpower relations are giving way to alignments defined by culture and civilization. Political boundaries increasingly are redrawn to coincide with cultural ones. Cultural communities are replacing Cold War blocs and the fault lines between civilizations are becoming the central lines of conflict in global politics. Because the roots of culture remain religious (as the old saw has it, always inquire whether an atheist is a Protestant, Catholic, Jewish, or Muslim atheist), a shift to political blocs based on culture and civilization means that religion displaces nation, relatively speaking, as a primary axis of human identity and a force in politics at all levels. That is Huntington's argument, barely paraphrased, and it captures a real tendency and its potentially destructive consequences at the opening of the twenty-first century.

The second wave of globalization through which we have been living has turned out to be wider but thinner and just as intractably dangerous as the globalization of the late nineteenth century. Transaction costs radically fell in commerce but that was perhaps only temporary, since the successes of globalization stimulated policies and social movements to counteract and undo it. On the one hand, the events of September 11 reversed the curve of transaction costs, radically raising the costs of transport, insurance, security, including cyberspace security, and triggered globally the redirection of money into military and intelligence budgets. That in itself will slow the pace of globalization. More importantly, globalization has broken down on the cultural plane. Free trade in culture, always the last item to be negotiated in world congresses, runs into the stubborn resistance of historic forms of life, of belief and understanding, of beauty and friendship, and this resistance places strict limits on universalizing communication. Americans, paradoxically a relatively insular people for whom culture is a commodity like any other to be bought and sold in the marketplace, have a hard time understanding this resistance. That failure became painfully apparent in Lower Manhattan and Washington in early September 2001.

Note

This chapter was originally published in *Prometheus* 20, no. 3 (2002): 289–93.

16

Is There a bin Laden in the Audience? Considering the Events of September 11 as a Possible Boomerang Effect of the Globalization of U.S. Mass Communication

René-Jean Ravault

René-Jean Ravault discusses the effects of the globalization of U.S. mass entertainment media on fostering an environment for terrorism. He explains how modern telecommunications can enable terrorists to remain isolated in a host country, and also how the images created by U.S. mass entertainment media create expectations and frustrations, unfortunately strong enough to result in severe violence.

American Media: A Double-Edged Sword

THE PRODUCTS OF AMERICAN information and entertainment media, as well as the promotional artifacts distributed by U.S. institutions for the export of American culture, overwhelm global communications.[1] These products show an inclusive, cosmopolitan, universal image of the United States.[2] Members of foreign elites exposing themselves to these products find them very appealing and are seduced by the American way of life so attractively depicted. Many of them attempt to get closer to the United States by trying to immigrate or obtaining a diploma from a U.S. university. Most of these people ultimately find happiness as integrated immigrants or as Western-educated citizens of their own country, but a few founder in the gap between the first impressions they constructed out of the American media and their day-to-day perception of "reality." They then justify their failure through an enlargement of their preprogrammed criticism of the American way of life.

Their deceptions and frustrations may be articulated and in some way legitimized and embellished through an emotional "rationale" provided by a return and an aggravation of the anti-American rhetoric inscribed in their local indoctrination. They can end up making terrorist gestures against the United States. This return rhetoric is often facilitated by the perverse use of telecommunications. Finally, the American media, originally conceived of to seduce immigrants and foreigners, are used by these misfits as a source of information and/or legitimization in their decision-making processes leading to their terrorist deeds which are often inspired by Hollywood horror and spy movies.

Media Globalization: Fostering Frustration

We today believe that we are now living in a global age because our means of communications allow us to get in touch with people located on the opposite side of the globe. We can get access, in real time, to data provided to us by databanks located in many countries around the world. However, if we look more critically, we can see that most people do not grow more open to the rest of the world than they—or their ancestors—were years, decades, and centuries ago. For instance, it could be argued that people using cell phones to get in touch with their loved ones have a greater tendency to ignore the presence of their fellow human beings immediately surrounding them in day-to-day activities and business life.

Thus telephones and the Internet may cause immigrants to slow their integration into the host country. They remain among the members of their own diaspora for a generation or two,[3] but now, thanks to telecommunications, they stay in touch with their friends and/or significant members of their interpersonal networks in their country of origin. They watch their home country's TV signals portraying entertainment, news, and religious programs from abroad instead of exposing themselves to local programs and local people. For instance, "telenovellas" from Brazil and Argentina, relayed through Mexico and TV satellites, are watched exclusively by recent immigrants from Latin America.

Remaining exposed to the language, culture, values, beliefs, and attitudes of the community of origin through consumption of imported mass communication products and/or the use of Internet and international telephone lines may contribute to an inadequate integration into the host society. The situation is aggravated if these communication products do not fit the American way of life or if significant members of the community of origin are hostile to the United States.

Most mass communication theoreticians believe that the owner of the media controls the content and, most importantly, its effect on the audience, whatever the cultural background of the audience members. However, a closer look shows that when foreign recipients take into account American-made mass communication products, they transform them simultaneously into significant and relevant "messages." The memory they keep of these products and the meaning they get out of them are coconstructed by the recipients' weltanschauung, or worldview.[4] This weltanschauung of foreign recipients has been shaped, structured, and programmed[5] through previous face-to-face, coercive, and seductive interactions with the significant members of their communication networks constituting their community of identification. Consequently, the way foreign recipients select American media and decode their contents depends much more upon the coercive and seductive power of the significant members of the interpersonal networks that structure their community of origin than on the alleged "might" of the American communication media and products.

Many students of the globalization of U.S. mass communication have criticized U.S. communication industries for promoting the American way of life and historic ideals, as well as the interests of capitalistic American enterprises.[6] Others, less critical of neoliberalism, have seen the globalization of U.S. media as a contribution to the triumph of democracy around the world.[7] In spite of criticism and dramatic failures,[8] the notion of creating empathy toward democracy, capitalism, and other American values through exposure to American media[9] has worked well and is still working well for some local elites in the Third World, especially in the Middle East.

Following exposure to American mass communication and education products, many students in the Middle East decide to go to the United States or other Western countries to polish their graduate education. For instance, when the shah of Iran was overthrown by the revolution of 1979, Iranian students constituted the largest body of foreign students in the United States. Some of them returned to Iran when the ayatollahs took over and helped decipher CIA documents in the student-occupied U.S. embassy in Tehran.

Indeed, most of the terrorists who were directly involved in hijacking the four commercial airplanes on the morning of September 11 sojourned a long time in the United States or other countries of the West. Some of them learned how to fly planes, but most of them studied there before getting involved in terrorist plans. During this time they became frustrated and angry to the point of getting in touch with terrorist organizations somehow connected to their religious network. The same itinerary, marked with a long sojourn in the West, seems to have been followed by the Pakistani extremist Ahmed Omar Saced Sheikh, the terrorist whom authorities suspect masterminded the plot to kidnap *Wall Street Journal* reporter Daniel Pearl. Sheikh was born and raised in London, England.[10]

A revealing history of what happened to some of these people before they became terrorists or Islamic fundamentalist ideologues is provided by

Jonathan Raban in an article published in the *New Yorker*.[11] According to Raban, Qutb's sojourn[12] in the United States, including exposure to local media, played an important role in his moral conditioning. This conditioning was the intellectual counterpart and prelude to the physical training terrorists received in al-Qaeda camps. Raban writes, "Like many homesick people, living outside their language in an abrasive foreign culture, Qutb aggrandized his loneliness into heroic solitude." When people are born and/or raised, at least for some time, in a context in which they find themselves belonging to an ethnic community, religion, and culture that is marginalized while the host nation seems to be very open-minded through its media and political rhetoric but is experienced as more or less closed in its day-to-day intercultural personal encounters, terrorism may become an answer to their frustrations. The situation worsens if the souvenir or the electronic contacts keeping them in touch with the significant leaders of their culture of origin "aggrandize their loneliness into heroic solitude," as Raban saw it.

Once a decision is made to become involved with terrorist organizations, exposure to the media and to the people of the host culture becomes something of a "spy game." Once such a drastic change has occurred, "boomerang theories," conceived of in international and especially wartime communication studies,[13] can help us understand how these potential terrorists use American media, be they mass media or telecommunications.

Since the end of World War II, a few theoreticians and politicians like Sukarno[14] and, more recently, Chirac[15] have pointed out that, in intercultural or transnational and global communication situations, the impact of internationally broadcast communication products conceived of within a specific community of interpretation or *épistémè* may or may not be received and interpreted by foreigners the way it was intended. A few researchers have convincingly explained this phenomenon. Shils and Janowitz[16] studied the way the Wehrmacht twisted Madison Avenue propaganda during World War II. Stewart Hall[17] pointed out the multiple possibilities of mismatch, distortion, and reversal between coding and decoding popular television in multicultural England. Hamid Mowlana[18] and Majid Tehranian[19] underlined how the westernized media of the shah and U.S. universities contributed inadvertently to the ayatollah's revolution in Iran. Tzvetan Todorov, a French semiotician and historian, demonstrated how the conquistador Cortés used his knowledge of Moctezuma's communication ecology in his successful and unlikely conquest of Mexico.[20] In my doctoral dissertation, I described how West Germany and Japan, between 1945 and 1980, used information about the American way of life and consumption provided to them by U.S. communication and cultural hegemony to accomplish their economic "miracle" on the back of the United States.[21]

The September 11 terrorist attacks demonstrate that global communications saturated with images of the United States can dramatically backfire when used by global terrorists for their own ends. There are some lessons to be learned that might help lessen the chance for future attacks.

Global Exhibitionists, Beware!

Being globally seen and overheard by unintended and unscrupulous audiences is more likely to be a potential source of worry, uncertainty, and danger than to elicit global admiration and fascination. This situation is especially dangerous when these audiences have been culturally, ethnically, and religiously programmed through the networks of coercion and seduction that crisscross their communities of origin and interpretation. One solution for the United States is to keep silent like the Swiss bankers, for whom "silence is golden." However, given the exhibitionistic impulse of the media, this wise advice is doomed to be rejected.

A more practical solution is to understand the origin and nature of the gap existing (or invented) between the expectations created in foreign audiences exposed to American media and the way immigrants or graduate students residing in the United States actually live. This is especially relevant when these foreigners have been indoctrinated with non-American values and lifestyles during their socialization and acculturation processes.

The media should not provoke frustration through a global exhibition of the American rich and famous. Other indicators for social success like human solidarity, loyalty to one's own friends, a global quest for equity and fairness, spiritual development, and happiness in solitude as well as in sociability should be equally promoted. The United States should not monopolize simultaneously all the powers—military, financial, economic, intellectual, spiritual, moral, and religious—leaving the disenfranchised with the only perceived option of killing themselves in terrorist acts.

Finally, students of international communication should not neglect the careful study of human and cultural factors. Ethnography research about the ritualistic aspects of day-to-day life should be part of the research and teaching curriculum in communications studies.

Notes

This chapter was originally published in *Prometheus* 20, no. 3 (2002): 295–300.

1. From Jeremy Tunstall, *The Media Are American: Anglo-American Media in the World* (London: Constable, 1977) to Daya Kishan Thussu, *International Communication: Continuity and Change* (London: Arnold, 2000).

2. René-Jean Ravault, "Communication dans le monde, un rêve américain," in Lucien Sfez, *Dictionnaire critique de la communication* (Paris: Presses Universitaires de France, 1993), 1:73–86.

3. Arjun Appadurai, *Modernity at Large: Cultural Dimensions of Globalization* (Minneapolis: University of Minnesota Press, 1996).

4. Lee Thayer, *Communication and Communication Systems* (Homewood, Ill.: Irwin, 1968).

5. Geert Hofstede, *Culture and Organizations, Software of the Mind: Intercultural Cooperation and Its Importance for Survival* (U.K.: McGraw Hill International, 1991).

6. Kaarle Nordenstreng and Tapio Varis, *Television Traffic: A One-Way Street* (Paris: UNESCO, 1974); A. Mattelart and A. Dorfman, *Donald l'imposteur* (Paris: Alain Moreau, 1979); Herbert Schiller, *Communication and Cultural Domination* (New York: Sharpe, 1976); *Mass Communication and American Empire* (Boston: Beacon, 1971); Herbert I. Schiller and K. Nordenstreng, eds., *National Sovereignty and International Communication* (Norwood, N.J.: Ablex, 1979); C. J. Hamelink, *Cultural Autonomy in Global Communications* (New York: Longman, 1983); Thomas L. McPhail, *Electronic Colonialism: The Future of International Broadcasting and Communication* (Newbury Park, Calif.: Sage, 1987); Edward S. Herman and Robert W. McChesney, *The Global Media: The New Missionaries of Global Capitalism* (London: Cassell, 1997).

7. Anthony Giddens, *Runaway World* (New York: Routledge, 2000, 32–33): "The Soviet and the East European regimes were unable to prevent the reception of Western radio and television broadcasts. Television played a direct role in the 1989 revolutions, which have rightly been called the first 'television revolution.' Street protests taking place in one country were watched by television audiences in others, large numbers of whom then took to the streets themselves."

8. Fred Casmir, ed., *Communication in Development* (Norwood, N.J.: Ablex, 1991); Gilbert Rist, *Le développement, histoire d'une croyance occidentale* (Paris: Presses de Sciences, 1996); Chris Barker, *Television, Globalization, and Cultural Identities* (Philadelphia: Open University Press, 1999).

9. Daniel Lerner, *The Passing of Traditional Society: Modernizing the Middle East* (New York: Free Press, 1964); Wilbur Schramm, *Mass Media and National Development* (Stanford: Stanford University Press, 1964).

10. *Newsweek*, March 4, 2002, 24.

11. *New Yorker*, www.new-yorker.com/FACT/?020204fa_FACT.

12. According to Raban, Sayid Qutb's *Milestones* (1964) is the essential charter of the Jihad movement, its *Mein Kampf* that inspired the Islamic kamikazes.

13. René Jean Ravault, "Some Possible Economic Dysfunction of the Anglo-American Practice of International Communication: A Theoretical Approach" (Ph.D. diss., University of Iowa, 1980) and related published papers (see n. 21). I demonstrated that foreign decision makers, diplomats, and violent actors informed their decision and planned their deeds against the United States out of mass communication products made accessible to them through the global export or overreach of American media. Seminal pieces were written, on the one hand, by Edward Shils and Morris Janowitz, "Cohesion and Disintegration in the Wehrmacht," in Bernard Berelson and Morris Janowitz, eds., *Reader in Public Opinion and Communication*, 2d ed. (New York: Free Press, 1966), 402–17; and, on the other, Tzvetan Todorov, *La conquête de*

l'Amérique, la question de l'autre (Paris: Seuil, 1982), which can be considered as the best manifestation of this boomerang effect theory. Shils and Janowitz studied how German counterpropaganda officers used Allied propaganda to maintain the cohesion of the Wehrmacht from 1942 to 1945 and pointed out: "The Nazis frankly believed that they could employ our propaganda efforts as a point of departure for strengthening the unpolitical resolve of their men. . . . The Germans followed the policy of stamping Allied leaflets with the imprint, 'hostile propaganda,' and then allowing them to circulate in limited numbers. . . . to employ them as a point of departure for counter-propaganda" (409–10). Tzvetan Todorov, studying how Mexico was won by Cortés in the first part of the sixteenth century, suggests that it is through the knowledge of the languages and cultures of the Aztecs and the Mayas that Cortés obtained, thanks to the Malinche—a woman of Mayan origin sold as a slave by her own tribesmen to the Aztec who eventually sold her to the Spanish conquistadores who led him to a better understanding of Moctezuma's attitudes and beliefs. A better understanding of the other's language and culture ultimately allowed him to triumph over his powerful enemy, who fatefully ignored Cortés's culture, language, and intent.

14. Sukarno, president of Indonesia, underlined the fact that the level of luxury, richness, quality of life, and so on, demonstrated in many American movies elicited envy in most Indonesian viewers.

15. Jacques Chirac, president of France, mentioned in an address he delivered in Cairo in December 2001 that he understood the Arabs, who were humiliated and described in a very partial way by global media.

16. Edward A. Shils and Morris Janowitz, "Cohesion and Disintegration in the Wehrmacht," in Bernard Berelson and Morris Janowitz, eds., *Reader in Public Opinion and Communication*, 2d ed. (New York: Free Press, 1966), 402–417. This classical piece of research in communication or psychological warfare should be read carefully in the light of what is going on in the present war against international terrorism.

17. Stuart Hall, "Encoding and Decoding in the Television Discourse," in Stuart Hall, Dorothy Hobson, Andrew Lowe, and Paul Williams, eds., *Culture, Media, Language,* Working Papers in Cultural Studies, 1972–1979 (London: Hutchinson, 1987), 7.

18. Hamid Mowlana, "Technology versus Tradition: Communication in the Iranian revolution," *Journal of Communication* 3 (1979): 107–12.

19. Majid Tehranian, "Development Theories and Messianic Ideologies: Dependency, Communication, and Democracy in the Third World" (paper presented at the International Association for Mass Communication Research Conference, Paris, 1982).

20. Todorov, *La conquête de l'Amérique.*

21. Ravault, "Some Possible Economic Dysfunctions"; "Information Flow: Which Way Is the Wrong Way?" *Journal of Communication* 31, no. 4 (1981): 129–34; "Resisting Media Imperialism by Coreseduction," *Intermedia* 13, no. 3 (1985): 3–37; "International Information: Bullet or Boomerang?" in David Paletz, ed., *Political Communication Research: Approaches, Studies, Assessments,* vol. 2 (Norwood, N.J.: Ablex, 1996).

Epilogue: "The Bell Rang and We Answered"

Peter Clarke

The many chapters in this book are admirably diverse and defy placement within research traditions. So rather than attempt to summarize them in his epilogue, Peter Clarke has chosen to sketch ideas about communication in crisis that the authors provoke, whether they intended to or not. These personal sketches, or commentaries, allow him to alert readers to unexpected treasures in the chapters. To conclude the epilogue, Clarke reveals the corpus of research into terrorism, before and after September 11, so readers can see how completely this book explores this terrain.

Commentary on the Chapters

A MEMORIAL WALL STANDS outside the Fire Museum of Memphis, Tennessee, presenting a towering sculpture of exhausted firefighters after a blaze. "The Bell Rang and We Answered," reads the inscription. This modest but memorable statement also describes researchers who leaped to study the terrorist attacks against icons of the nation's commercial and military might. Social scientists of many stripes and colors answered an instinctive need to comprehend and illuminate violence unprecedented in the American experience.

The present volume concentrates on communication during and following 9/11. Chapters share a bounty of fascinating details and far-reaching insights. Let me cast this impressive work within two contexts: one narrowly framed and the other more broadly conceived. I begin with meta-stories that I believe the contributors implicitly convey, issues about communication in a crisis that sometimes lurk between the lines of their reports. Arguable though my personal readings may be, I hope they provoke readers to peer beyond the authors' data to consider intriguing implications for future research. I conclude with observations about the larger flow of research into terrorism, before and following September's raw events. These comments draw on my analysis of two leading bibliographic databases in the social sciences.

John Carey and William Dutton and Frank Nainoa remind us that media have swelled to saturate all of life's venues—sidewalks, office cubicles, and airport waiting rooms, as well as homes and automobiles. No part of the day is sheltered. Media are either installed everywhere or portable. We can expect such an infrastructure to remain robust, even when subjected to exceptional stress, like 9/11. Cell phones hastened the pace of people's awareness of events and reactions to them. Inexpensive, miniature, and wireless technologies performed like methamphetamine. The twitchy behaviors these technologies unleashed that day appeared highly adaptive, for the most part. Could the same be said, one wonders, over the longer haul and under less menacing conditions? When do communication devices inform and excite our reactions too quickly for our own well-being?

Everett Rogers's data confirm that reciprocal linkages may trump linear, directional ties between receivers and generators of communication, contradicting traditional causal models for capturing communication processes. Conventions of theorizing in behavioral research must bend to the staccato of different ways people actually tune into profound events. The search for a convergent or dominant pattern may be fruitless.

Elisia Cohen, Sandra Ball-Rokeach, Joo-Young Jung, and Yong-Chan Kim, as well as René Jean Ravault, help us appreciate how far scholars have traveled from the last century's analytic polarities pitting mass against intimate cultures. In the face of intense and external attack, a burst of mediated communication on September 11 activated latent collective identities and a sense of mutuality, instead of driving people numbly into private and alienated worlds. In short, machine-based media and a community's social capital may be more interdependent than some scholars have recognized. And while America exports a popular culture that many intellectuals disdain as seamless and shallow, people manage to practice indigenous forms of creativity and forge their own, sometimes nasty, interpretations of news and entertainment.

Pille Vengerfeldt and Joachim Haes give us perspectives from Europe. Perhaps we can use Vengerfeldt's Estonia as a petri dish for detecting patterns of public opinion that may have cropped up elsewhere. Other states and societies may have varied along the themes of grief, laying blame, and offering succor, expressions that caught Vengerfeldt's attention. Politico-economic differences between cultures may also explain how quickly these sentiments dissipated as American policies for dealing with terrorism evolved after 9/11. Data offered by Haes invite us, unintended, to grasp a cunning detail in the terrorists' planning behind that day. The hour of attack commanded maximum attention, stretching across Western Hemisphere and European news audiences. The vast majority of people in postmodern cultures were awake and entrained by their daily news cycle.

James Katz and Ronald Rice document how people remembered that day as a series of their own communicative acts. Participants' narratives about 9/11 were anchored by seeing televised images, telephoning others, securing an Internet connection, and the like. The verbs of communication dominated people's vocabulary of experience. Perhaps acute occasions inevitably frame people's memories this way; perhaps, though, 9/11 was unique.

Paul Rappoport and James Alleman's account of how decisively 9/11 established new levels of audience reach for Internet news sites invites many speculations. Here is one: an unprecedented number of people got a crash course in empowered news consumption. They navigated comfortably across competing sources and among hyperlinked pages, compared reports for completeness and other qualities, extended their reading and viewing into nontraditional dayparts (or parts of the day) of the news cycle, and connected to a news tool that also served as a communication link with other people. Did these experiences, to raise a single possibility, spawn critical faculties that people now bring to bear when they follow daily events in conventional print and broadcast media?

Patrick Martin and Sean Phelan compare television and Internet message boards in their use of language to represent Islam following 9/11. Their analysis could serve as a prototype for monitoring of communications, in the service of greater public understanding about vital issues like war and terrorism. How better informed we might become if given periodic reports about trends in "official" language, such as favored by television news, and developments in vernacular expression as found in chat rooms. When do these discourses frame events differently, and when do they align? Wouldn't such studies tempt investigators to raise fresh hypotheses about agenda-setting and the formation of public opinion?

Menahem Blondheim and Tamar Liebes ask for renewed debate over the course of action that media should follow when covering terrorism. How does an attack spiral into a "disaster marathon," they ask. Three factors contribute to a descent from relative order to chaos: the starkness of special effects, including the visibility of death; the orchestration of anxiety by commanding public attention across time; and mystery surrounding the perpetrators and their aims. September 11 nearly had it all. If we are to fashion any rules for treating terror as spectacle, the government, private media, journalists, and concerned citizens will need to become involved. Jeremy Harris Lipschultz's discussion lends urgency to the debate about rules by reminding us that where journalists converge on certain frames for understanding recurring events like terrorism, public discourse usually follows—for lack of alternative schemas.

Fiona McNee points out that real events, even terrorism, inspire fictional reproductions—novels, television dramas, live theater, films. Translation from nonfiction to fictional genres can be revealing. When do narrative artists degrade the stories that life throws off, slathering them with populism, sentimentality, jingoism, hubris, or other trivializations? How does a fictional representation preserve the audience's options for constructing meaning? When does storytelling grow heavy-handed or preachy? McNee opens a window onto these issues by examining *West Wing's* use of 9/11 as metaphor, airing its treatment just twenty-two days after the attacks.

Two accounts of how voice and data services were restored following 9/11 highlight different fundamental principles. Mitchell Moss and Anthony Townsend confirm that human ingenuity and shrewd management are more indispensable than physical assets. Recovery was eased where institutions had rehearsed disaster plans, had arranged backup or redundant systems, and had embraced adaptive technical protocols. For this and future terrorist assaults, it is vital that decision makers disperse vital communication hubs. They must swiftly gather repair crews from afar and be willing to commit vast sums on short notice. These are such simple ideas. Yet we sometimes forget they are among the fruits of a competitive, free society. Jonathan Liebenau's report inspires an analogy. As windstorms strip away weak and decaying ground cover, disasters uncover frailties in communication networks. Where horticulturists and plant breeders develop new species of shrubs and trees to withstand nature's fury, engineers modify technical and institutional systems and their deployment. Tragic events are, from this perspective, part of a grand ecology that may, painfully, improve the human condition.

Finally, James Carey refocuses the microscope through which most of this volume's chapters examine 9/11, to achieve a wider-angle view. He casts the attacks as a seismic break from glib rhetoric about globalization. Optimistic, even aggressive claims about a planet winding its way toward "one civilization" have melted before posturing by conflicting political and spiritual systems and the realization that worldwide inequalities in income are growing. It remains to be seen, I suspect, whether we attribute the tectonic changes Carey notes mainly to 9/11, or to America's exercise of widened international prerogatives.

The Corpus of Terrorism Research

Of course, the chapters in this volume are but a fraction from the behavioral sciences literature examining 9/11 and its aftermath. We can sense outlines of the larger creative effort by examining two of the most important bibliographic databases in the social sciences, *PsycInfo* and *Sociological Abstracts*.

The amount and character of research these sources have documented provide a backdrop against which we can better appreciate the chapters that appear here.

First, terrorist attacks against the World Trade Center and the Pentagon revved the engines of scholarship. For example, by early March 2003 *PsycInfo* returned more than two hundred entries to a search using September 11 and its equivalents as key words—or approximately thirteen publications per month since the attacks occurred, allowing a lag for studies to appear. Research about 9/11 cited in *Sociological Abstracts* has also been vigorous, if somewhat less so, at seven to eight works per month. By comparison, the subjects of terrorism and terrorists during a dozen years before the attacks drew approximately two publications per month in the psychological literature and four per month in sociological outlets. Altogether, therefore, the data chart a threefold burst in intellectual activity, before to after 9/11. And attention to 9/11 supplemented inquiries into terrorism in general, which continued undiminished during the attacks' aftermath. Clearly the academy has not neglected the nation's newest and most urgent peril.

To a casual observer, perhaps, this surge in research matched the unprecedented nature of 9/11. For the first time in many years, the United States appeared naked against adversity and trauma. Equally dramatic, the foe transcended state boundaries and dodged into shadows to escape our retribution. Cells of operatives might lurk anywhere in America, poised to strike again. No wonder, one might speculate, intellectuals in the social sciences rose to examine such a singular sociopolitical phenomenon.

A closer look at the social scientific outpouring leads to a different interpretation, however. I will briefly argue that communication research about 9/11 actually resembles the tradition of scholarship about terrorism, rather than breaking with the past as al-Qaeda's attacks seemed to do. In short, the academy mustered uncommon energy to study September's tragedy and its aftermath. But for the most part, contours of its output have traced the renderings of earlier terrorist events, instead of deviating from this body of work.

Before getting to results, let me be modest about my examination of *PsycInfo* and *Sociological Abstracts*. I scratched just the surfaces of the research they report, noting the key words that indexed entries in the two databases. Deeper and more textured readings of the 1,264 citations I retrieved might easily come to different conclusions. Nonetheless, my discoveries help map the conceptual terrain that this body of research has explored, and against which we can view the present contributions.

I began by delimiting two slices in time, 1989–2000 and 2001–2003. Within the earlier period, I used "terrorist/terrorists" and "terrorism" as locators.[1] To find the postattack literature, I used "September 11/Sept. 11" as locators. Then I introduced a dictionary of concepts representing touchstones in the empirical study of communication. Research entries survived this winnowing, where they exhibited at least one of the dictionary's keywords. The chart below presents my dictionary's terms, arbitrary and incomplete as they may be, separated into four subthemes (more on those below).

When deployed together, terms in the chart narrowed citations by approximately one-half. Thus, according to my perimeter of keywords, communication studies represented half of the social scientific research into terrorism—at least the portion of such research that gained notice by the two bibliographic databases I studied.

Even more interesting, the rate of shrinkage—from the totality of studies into terrorism to the subset that focused on communication—remained constant from before to after 9/11. It appears, therefore, that September's tragedy mobilized communication scholars to the same degree as other social scientists. The resulting complexion of research into terrorism did not change much, at least at this coarse level of granularity. Spectacular though 9/11 was, the scholars' lens has not cast the day's events as a singularly communicative occasion, qualitatively apart from other political terror.

This portrait of consistency across time remains even after a more penetrating look. By separating my dictionary into four conceptual themes, I sought to unpack the kinds of knowledge we can gain about the communication of terrorism. Studies that focus on mass channels uncover important facts about the engines that drive popular sentiment in our culture, and how perpetrators manipulate such tools. Research into personal channels opens windows into people's idiosyncratic responses to terrifying events. Inquiries that focus on message components allow us to gain insights into the visual and textual vocabulary of terror. Finally, studies that include processes link political violence to mechanisms of human behavior that help explain many different phenomena.

TABLE E.1
Communication Themes and Key Words

Conceptual Themes	Communication Key Words
Mass channels	Broadcasting, cable, cartoon, commentary, coverage, editorial, Internet, magazine, media, medium, news, newspaper, press, radio, television, web
Personal channels	Address, cell phone, conversation, diary, expression, speech, talk, telephone, thinking, thought, writing
Message components	Image, information, knowledge, language, linguistic, meaning, message, metaphor, narrative, picture, story, video
Processes	Agenda setting, attention, attribution, communicate, communication, communicator, forgetting, frame, framing, inform, informing, learning, memory, persuade, persuasion, recall, recognition, remembering, retention

TABLE E.2
Percentages of Communication Studies That Included Each Theme,
Prior to and Following the 9/11 Attacks

Conceptual Themes	Pre-9/11 (%)	Post-9/11 (%)
Mass channels	44	29
Personal channels	25	32
Message components	47	49
Processes	40	33

Note: Percentages total >100%, due to multiple use of themes within publications. Data are based on 404 pre- and 190 post-9/11 works.

The table above shows results from these separate searches in the literature. Findings impress me by their similarities. For the most part, differences between the left- and right-hand columns are in the single digits, trivial changes from pre- to post-9/11.

One could, of course, argue that attention to mass channels declined somewhat following the attacks. But persistence in scholarly interests, I think, outweighs any differences—between the "good old days" when terrorism seemed contained on foreign soil, to today, when this malignancy camps on America's doorstep.[2]

Provisionally, therefore, we should consider the chapters in this volume against a stable backdrop of subjects about terrorism that communication scholars have been pursuing for more than a decade. Collectively, the contributors explore all the corners I have identified. Readers will find hypotheses and findings about mass channels, personal channels, message components, and processes sprinkled liberally across these pages. The chapters represent not just dutiful but far-reaching answers to the bell that sounded on September 11.

Notes

1. The rates of interest in terrorism revealed by citations in *PsycInfo* and *Sociological Abstracts* remained relatively stable between 1989–1990 and 1999–2000.

2. I recognize that detecting shifts in scholarly attention depends critically on one's rules for selecting search terms and for categorizing them. Other clumps of locators might unearth trends or nuances that have eluded me.

Index

interpretive and introspective analysis,
   xix–xx
interpretive frames, 114–15
"Isaac and Ishmael," 115–16

jokes, use in chat rooms, 142, 144

Kennedy (U.S. President), 10–11

Lehman Brothers, 58–59, 64, 66
"Let's roll," 74, 77

MARC. *See* Mutual Aid and Restoration
   Consortium
MARC-II, 51
Media: fictional, 113–22; performance,
   12–13
media event, 185–97; September 11,
   2001, 189–92; September 11, 2002,
   192–95
media globalization, 206–7
messageboard discourse, 167–84
metamorphosis project, 31
metricom use during 9/11, 63
microwave use during and after crisis,
   50, 66
Middle East, terror, 103–4
mobile phones. *See* cell phones, wireless
movie attendance, 3
MSNBC.com usage, 151
multimedia ecology, of wireless, 75
Mutual Aid and Restoration Consortium
   (MARC), 49, 51

narrative effects, of disaster marathon,
   191–92
nation building, 200–201
national narrative, 201–202
national trends, 59
NBC, West Wing series, 115–16
neighborhood conversations, 38
network failures, 45–53
network newscasts before 9/11, 91–112
Network Reliability and Interoperability
   Council (NRIC), 51–52
network TV discourse, 167–84

New Mexico, news diffusion study, 18–24
new symbolism of 9/11, 202–204
news event, 19, 27–28
newspapers: learning of the crisis, 22
news websites: learning of the crisis, 24;
   traffic during crisis, 56–57
Northridge earthquake, 46, 64, 67
NRIC. *See* Network Reliability and
   Interoperability Council

online commentary forum, use in
   Estonia, 136
online discourse, 167–84
online news. *See* Internet and web
organizational participation, 38

Palestinian terror, 103–4
Pan Am Flight 103, 104–5 107
parasocial interaction, 27
Pearl Harbor, comparisons to, 177–79,
   200
person-to-person communication, 22
personal effects
physical causes of failure, 49
phone. *See* telephone
portable radios, 58
Postimees newspaper in Estonia, 136–37
Postimees online, 142
prayer, 27
printing press, as unifier of nations, 201
propaganda, twisting of, 208

Qutb's sojourn, 208

radio: learning of the crisis, 22, 128;
   portable, 58; robustness, 8; use
   during crisis, 3–4, 22, 35; use after
   crisis, 4, 36
recovery of network infrastructure,
   65–66
recovery mechanism, fictional media as,
   113–22
redundancy of media, 12
relocating displaced firms, 64–65
repeater failure, 57–58
research methodologies, xvii–xxi

About the Contributors

James Alleman is an associate professor in the Department of Interdisciplinary Telecommunications, College of Engineering, University of Colorado, Boulder. He was most recently a visiting professor and research director at the Columbia Institute for Tele-Information at Columbia University in New York. Prior to his appointment at the University of Colorado in 1991, Alleman was associate professor and director of the International Center for Telecommunications Management, College of Business Administration at the University of Nebraska, Omaha. From 1978 to 1989, Alleman worked in a variety of policy and research positions at GTE. He is a past president of the International Telecommunications Society, and coeditor (with Eli Noam) of *The New Investment Theory of Real Options and Its Implications for Telecommunications Economics* (1999).

Sandra J. Ball-Rokeach is professor of communication and director of the Communication Technology and Community Program at the Annenberg School for Communication at the University of Southern California. She is principal investigator of the Metamorphosis: Transforming the Ties That Bind research project funded by the Annenberg Center for Communication, the Annenberg School for Communication, and First Five L.A. She has authored numerous published works dealing with communication technology and community, human values, inequality, strategies of social change, and collective and interpersonal violence. Ball-Rokeach received her Ph.D. in sociology from the University of Washington. She was a Fulbright scholar at Hebrew University in Jerusalem and a Rockefeller Fellow at the Bellagio Study Center in northern Italy.

Menahem Blondheim teaches in the Departments of Communication and American Studies at the Hebrew University of Jerusalem and serves as director of the university's Smart Family Foundation Communication Institute. He has worked in the media technology sector of Israel's high-tech industry.

James William Carey is CBS Professor of International Journalism and chair of the Interdepartmental Committee on Communications at Columbia University.

John Carey is managing director of Greystone Communications, a media research and planning firm. He conducts in-home ethnographic research, focus groups, planning studies, and laboratory-based usability studies of new communication services. Recently he conducted studies of broadband web users, digital satellite radio service for cars, software on demand, digital cable services, TV use in prime time, and personal video recorders. Clients have included American Express, AT&T, A&E Television Networks, Cablevision, Corporation for Public Broadcasting, Hughes Electronics, NBC, the *New York Times,* Statistical Research Inc., Telus Communications, and XM Satellite Radio, among others. Carey is also an adjunct professor in the Graduate School of Business at Columbia University, where he teaches Demand for New Media, and an affiliated research fellow at the Columbia Institute For Tele-Information. He holds a Ph.D. in communication research from the University of Pennsylvania.

Peter Clarke, Ph.D. (University of Minnesota), holds two appointments at the University of Southern California: professor of preventive medicine and of communication. Clarke's current interests center on improving human nutrition through programs that build the capacity of food rescue efforts at the local level. In addition to his research and work in social action, Clarke has chaired or served as dean of four academic programs in communication at three universities: the School of Communications (University of Washington); the Department of Journalism and, later, the Department of Communication (University of Michigan); and the Annenberg School for Communication (University of Southern California). He has published more than forty articles in professional journals and edited works such as *The Computer Culture* (1984), *New Models for Communication Research* (1973), and seven volumes of the *Annual Reviews of Communication Research.* His most recent book (with Dr. Susan H. Evans) is *Surviving Modern Medicine* (1998).

Elisia L. Cohen recently earned a Ph.D. at the Annenberg School for Communication at the University of Southern California, where she was a research assistant for the Metamorphosis: Transforming the Ties That Bind project. Her work focused on several aspects of public communication, including public argument, political and health communication campaigns, and the role of media and new communication technologies in society. Specifically, her recent research explored how media and interpersonal storytelling shapes how individuals construct a sense of community in urban environments. She has an M.A. in communication studies from Wake Forest University and a B.A. with university honors from the University of Louisville in political science. She currently is an assistant professor at St. Louis University.

William H. Dutton is director of the Oxford Internet Institute and professor of Internet studies at the University of Oxford, where he is also a fellow in Balliol College. Since 1974, his work has focused on the political and social aspects of information and communication technologies. Dutton formerly was at the Annenberg School for Communication at the University of Southern California.

Joachim W. H. Haes is a project manager at the University of Lugano in Switzerland. His current research deals with the social acceptance and proper communication of organ donations. Before coming to Lugano, Haes was a research assistant with the Institute for Media and Communications Management in St. Gallen and a freelance journalist for several German media. He holds an undergraduate and graduate degree in economics from Bonn University, a master's in Communication Management from the Annenberg School at the University of Southern California, and a doctorate in economics from the University of St. Gallen.

Joo-Young Jung is a researcher in the social implications of communication technologies and in the globalization of communication behaviors. She was a research assistant for the Metamorphosis: Transforming the Ties That Bind project funded by the Annenberg Center for Communication, the Annenberg School for Communication, and First Five L.A. Her recent works focus on how various social factors interact to affect the ways in which people adopt and use new communication technologies. Jung is a magna cum laude graduate of Yonsei University in Seoul, receiving a B.A. in mass communication. She received an M.A. and a Ph.D. from the Annenberg School for Communication at the University of Southern California.

James E. Katz is a professor in the Department of Communication at Rutgers University. Katz has won postdoctoral fellowships at Harvard and MIT and served on the faculties of the University of Texas, Austin, and Clarkson University. He has been granted national and foreign patents on his inventions in telecommunication technology. His coedited book, *Perpetual Contact: Mobile*

Communication, Private Talk, Public Performance (2002) is being translated into Japanese, and his book *Connections: Social and Cultural Studies of the Telephone in American Life* (1999) has been cited in *Choice* as a landmark study. The fruits of his collaborations with Ronald E. Rice include the recent books *Social Consequences of Internet Use* (2002) and *Internet and Health Communication* (2000).

Yong-Chan Kim received a Ph.D. from the Annenberg School for Communication at the University of Southern California. He is a research associate with the Metamorphosis: Transforming the Ties That Bind project funded by the Annenberg Center for Communication, the Annenberg School for Communication, and First Five L.A. His work has focused on ecological relationships among communication technologies, media organizations, and urban communities as three key components of the contemporary communication environment. A Korean native, Kim earned a B.A. and M.A. in mass communication at Yonsei University in Seoul, and later an M.A. in organizational communication at the State University of New York at Albany.

Jonathan Liebenau is currently visiting professor of management and electrical engineering at Columbia University, where he teaches courses on innovation management, managing technological innovation, technology management, and a unique master's course, Resilient Communications Networks. He is affiliated with the Columbia Institute for Tele-Information, where he directs a project called Network Resiliency Strategies. He has taught at the London School of Economics since 1980 and is currently a member of the Department of Information Systems there. Liebenau earned his Ph.D. at the University of Pennsylvania and is the author of numerous books and articles in the areas of technology policy, information systems theory, and business history.

Tamar Liebes is professor of communication and chair of the Department of Communication and Journalism at the Hebrew University of Jerusalem. Her recent books are *Reporting the Arab Israeli Conflict: How Hegemony Works* (1997); *American Dreams, Hebrew Subtitles: Globalization from the Receiving End* (2003); and *Media, Ritual, Identity* (1998) (coedited with James Curran).

Jeremy Harris Lipschultz (Ph.D., Southern Illinois University, 1990) is the Robert Reilly Diamond Professor of Communication at the University of Nebraska-Omaha. He is coauthor of *Crime and Local Television News: Dramatic, Breaking, and Live from the Scene* (2002), and author of *Free Expression in the Age of the Internet: Social and Legal Boundaries* (2000) and *Broadcast Indecency: FCC Regulation and the First Amendment* (1997). An award-winning broadcast journalist in the 1980s, he now authors the annual update "New Communication Technologies" for the book *Communication and the Law.*

Patrick Martin, M.A., is a researcher on a European Union–funded project in discourse analysis, corpus linguistics, and software engineering that seeks to combat racist content on the Internet. His doctoral thesis and other publications are concerned with new communication technologies as a resource for outsider belief communities. He is based in the School of Communications and the School of Applied Languages and Intercultural Studies, Dublin City University.

Fiona McNee has qualifications in both law and communication at a postgraduate level. Having practiced as a commercial lawyer in the fields of intellectual property and new media, she now works in the Australian public sector. Her current research interests include convergence in the entertainment and media industries, and the social impacts of mass communication.

Mitchell L. Moss is the director of the Taub Urban Research Center and the Henry Hart Rice Professor of Urban Policy and Planning at New York University's Robert F. Wagner Graduate School of Public Service. Moss has written extensively on cities and telecommunications, and the National Science Foundation has supported his research. He received his B.A. from Northwestern University, M.A. from the University of Washington, and Ph.D. from the University of Southern California.

Frank Nainoa is a graduate of the Master of Communication Management Program in the Annenberg School for Communication at the University of Southern California. He currently is a manager at Verizon.

A. Michael Noll is a professor at the Annenberg School for Communication at the University of Southern California and was dean of the school for an interim period from 1992 to 1994. Noll spent nearly fifteen years performing basic research at Bell Labs and is one of the earliest pioneers in the use of digital computers in the visual arts. In the early 1970s, he was on the staff of the president's science adviser at the White House and later worked at AT&T identifying opportunities for new products and services. Noll is affiliated with the Columbia Institute for Tele-Information at Columbia University and the Media Center at New York Law School. He has published over ninety professional papers and nearly fifty editorial opinion pieces. He holds six patents and has authored nine books on various aspects of telecommunications.

Sean Phelan is a Ph.D. candidate in the School of Communications, Dublin City University, with emphasis on political discourse, critical theory, and media analysis. His other publications on September 11 focus on the contrasting discourse practices of the Irish and British TV media and on the reaction of the Irish print media to the attacks.

Paul N. Rappoport is associate professor of economics at Temple University. He is also a principal and senior academic consultant with the economics consulting firm, Econsult. He has over twenty-five years of experience in data analysis, modeling, and statistical assessment, with a specialization in telecommunications demand analysis. He was responsible for the development of Bill Harvesting, a national database of actual communication bills, a small business panel (which focused on telecommunications and energy), and a large consumer national telecommunication database. His current research interests include the construction of Internet metrics, modeling the digital divide, specifying and modeling business broadband, forecasting Internet demand, and measuring the nature of network externalities. He received his Ph.D. from Ohio State University in 1974.

René-Jean Ravault has a Ph.D. in mass communication from the University of Iowa at Iowa City. Ravault has been teaching since 1980 in the Department Of Communication Studies at the University of Quebec in Montreal at the B.A., M.A., and Ph.D. levels. He has been a consultant for the Canadian federal and the New Brunswick provincial governments analyzing and evaluating the efficiency of policies on multiculturalism and bilingualism. For the last twenty years, his main area of research and publication has been international and transcultural communications, comparative studies of theories and paradigms used in different cultural setting in order to understand how human communication works. His main concern lies with how foreign recipients of American-made mass communication products transform them into "messages" that are significant and relevant to their own decisions regarding international business, diplomatic, and, nowadays, terrorist activities.

Ronald E. Rice is a professor and also chair of the Department of Communication at Rutgers University. Rice earned his Ph.D. in communication research from Stanford University and is the author of more than one hundred peer-reviewed articles. He has conducted research and published widely in communication science, public communication campaigns, computer-mediated communication systems, methodology, organizational and management theory, information systems, information science and bibliometrics, and social networks. His publications have won awards as Best Dissertation from the American Society for Information Science, half a dozen times as Best Paper from International Communication Association divisions, and twice as Best Paper from the Academy of Management divisions. He is among the top-cited scholars in both the communication and the information science disciplines.

Everett M. Rogers is Regents Professor in the Department of Communication and Journalism, University of New Mexico. He is best known for his book *Diffusion of Innovations* (5th ed., 2003). Rogers has been involved in teaching and research in universities for the past forty-six years. He has conducted several studies of the diffusion of news events over the years.

Anthony Townsend is a research scientist at New York University's Taub Urban Research Center and a faculty member in the Urban Planning Program at NYU's Wagner School. He is completing a doctorate in urban studies at MIT and has developed wireless communications systems in major urban areas. He is a member of the Editorial Board of Environment and Planning.

Pille Vengerfeldt has an M.A. in media and communications as well as a B.A. in public relations from the University of Tartu in Estonia. She is doing her Ph.D. in media and communications on the issues of new media. She is a visiting fellow on a Marie Curie Fellowship at Dublin City University. She teaches undergraduate and graduate courses on topics related to the information society. Her research interests are in new media, specifically issues of online communities, different roles of the Internet in people's everyday lives, and different levels of inclusion and exclusion in the information society.